# The Song of Roland

## FORMULAIC STYLE AND POETIC CRAFT

*Published under the auspices of the*
CENTER FOR MEDIEVAL AND RENAISSANCE STUDIES
*University of California, Los Angeles*

*Publications of the*
CENTER FOR MEDIEVAL AND RENAISSANCE STUDIES, UCLA

1. Jeffrey Burton Russell: Dissent and Reform in the Early Middle Ages

2. C. D. O'Malley: Leonardo's Legacy

3. Richard H. Rouse: Serial Bibliographies for Medieval Studies

4. Speros Vryonis, Jr.: The Decline of Medieval Hellenism in Asia Minor and the Process of Islamization from the Eleventh through the Fifteenth Century

5. Stanley Chodorow: Christian Political Theory and Church Politics in the Mid-Twelfth Century

6. Joseph J. Duggan: The Song of Roland: Formulaic Style and Poetic Craft

JOSEPH J. DUGGAN

# The Song of Roland

FORMULAIC STYLE AND POETIC CRAFT

University of California Press

Berkeley    Los Angeles    London

1973

University of California Press
Berkeley and Los Angeles, California
University of California Press, Ltd.
London, England
Copyright © 1973, by
The Regents of the University of California
ISBN 0–520–02201–7
Library of Congress Catalog Card Number: 75–186101
Printed in the United States of America
Designed by Theo Jung

*To Mary Boyce Duggan*

# Acknowledgments

I WOULD LIKE to express my thanks to the colleagues who supported me with their encouragement while this book was being written, to Robert Alter, Louise Clubb, Phillip Damon, Janette Richardson, Thomas G. Rosenmeyer, and, above all, Alain Renoir. As early as 1963, when computer applications to literary studies were still in their infancy, Eleanor Bulatkin encouraged me to develop a way of isolating formulas through data processing methods. I am indebted also to Gio Wiederhold, Laura Gould, and Regina Frey, whose programming skills were indispensible to my undertaking, and to the Committee on Research and the Computer Center of the University of California, Berkeley, both of which gave generous financial aid. A grant from the National Endowment for the Humanities allowed me precious time for completing the basic research. Ian Short, Phillip Damon, and Manfred Sandmann read the manuscript in full and offered advice which improved it immeasurably; for the shortcomings which subsist, they are, of course, in no way responsible. My debt of gratitude to Mary Kay, Marie Christine and Kathleen Duggan for their unfailing patience and cheerfulness over the past four years, despite the many inconveniences and disruptions of family life caused by the preparation and writing of this book, cannot be sufficiently acknowledged.

# Contents

1: The Problem and the Method   1

2: Formulaic Language and Mode of Creation   16

3: The Episode of Baligant: Theme and Technique   63

4: *Roland*'s Formulaic Repertory   105

5: *Roland*'s Motifs and Formulas and
the Evolution of Old French Epic Style   160

6: Consequences   213

Index   223

# 1: The Problem and the Method

THE OXFORD MANUSCRIPT of the *Chanson de Roland* is at the base of every general theory concerning the origins and nature of the Old French epic. Gaston Paris, Joseph Bédier, Ferdinand Lot, Ramón Menéndez Pidal, Jean Rychner, Italo Siciliano, all scholars who have had pretensions toward an overview of the epic genre, have concentrated their analytic powers on this text, and sometimes to the neglect of other poems of great worth. It is the keystone of any theory which pretends to support, with the strength of its evidence, the immense weight of well over a hundred *chansons de geste*. This is partly because the language of the poem of which Oxford is a copy reveals it as one of the earliest Old French texts, situated on the brink of the twelfth century, before the great mass of works in the vulgar language which illuminate the secular side of the revival of letters. More ancient than the other epics, it may represent a more archaic technique and be closer to the origins of the genre than any other extant song. On the other hand the poet's artistic mastery has led some to place the Oxford *Roland* apart from the bulk of eleventh- and twelfth-century *chansons de geste*. Is the content of this manuscript to be considered typical or atypical of the epic production of its time?

While seeking an answer to this question one must proceed with more than ordinary prudence, for many scholars who concern themselves with Old French literature are particularly attached to the *Chanson de Roland* and are quick to take offense when they believe that its esthetic excellence is being impugned. This situation has immeasurably complicated the controversy be-

1

tween "individualists" and "traditionalists," the former generally considering their opponents' views to be violations of the poem's artistic integrity. There is a complementary tendency to accept statements about *Raoul de Cambrai,* the *Charroi de Nîmes, Gormont et Isembart* or any one of several dozen other *chansons de geste* which would never be admitted or even formulated about *Roland.*

On the other hand, if *Roland* criticism has been tempered by this particular atmosphere of scholarly sensitivity, the restraining effect has been counterbalanced by a more positive result: one can be fairly certain that any theory which stands up under this assessment is a sound one. It is necessary, then, and perhaps even beneficial, that every estimation of the Old French epic, whether it is primarily stylistic as is the present study, or historical and linguistic like the bulk of the scholarly *Roland* bibliography, should test itself against the majesty of the Oxford version. This poem, universally esteemed, so often extolled, has been the downfall of more than one system. It is therefore with a touch of apprehension and with a vivid awareness of the inadequacies, in many respects, of my own method, that I begin this study of the Oxford *Roland*'s style viewed against the backdrop of the twelfth-century *chanson de geste.*[1]

In considering the *Roland*'s mode of creation, what alternatives lie before us?

Defenders of the thesis that the poem is a clerical creation have argued that it is too well put together, too near perfection, to be the product of an unwritten, traditional, spontaneously composed literature,[2] the mere recording of an oral recitation.[3] One

---

[1] Henceforth when *Roland* is mentioned, the reference is to Raoul Mortier's conservative edition of the Oxford manuscript in *Les Textes de la Chanson de Roland,* vol. I: *La Version d'Oxford* (Paris: Editions de la Geste Francor, 1940). When the other manuscripts are in question, they will always be clearly distinguished from Oxford.

[2] The term "literature" may seem out of place in this context, but as long as no term in general critical usage designates the body of orally-composed poems, the word "literature", properly qualified, must serve the purpose.

[3] See especially Maurice Delbouille, "Les Chansons de geste et le livre,"

must, then, consider the eventuality that the *Roland* is simply, as has been believed by many commentators since Philip-August Becker, the creation of one cultivated author, just as *La Vie inestimable du grant Gargantua* was created by Rabelais from legendary material.[4] While admitting the presence of formulaic language in the *chansons de geste,* including *Roland,* contemporary individualism stoutly refuses to concede that formulas are in themselves indicative of either traditional elaboration or improvisational technique.

It is possible, too, that a man of great genius took an existing oral poem, product of an unwritten poetic tradition, and revised it in the process of setting it down in writing, transforming it from a rude song of battles into a well constructed and highly idealistic work, close forerunner of Oxford. Since it has become evident in the years since the publication of Rychner's *La Chanson de geste: Essai sur l'art épique des jongleurs*[5] that individualists are going to have to make their peace one day with traditionalism, there has been a tendency to work toward some sort of middle view rather than accept outright that oral, spontaneous composition could have resulted in a poem of *Roland's* scope and skill. Among the partisans of this compromise position must be ranged, paradoxically, Professor Rychner himself, who hesitates to include *Roland* in the same class as the other twelfth-century epics, which he sees as products of oral improvisation. ". . . A supposer qu'il y ait eu des chants épiques sur Roncevaux antérieurs à la chanson d'Oxford, leur mise par écrit a dû être très créatrice, coïncider, en fait, avec un acte de création poétique."[6]

---

in *La Technique littéraire des chansons de geste: Actes du Colloque de Liège (septembre 1957)*, Bibliothèque de la Faculté de Philosophie et Lettres de l'Université de Liège, CL (Paris: Société d'Edition "Les Belles Lettres," 1959), pp. 295–428, and Italo Siciliano, *Les Chansons de geste et l'épopée: Mythes, Histoire, Poèmes* (Turin: Società Editrice Internazionale, 1968).

[4] Whether the supposed sources of *Roland* were oral or written does not directly concern us in the consideration of this hypothesis.

[5] Geneva: Droz, 1955.

[6] *La Chanson de geste,* p. 36.

Pierre Le Gentil, in a series of lucid articles, expresses a similar belief that the intermediate point of view is closer to the truth than either extreme and that *Roland* is probably both the culmination of an oral tradition and the work of a great individual.[7] He admits the existence of traditional legends anterior to Oxford, but supposes a sudden mutation in the tradition brought about by a poet of genius who is responsible for the high artistry of the extant song. As for the question of writing *versus* improvisation, Le Gentil leans toward the former, but "reconnaître à Turold des qualités hors de pair, ce n'est pas nier qu'il ait usé d'un style de caractère 'traditionnel.' C'est dire plutôt qu'il a si parfaitement assimilé ce style qu'il s'en est rendu maître et en a obtenu le maximum d'efficacité artistique."[8]

One of the few European exponents of pure traditionalism[9] is the late Ramón Menéndez Pidal, whose *La Chanson de Roland y el neotradicionalismo*[10] led to an upward revaluation of historical evidence for the existence of a poetic Roland tradition dating back to the event of August 15, 778. For the great Spanish master, traditional elaboration consists in the passing down, from

[7] "A propos de l'origine des chansons de geste: le problème de l'auteur," in *Coloquios de Roncesvalles* (Saragossa, 1956); "A propos de *la Chanson de Roland et la Tradition épique des Francs* de Ramón Menéndez Pidal," *Cahiers de Civilisation Médiévale*, VI (1962), 323–333; "Les chansons de geste et le problème de la création littéraire au moyen âge: 'remaniement' et 'mutation brusque'," in Maxime Chevalier, Robert Ricard, and Noël Salomon, ed., *Mélanges offerts à Marcel Bataillon par les hispanistes français*, Annales de la Faculté des Lettres de Bordeaux, supplement to *Bulletin Hispanique*, LXIV (Bordeaux: Féret et Fils, 1962); "Réflexions sur la création littéraire au moyen âge," *Chanson de geste und höfischer Roman* (Heidelberg: Carl Winter Verlag, 1963), pp. 9–20; "La Chanson de geste: le problème des origines," *Revue d'Histoire Littéraire de la France*, LXX (1970), 992–1006.

[8] *Mélanges Bataillon*, p. 496.

[9] One would have to include in this category René Louis: see his "L'épopée française est carolingienne," in *Coloquios de Roncevalles*, pp. 327–460.

[10] Madrid: Espasa-Calpe, 1959. All references will be to the second edition, translated by I.-M. Cluzel and revised with the collaboration of René Louis, *La Chanson de Roland et la Tradition épique des Francs* (Paris: Picard, 1960).

performer to performer, of the poetic text more or less intact. This poetry "lives through its variants" in as much as the slight changes made by each singer maintain it in a state of continuous reelaboration, sometimes to the esthetic detriment of the traditional poem, but often for its betterment. Menéndez Pidal differs from Rychner and from the American traditionalism represented by Albert B. Lord[11] in that he does not conceive of the performance as a spontaneous re-creation through the medium of formulaic phraseology.[12]

Lord has articulated better than any traditionalist before him the sociological, mythic, and linguistic elements which set oral literature apart from poems whose creation is synonymous with their being written down. After a long acquaintance with the actual performance milieu of the Yugoslavian epic, he has described in detail the process of singers' apprenticeship, during which they learn how to re-create, by means of formulaic phrases in which are couched the standard actions of epic plot, the long verse narratives of the oral tradition. Through the formulas and through the construction *while singing* of larger narrative segments, the motif and the theme, singers are able to perform long epic songs after having heard them sung by others only once. For Lord the mechanism of oral tradition does not entail memorization of the poetic text: the singer retains the sequence of events in the plot from the performance he has overheard. His own version will be a re-creation of each poetic line, motif, and theme, with the insertion or omission of as much material as he deems fit; he employs formulas of his own choosing which may or may not coincide with those of the source performance. Lord admits

[11] See, above all, *The Singer of Tales,* Harvard Studies in Comparative Literature, XXIV (Cambridge: Harvard University Press, 1960), the classic formulation of the oral-formulaic theory and a culmination of the pioneering work of Milman Parry.

[12] See "Sobre las variantes del códice rolandiano V4 de Venecia," *Cultura Neolatina,* XXI (1961), 10–19; also "Los cantores épicos yugoeslavos y los occidentales: el *Mio Cid* y dos refundidores primitivos," *Boletín de la Real Academia de Buenas Letras de Barcelona,* XXXI (1965–1966).

the possibility of a transitional *poet*, one trained to sing oral-
formulaic poems who has later learned to write, but he regards
the transitional *poem* as a contradiction in terms: a poem is
created either orally or in writing, and no matter how much
traditional material the writing poet incorporates into his work,
that work is still a product of written creation.[13]

Needless to say, the polemic which has involved so many per-
ceptive scholars is not without relevance for an esthetic apprecia-
tion of the poem itself. One cannot validly interpret a literary
work without at least a rudimentary knowledge of the circum-
stances of its creation. If the individualists are correct, then the
*Roland* should be read in the light of a tradition of written com-
position which stretches from Virgil's *Aeneid* to the *Roman
d'Enéas* and beyond.[14] But should traditionalism prevail, many,
perhaps most, of the analytic methods developed for a written
culture would have to be reexamined and their relevance to
*Roland* criticism placed systematically in question. A technique
of oral creation implies, after all, an esthetics in sympathy with
what is known of this technique. Before the question of esthetics
lies that of the mode of creation. The second cannot be considered
in isolation from the first.

I have not attempted to present an exposition of past *Roland*
scholarship,[15] but only to outline the three main points of view
concerning the poem's mode of creation in so far as they affect a

[13] *Singer of Tales*, p. 129.

[14] I am by no means equating individualism with advocacy of classical
or medieval Latin origins or models, either for the *Roland* or for the *chanson
de geste* in general. But the *Aeneid* and the vernacular *romans d'antiquité*
would, if individualism were vindicated, provide a body of literary works
through which one could construct a poetic context for criticism of *Roland*.
For a fuller discussion, see "Virgilian Inspiration in the *Roman d'Enéas*
and the *Chanson de Roland*," in Rosario P. Armato and John M. Spalek, ed.,
*Medieval Epic to the "Epic Theater" of Brecht*, University of Southern
California Studies in Comparative Literature, I (Los Angeles: University
of Southern California Press, 1968), pp. 9–23.

[15] Menéndez Pidal provides a history of the main questions, seen through
his particular optic, in *La Chanson de Roland et la tradition épique des
Francs*, pp. 3–50.

critical reading. My own contribution will be in part evaluative, but to a great extent descriptive, and necessarily so, for the question of formulaic composition in the *chanson de geste* and its significance has been considered in a rarified atmosphere.[16] There can be little agreement concerning such matters as the jongleur's improvisation of his songs, the fluidity or fixity of transmitted works, and the greater or lesser degree of dominance exercised by stylized elements on the poet's art, until we have a more exact, comprehensive view of the role played by formulas in the texture of each poem.

For this reason I have given much thought to the development of a method for ascertaining the extent to which formulaic style pervades a given poem.[17] The approach I finally settled on, which takes advantage of the high speed and accuracy of electronic data processing machines, can be extended beyond the limits of a single poem, but the longer the totality of verses to be considered, and the more disparate their orthographical conventions, the less sure it becomes. It consists in generating, by means of a large electronic computer, a concordance of the poem to be studied. Not any concordance will do: individual concorded words must be arranged according to the alphabetization of the words which follow them in the poetic line, so that a concordance of groups of words, and not simply one of individual words divorced from their context, is obtained. A phrase coextensive with the hemistich and substantially identical with another phrase in the poem—and, allowing for the inconsistency of Old French spelling, similar phrases will generally be found next to each other on the concordance page because of the alphabetizing feature— can be regarded as a formula since it conforms to Parry's definition as "a group of words which is regularly employed under

[16] In this regard Maurice Delbouille complained—rightly so—of "la fragilité des éléments sur quoi reposent tant de développements hypothétiques donnés au lecteur pour des faits assurés." "Les Chansons de geste et le livre," p. 308.

[17] Throughout this work the term "formula" without qualification refers to semantically stylized hemistichs and not to syntactic formulas.

the same metrical conditions to express a given essential idea."[18]

The word-group concordance method has its difficulties. I would be the last to claim that it presents the scholar with an already constituted list of all the formulas in the work he is studying. This is not the case with Old French, at least, nor with any other language whose spelling is not standardized; the more uniform the orthography, the closer one approaches an automatically produced listing of the poem's formulas. But even with a work like the *Chanson de Roland*, where words differ greatly in their spelling, the word-group concordance renders formulaic analysis vastly more simple than the intuitive process of reading the poem several times and underlining what one perceives to be identical phrases, or the *fichier* method of inscribing each hemistich on a separate index card and collating the results. Let me give some examples of orthographic difficulties so as not to lose the reader amid a wealth of abstractions.

The Old French word *barons* may be spelled *baruns* in an Anglo-Norman text such as *Roland*, and as a matter of fact the Oxford scribe uses both spellings. This seemingly slight alteration results in the formulas *barons franceis* and *baruns franceis* being located on different pages in the "b" section of the *Roland* concordance. *Sun cheval brochet* and *sun ceval brochet* are likewise separated in the "c's". But in both of these cases, one realizes, while examining the formulas distinguishable in the "f" section under the word *franceis* and in the "b's" under *brochet* that *barons franceis/baruns franceis* and *sun cheval brochet/sun ceval brochet* are both single formulas with orthographic variations. It is particularly useful to search under such words as *il, le, de,* or, as might have been done with one of the examples just cited, *sun,* because these function words are subject to little or no orthographic variation, and are thus much more

[18] Milman Parry, "Studies in the Epic Technique of Oral Verse-Making. I. Homer and Homeric Style," *Harvard Studies in Classical Philology*, XLI (1930), 80. All Parry's published work is now reprinted in Adam Parry, ed., *The Making of Homeric Verse: the Collected Papers of Milman Parry* (Oxford: Clarendon Press, 1970).

likely to gather together all the versions of a given formula than are words which occur less frequently. They will, of course, change with case and number, but these mutations present little difficulty, as they are totally predictable.

One must, on the other hand, take care not to overcompensate for variable spelling by listing the formula as it is found under the entries for both *sun* and *brochet*, for example. To circumvent this possibility, which would result in too high an estimation of formulas, I took two precautions. No matter where in the concordance a formula was discovered, I recorded it as a formula only on that page where the occurrence of its first significant word was recorded. Thus, to continue with the same examples, it may have occurred to me that *baruns franceis* was a formula to be joined with the group *barons franceis* while I was perusing the entries for the word *franceis*, but I then turned back to *barons* and made a notation incorporating *baruns franceis*, *barons* being the first significant word (noun, adjective, verb or adverb) in the formula. I chose this particular form for my method, although one could just as easily count the formulas under their first word, or their last word, as long as some consistent procedure is followed to avoid duplication.

To verify the effectiveness of this safeguard, I took a second precaution. After the concordance was consigned to paper, I also had the computer instructed to produce a complete copy on perforated cards, so that for each formula found in the paper concordance, a corresponding card could be picked out and laid aside as a discrete physical counterpart of the formula. For one occurrence of the phrase *barons franceis*, therefore, there was a perforated card bearing the information: *a sa voiz grand et halte:/ "Barons franceis, as chevals e as armes!"* AOI. *2986.* Like all the entries, this one contains a preceding and a following context and an "address" or indication of line number. When the process of picking out the formulas was complete, all the cards were processed by a card sorting machine, which automatically placed them in the order of their line numbers. It was then a simple matter to check that no formula appeared twice in succession in the packet of cards, since this would have constituted a duplication in the formula list. With both these precautionary measures I was able to procure as complete a set of formulas as possible for the *Chanson de Roland*[19] and other epic texts.

By a formula I mean a hemistich which is found two or more times in substantially the same form within the poem.[20] Formulas are not rigidly fixed phrases. The poets' technique includes the faculty of adapting the formula to its immediate context, as will be shown in detail in Chapter IV. If two expressions differ in their essential idea, I have not considered them to be examples of the same formula. Since the idea content of a phrase is determined largely by words of considerable semantic weight—nouns, verbs, attributive adjectives, adverbs—I have considered it indispensible that, to be reckoned as formulas, the hemistichs in question can differ lexically only in their function words: pronouns, prepositions, conjunctions, possessive and demonstrative adjectives, interjections, and definite and indefinite articles. One exception to this guideline has been made: during the course of my investigation I remarked that an inordinately high number of phrases, always found in the second hemistich position, differed only in their terminal words. There was obviously a point of technique involved. The poets were manipulating formulas in a special way designed to facilitate the presentation of certain common motifs

[19] See *A Concordance of the Chanson de Roland* (Columbus: Ohio State University Press, 1970).

[20] Michael Nagler has proposed an interesting pre-verbal conception of the formula in "Toward a Generative View of the Homeric Formula," *Transactions and Proceedings of the American Philological Association,* XCVIII (1967), 269–311. I concur that formulas are the actualisation of, as Nagler puts it, a "central Gestalt . . . which is the real mental template underlying the production of all such phrases." Further work is needed to differentiate formulas from the other repeated phrases of language which presumably are also the actualisation of a pre-verbal configuration. Nagler's theoretical work may eventually provide a deeper understanding of the psychological processes behind the text. It does not, of course, alter the fact that formulas are *perceived* as repetitions by the scholar and are subject to statistical description like any other linguistic phenomenon.

in more than one assonance. Therefore I have counted as formulas those second hemistichs which express the same essential idea but which are endowed with assonantal flexibility through the substitution of semantically equivalent (I hesitate to say "synonymous") words—nouns, verbs, attributive adjectives, adverbs —in the final position.

Inversion of word order and paradigmatic changes—a singular alternating with a plural, a present tense with a past—have been admitted. They are indispensable for the jongleur's technique, as will be seen, especially in conjunction with slight lexical adjustments in the process which I call metrical compensation.

I recognize that some stylized word combinations are not neatly contained within the boundaries of the hemistich. Thus *des Francs de France* (*Roland*, v. 177) is related to the designation of the Franks in *pernez mil Francs de France, nostre tere* (*Roland*, v. 804), where *Francs* is in the first hemistich and *de France* in the second. Such combinations have not, however, been included in my tally of formulas. A formula is not *any* repeated sequence of words, but only a sequence which has a reality within the requirements of a system of versification. A quantitative study has no meaning unless the units which are being measured are definable in exact terms. To include a phrase like *Francs de France*, one whose occurrences straddle the caesura, would entail the admission of all repeated word sequences, independently of the verse rhythm. The number of such combinations is small, but their inclusion would lead to troublesome problems of definition— what would be the minimum admissible length, for example?— and I am not convinced that they are formulas at all. In addition, one of the two hemistichs containing the phrase in question may itself be formulaic, which is the case with *pernez mil Francs de France, nostre tere*, whose second hemistich is formulaic, as is shown by the occurrence *en France, la lur tere* (*Roland*, v. 50) and *de France, la lur tere* (v. 808). This situation would complicate the counting immeasurably: can the same words be counted twice? Is there such a beast as a quarter formula? The hemistich is a semiautonomous unit of versification which has a syntactic and semantic integrity of its own. When the jongleurs use repeated phrases, they almost invariably consist of entire hemistichs and not fractions thereof. While this question has not, to my knowledge, been discussed in the critical literature on the *chansons de geste*, scholarly practice has accorded formulaic status almost exclusively to the integral hemistich, and I concur with that practice.

On the other hand, even sympathetic critics are not all in accord about the precise functional nature or scope of formulaic language. Edmund de Chasca, while appreciating the work of Parry and Lord and revealing a willingness to build upon it, denies that all repeated phrases within an oral poem are necessarily formulaic. He first cites Menéndez Pidal's criticism of the Curtius school with respect to its unwillingness to distinguish between ordinary clichés of thought and literary *topoi*:

No distinguen entre aquello que se lo ocurre espontáneamente a cualquiera, a todos, y lo que lleva un sello personal; no pone[n] aparte las expresiones espontáneas, impuestas por la naturaleza misma de las cosas, por la lógica del pensamiento o de la imaginación, y el tópico literario, caracterizado por contener alguna singularidad de forma interna o externa, inventado por un autor, sea conocido o anónimo.[21]

Chasca draws an analogy between *topoi* and formulas and applies Menéndez Pidal's criticism to formulaic analysis, observing that great care should be taken to distinguish between "true" and "false" formulas. But the analogy is inappropriate.[22] The

[21] *El Arte juglaresco en el "Cantar de mio Cid"* (Madrid: Editorial Gredos, 1967), p. 40.

[22] It is nevertheless shared by Lionel J. Friedman who arrived at the irenic thought that "the traditionalist *themes* and *motifs* strikingly resemble Curtius' *topoi*. . . . Motif and *topos*, formula and cliché will probably one day coincide, so that individualists and traditionalists may lie down together, peaceful in the knowledge that they have unearthed little about origins but much more about medieval methods of composition." Review of Renate Hitze's *Studien zu Sprache und Stil der Kampfschilderungen in den "chansons de geste"* (*Romance Philology*, XXII (1969), 334–336). Robert Scholes and Robert Kellogg, in *The Nature of Narrative* (New York: Oxford

*topos* is a particular commonplace of thought which may be expressed in a variety of words; it is detected through its presence in writings from different periods. Menéndez Pidal's caution against those who mistake an ordinary cliché of thought for a *topos* is no doubt justified, and without it topical criticism would founder in a sea of vague, unprovable, and often highly improbable "causal" relationships. But the formula, unlike the *topos,* is a group of specific words; it represents a thought, but so do other groups of words which the poet chooses not to use; it is often shared by other poets and can have a life of its own within the oral tradition, but its function is defined basically by its habitual use within the technique of one poet. Chasca's distinction between "false" formulas, clichés of language common to singer and non-singer alike, and "true" formulas, presumably containing *alguna singularidad de forma interna o externa,* has no application to the formal study of epic, the analysis of whose technique is based not upon a qualitative distinction between cliché of language and literary repetition, but simply upon the usefulness to the singer of any habitually repeated phrase. It matters not one whit to the poet whether his nonsinging acquaintances employ a given expression or whether it belongs to the common fund of language patterns.[23] If that expression is useful to him for telling his story at a sustained pace before an audience, he will use it repeatedly, and it will thereby constitute a formula.

---

University Press, 1966), pp. 26–27, also propose that the term *theme,* used by Lord to denote the narration of a standard action (Rychner's and my *motifs*), be replaced by *topos,* since *theme* is already in wide usage with far different meanings. I prefer to leave the term *topos* alone. A precise vocabulary for the elements of narrative would distinguish, in the terminology, oral techniques from the devices of literate poets. The *topos,* as employed by Curtius, implies literary influence and a learned milieu. Its use in the criticism of oral poetry would only add to the instability of an already fluid terminology.

[23] I do believe that formulas are linked to oral composition and are incorporated into the special linguistic community of traditional technique. What I object to here is the assumption that if a group of words make up a cliché of language, they cannot be considered to constitute a formula.

Professor Italo Siciliano, in his *La Chanson de geste et l'épopée:
Mythes, Histoire, Poèmes*,[24] has put forth the idea that because re-
peated phrases are found in all types of poetry, it is not in formu-
laic composition that one will find a key to the genesis of the epic
genre. Unfortunately his view ignores the statistical reality of
the formula and shows a total lack of acquaintance with most
of Parry's work, and above all with his painstaking comparison
between the formulaic poetry of Homer and the repetitions found
in later Greek poetry and in Virgil. It is obvious from the phrases
of Virgil and the *Roman d'Enéas* cited by Professor Siciliano that
he too thinks of the formula as a cliché of thought rather than
as a group of particular words. He concludes that formulas are
prevalent only in battle scenes or to introduce speeches and
meals,[25] and seems to view them as a kind of lazy man's style, to
be turned on or off according to whether the poet is presenting a
scene of great thematic significance or merely filling in the back-
drop of common actions which can be described in no other way
than with repeated phrases.

These misconceptions are not atypical,[26] and although the

---

[24] Pp. 131–133.

[25] *La Chanson de geste et l'épopée*, pp. 131–133, 166n.

[26] In an article entitled "Notes on the Development of Formulaic Lan-
guage in Romanesque Poetry," in Pierre Gallais and Yves-Jean Riou, ed.,
*Mélanges offerts à René Crozet* (Poitiers: Société d'Etudes Médiévales,
1966), I, 427, Eugene Vance asserts that "a survey will reveal that no more
than ten to fifteen percent of the overall text of the Oxford manuscript may
be called 'formulaic.'" No reference is given to substantiate these figures,
presumably an intuitive estimate. The author goes on to speculate about
the distribution of formulas in the poem, saying that passages describing
weaponry, the movements of armies, and the actions of minor figures, par-
ticularly in combat, tend to be heavily formulaic, while passages of height-
ened interest such as those depicting Oliver's and Roland's deaths or
Charlemagne's reaction to his nephew's horn call rely only slightly on
formulas. This is inaccurate, and significantly the author omits it from his
*Reading the Song of Roland* (Englewood Cliffs, N.J.: Prentice-Hall, 1970).
One more example will suffice to illustrate an attitude which is little short
of universal among *chanson de geste* scholars. Julian Harris, discussing
"'Pleine sa hanste' in the *Chanson de Roland*," in Urban T. Holmes and
Kenneth R. Scholberg, ed., *French and Provençal Lexicography: Studies*

studies of Parry, Lord, and Rychner have established the all-pervasive character of the formulaic language and revealed that it is *the* language of oral poetry rather than a lower style unfit for the construction of literarily excellent scenes, the lack of concrete, comprehensive, and verifiable evidence has contributed to the perpetuation of misunderstandings. For this reason, rather than discuss only "representative" or especially significant phrases, I will consider quantitatively, in the following pages, the totality of formulas perceivable in the Oxford *Chanson de Roland,* so that an overall view may be had of at least one *chanson de geste,* before going on to discuss the way the poet employed them to compose his song, about whose literary excellence twentieth-century critics are in general agreement.

----

*Presented to Honor Alexander Herman Schutz* (Columbus: Ohio State University Press, 1964), pp. 100–117, writes: "Rychner has pointed out how the second-rate *chansons de geste* were made up largely of set expressions. Our expression, filling the first part of a decasyllabic line as it did and having a fine epic sound, was naturally used over and over by jongleurs who were incapable of inventing new ones." (p. 101) Professor Harris is applying the values of good literate authors to the *chansons de geste,* and not finding them reflected therein, concludes that the jongleurs (the *Roland's* excepted) lacked ability and originality.

# 2: Formulaic Language
# and Mode of Creation

THE THREE ALTERNATIVE modes of creation with which the critical tradition presents us for the archetype of the Oxford manuscript are: individual creation by a literate poet; fusion of a preexisting oral poem into a composite creation; or direct oral dictation of the first written version behind Oxford, which would then have been transmitted with only slight scribal variations.

A starting point for discussion of these three possibilities is the proposition that formulaic language and oral composition are inseparably linked. This statement is meant not as an *a priori* postulate, but rather as a conclusion based upon quantitative evidence. Before describing the sequence of deductions from which it is drawn, however, I would like to review previous comparisons made between long narrative poems in regard to their relative repetitiousness.

Several scholars have attempted to determine the formulaic density of whole poetic works, both oral and written, in differing national traditions, through the method, initiated by Milman Parry, of choosing short samples of the poems in question and underlining those phrases verifiable as semantic and syntactic formulas on the basis of the whole poetic material.[1] Since I am

---

[1] Robert E. Diamond is, to my knowledge, the only scholar who has improved upon this method to date. His study of "The Diction of the Signed Poems of Cynewulf," *Philological Quarterly*, XXXVIII (1959), 228–241, is limited to *Elene*, *Juliana*, the *Fates of the Apostles*, and *Christ II*,

dealing mainly with semantic formulas in this study, I will con-
sider here the information available for this type of formula and
leave aside for the moment the question of syntactic formulas,
termed by Lord "formulaic expressions."

There has been general agreement that any group of words
bounded on either side by a natural pause or caesura and re-
peated in substantially the same form (allowing for inversions,
paradigmatic variations and a few other admissible modifications)
should be counted as a formula.[2] Parry found that 50 and 54
percent of the first 25 lines of the *Iliad* and the *Odyssey*, respec-
tively, were made up of formulas.[3] To find repetitions, he searched
all 27,000 lines of the Homeric corpus as a referent for each
sample. Lord applied an analogous test to 15 lines of the *Song
of Bagdad*, recorded from the performance of Salih Ugljanin of
Novi Pazar, Yugoslavia, on the phonograph records of the Milman
Parry Collection of South Slavic Texts at Harvard University,
and uncovered formulas in 65 percent of the sample.[4] For veri-
fication he used 11 different songs by the same performer, total-

---

they being both the subject of the study and the referent. This approach is,
as we shall see, methodologically sound. In addition, he checked a random
sample of 456 "verses" (two "verses" make up a line in the terminology of
Old English metrics) against the whole Anglo-Saxon Poetic Records, and
uncovered 62.7 percent formulas. Less happily he relied on random samples
in his later study of *The Diction of the Anglo-Saxon Metrical Psalms*
("Janua Linguarum," Series Practica, X; The Hague: Mouton, 1963), dis-
cussed in greater detail below.

[2] The prime test of any formula is that it be useful to the poet in sustain-
ing his narrative, and occurrence within the text even as infrequently as
twice is proof of a hemistich's utility. Those occurring more often are even
more useful. Lest the reader remain sceptical, when quantitative analysis
is carried out for the purpose of comparing one poem's repetitions to an-
other's, the practice of counting phrases occurring twice is methodologically
justified as long as they are counted in all the works which enter into the
comparison, as is the case with the present study.

[3] "Studies in the Epic Technique of Oral Verse-Making. I: Homer and
Homeric Style," *Harvard Studies in Classical Philology*, XLI (1930), 73–147,
esp. 118–121; reprinted in *The Making of Homeric Verse: the Collected
Papers of Milman Parry* (Oxford: Clarendon Press, 1970), pp. 266–324.

[4] *The Singer of Tales* (Cambridge: Harvard University Press, 1960), p. 46.

ing 12,000 lines. On the basis of the entire Anglo-Saxon Poetic Records, Francis P. Magoun, Jr., found the first 25 lines of *Beowulf* to be 61 percent formulas,[5] and with the same referent 20 lines of the *Meters of Boethius* and 153 lines of the *Metrical Psalms* were estimated to be 50 and 60 percent formulaic respectively by Larry D. Benson and Robert E. Diamond.

The evidence in other studies has been based only on the poem under consideration rather than on an entire corpus or on several pieces, but unfortunately this method has been followed only for works which were considered, on external evidence, *not* to belong to the oral tradition: the Middle English *Havelok the Dane* and *Sir Gawain and the Green Knight*, the Old English *Daniel*, the verse part of Andrija Kačič-Miošić's history of the South Slavs (*Razgovor ugodni naroda slovinskoga*, 1759), and Matija Antun Reljkovič's satirical poem *Satir*. *Havelok's* two samples were 18 and 30 percent formulas, *Daniel's* 22 line sample 19 percent, while in *Sir Gawain* only one formula appeared in 18 lines. Thirty lines of the Slavic historical work were 27 percent formulas, and nine verses of *Satir* yielded none.[6]

Two serious difficulties arise from this survey of previous quantitative formula analyses. The first derives from the length of the material upon which one bases the evidence for the sample. Obviously the more lines one searches for identical phrases, the more formulas one is likely to uncover in the sample: the difference in formula densities based upon evidence from 27,000 lines and from 12,000 lines is substantial. The results have little meaning, then, *on a comparative basis*, unless one adjusts the larger figure by counting only those formulas discovered in the first 12,000 of the 27,000 lines. The purpose of the research we are considering here was to draw inferences about specific works on the basis of analogies with poems in various languages. There are three

[5] "The Oral-Formulaic Character of Anglo-Saxon Narrative Poetry," *Speculum*, XXVIII (1953), 446–467.

[6] Albert B. Lord, "Homer as Oral Poet," *Harvard Studies in Classical Philology*, LXXII (1968), 20–24.

absolute figures involved in the proportions upon which the analogies are based: the length of the sample, the number of formulas in the sample, and the number of lines in the referent which was searched to find evidence for these formulas. That the third figure is not included in the actual calculation of percentage does not lessen its significance. If samples are to be dependable, then the number of lines upon which the evidence for formulas is based must be identical in each case. Otherwise inferences drawn from the relative densities of the samples have no meaning.

My second, more fundamental, objection is to the size and choice of samples. The shorter the random sample, the less chance that it will reflect the characteristics of the entire text under consideration, and random samples taken from one place in the poem and counted in two-digit amounts are hopelessly inadequate. Public opinion polls use samples and are more often than not astonishingly accurate, but this is precisely because only samples which are microcosms of the whole are chosen, so that they faithfully reflect its qualitative make-up. Random samples—and the beginning of a poem, chosen because it happens to come first and not on account of its subject matter, is a random sample—cannot be relied upon to the same degree unless the sampling is conducted upon statistically valid principles. In the research conducted on formula density to date, the samples have been random, concentrated, and small. Corroboration for their unreliability is not difficult to find. In the *Singer of Tales*, Albert B. Lord picked a sample of the first 10 lines of the *Roland*'s laisse 105, and found 12 formulas, or 60 percent of the hemistichs sampled.[7] He could just as easily have chosen the 27 verses of laisses 34 and 35, an even longer sample, in which case the percentage would have dropped to 15, or the 23 verses of laisses 99 to 101, where the result would have been 76 percent, five times higher. Lord at no time claimed that the *Roland* as a whole was 60 percent formulas; he prudently argued that the presence of a passage 60 percent formulaic is a

[7] P. 202.

strong indication that the whole contains many formulas. Never-
theless, it is desirable that whatever method is employed be capa-
ble of revealing the quantity of formulas in the poem, and Parry's,
Lord's, and Magoun's figures have been interpreted by others as
statements of formulaic density for the poems in question. For
a random sample to be a realistic segment of the whole, it should
be much longer than those previously employed, as the figures
given below for hundred-line sections of the *Roland* demonstrate.[8]
In the case of *Roland* only the results for four-hundred-line seg-
ments approach within five percentage points of the figure for
the whole poem. Presumably this is also true for poems in other
national traditions. If, on the other hand, one elects the alterna-
tive of a smaller sample carefully chosen on the basis of its
subject matter, and attempts to select a typical passage, a micro-
cosm of the whole, the problem is no less thorny. Only 92 of
*Roland's* 290 laisses fall within the range of accuracy of the four-
hundred-line segments.[9] Certainly the motif which, from the
standpoint of subject matter, is most typical of the epic, the single
combat, is on the average more formulaic than the entire poem.
But if one then resigns oneself to taking a four-hundred-verse
sample, the methodological difficulty changes but by no means
disappears. It is, in fact, compounded beyond measure on the
level of verification, since a single man cannot practically search
for repetitions of four hundred separate lines (for the Old French
epics this would mean 800 potential formulas) without mecano-
graphic help. If electronic data processing equipment is employed,
it is no more difficult to give up sampling altogether and deter-
mine the real percentage of verifiable formulas for the whole work.
I have learned from frustrating experience that the computer-
aided method is indeed the only practical and accurate way of
accomplishing this task. When it is applied, the first difficulty
discussed above, that of the varying number of lines searched
in order to detect formulas, is also circumvented, for with this
method the size of the population and the size of the referent are

---

[8] See p. 37.                              [9] *Ibid.*

identical, both being equal to the entire poem. Statistics collected
on this basis can be compared without adjustment, because the
relationship between the referent and the population is always
constant.

The results of sampling are summed up in the following table:

| poem | length of sample(s) | referent | length of referent | percentage of formulas |
|---|---|---|---|---|
| Satir | 8 lines | | 2203 lines | 0 |
| Sir Gawain | 18 lines | entire poem | 2530 lines | negligible |
| Havelok | ? | entire poem | 3001 lines | 18, 30 |
| Daniel | 22 lines | entire poem | 4019 lines | 19 |
| History of Slavs | 30 lines | verse sections of part two | 3208 lines | 27 |
| Metrical Psalms | 153 lines | Anglo-Saxon Poetic Records | 30,000 lines | 50 |
| Iliad | 25 lines | Homeric corpus | 27,000 lines | 50 |
| Odyssey | 25 lines | Homeric corpus | 27,000 lines | 54 |
| Meters of Boethius[10] | 20 lines | Anglo-Saxon Poetic Records | 30,000 lines | 60 |
| Roland | 10 lines | entire poem | 4002 lines | 60 |
| Beowulf | 25 lines | Anglo-Saxon Poetic Records | 30,000 lines | 61 |
| Song of Bagdad | 15 lines | songs of the same singer | 12,000 lines | 65 |

In all these cases the actual formulaic density is unknown, al-
though one is at liberty to assume that a poem whose random
sample yields more than 50 percent formulas is more likely to be
a product of the oral tradition than one for which the sample is
27 percent formulaic or less. Nonetheless the degree of proba-
bility for such an assumption is slight.

The computer-aided method of determining the formulaic con-
tent of an entire poem on the basis of repetitions within the poem
itself has produced more consistent results. In addition to the

---

[10] For a discussion of the validity of the figures for this poem, see below,
pp. 31–33.

*Couronnement de Louis*, to which I have devoted a previous study,[11] and *Roland*, I applied it to *Gormont et Isembart*, the *Chanson de Guillaume*, the *Charroi de Nîmes*, the *Prise d'Orange*, *Raoul de Cambrai*, the *Pèlerinage de Charlemagne à Jérusalem et à Constantinople*, the *Moniage Guillaume* (longer version, sometimes called *Moniage II*), the first 2700 verses of the *Siège de Barbastre*, *Buevon de Conmarchis*,[12] the first 2695 verses of the *Roman d'Enéas*,[13] and the decasyllabic *Roman d'Alexandre* from the Venice manuscript.[14] Most of these poems employ a

[11] "Formulas in the *Couronnement de Louis*," *Romania*, LXXXVII (1966), 315–344. The text used was E. Langlois, ed., *Le Couronnement de Louis* (2nd ed.; Paris: Champion, 1925).

[12] The method employed for the *Siège de Barbastre* and *Buevon de Conmarchis*, though just as effective as the word-group concordance method described in Chapter I, differed from it in its mechanics. It consisted in analysing each hemistich of the two poems into a code based on semantic fields and then concording on the basis of the code. I later abandoned this method for the present one because the latter requires no preliminary analysis. See my dissertation, "Formulaic Language in the Old French Epic Poems *Le Siège de Barbastre* and *Buevon de Conmarchis*," Ohio State University, 1964.

[13] This number was chosen to provide a romance of equal length with the *Couronnement de Louis*. Likewise for the *Siège de Barbastre* I only tested the part which inspired Adenet's *Buevon de Conmarchis*. I realized only later that the size of the text is irrelevant if the population and the referent are identical.

[14] The following editions were employed: Alphonse Bayot, ed., *Gormont et Isembart* (3rd ed., Classiques français du moyen âge, XIV; Paris: Champion, 1931); Duncan McMillan, ed., *La Chanson de Guillaume* (2 vols., Société des anciens textes français; Paris: Picard, 1949–1950); J.-L. Perrier, ed., *Le Charroi de Nîmes* (CFMA, LXVI; Paris: Champion, 1931); Blanche Katz, ed., *La Prise d'Orenge* (New York: King's Crown Press, 1947); Paul Meyer and Auguste Longnon, eds., *Raoul de Cambrai, chanson de geste* (SATF; Paris: Firmin Didot, 1882); Eduard Koschwitz, *Karls des Grossen Reise nach Jerusalem und Constantinopel* (7th ed.; Heilbronn: 1925); Wilhelm Cloetta, ed., *Les deux rédactions en vers du Moniage Guillaume* (2 vols., SATF; Paris: Champion, 1906–1911); J.-L. Perrier, ed., *Le Siège de Barbastre* (CFMA, LIV; Paris: Champion, 1926); Albert Henry, ed., *Les Œuvres d'Adenet le Roi*, II, *Buevon de Conmarchis* (Bruges: "de Tempel," 1953); J.-J. Salverda de Grave, ed., *Enéas, roman du XIIe siècle* (2 vols., CFMA, XLIV, LXII; Paris: Champion, 1925–1931); Milan S. LaDu, ed., *The Medieval French Roman d'Alexandre*, I (Princeton University Press, 1937).

ten-syllable line, the exceptions being *Gormont et Isembart* and
*Enéas,* both octosyllabic, and the dodecasyllabic *Pèlerinage, Siège*
and *Buevon.* The figures for the 13 poems are given below:

| poem | hemistichs | repeated hemistichs | percentage of repeated hemistichs | approximate[15] date | versification |
|---|---|---|---|---|---|
| *Buevon* | 7762 | 1187 | 15 | 1269–1285 | dodecasyllabic |
| *Enéas* | 5390 | 953 | 16 | 1150–1160 | octosyllabic |
| *Alexandre* | 1614 | 277 | 17 | 1150 | decasyllabic |
| *Pèlerinage* | 1740 | 402 | 23 | 1100 | dodecasyllabic |
| *Siège* | 5314 | 1221 | 23 | 1180 | dodecasyllabic |
| *Moniage* | 13258 | 3308 | 24 | 1180 | decasyllabic |
| *Gormont* | 1318 | 380 | 29 | 1068–1104 | octosyllabic |
| *Charroi* | 2972 | 851 | 29 | 1135–1165 | decasyllabic |
| *Guillaume* | 7108 | 2172 | 31 | 1075–1125 | decasyllabic |
| *Raoul* | 11110 | 3630 | 33 | 1190 | decasyllabic |
| *Couronnement* | 5390 | 2021 | 37 | 1131–1150 | decasyllabic |
| *Prise* | 3774 | 1464 | 39 | 1150–1165 | decasyllabic |

Only those hemistichs repeated within a given poem in substan-
tially the same form have been counted as formulas. If all the
hemistichs of all twelve poems were to be compared to each other
(66,750 possible formulas), more formulas would be detected,

The Aebischer and Favati editions of the *Pèlerinage de Charlemagne,* the
Régnier edition of the *Prise d'Orange* and that of the *Charroi de Nîmes* by
G. de Poerck *et al.* were all published after I had made the concordances
to these poems.

[15] Dating is based on the following authorities: *Buevon:* Albert Henry,
*Les Œuvres d'Adenet le Roi,* I, 47; *Enéas:* Salverda de Grave, *Enéas,* I, xix–
xx; *Alexandre:* E.C. Armstrong, ed., *The Medieval French Roman d'Alex-
andre,* II, x; *Pèlerinage:* Koschwitz, *Karls des Grossen Reise,* p. xxv; *Siège:*
Raymond Weeks, "The *Siège de Barbastre,*" *Romanic Review,* X (1919),
287; *Moniage:* Cloetta, *Les deux rédactions en vers,* II, 269; *Gormont:*
Ferdinand Lot, "Encore *Gormond et Isembard,*" *Romania,* LIII (1927), re-
printed in Robert Bossuat, ed., *Etudes sur les légendes épiques françaises*
(Paris: Champion, n.d.), p. 342; *Charroi:* Jean Frappier, *Les Chansons de
geste du cycle de Guillaume d'Orange,* II (Paris: SEDES, 1965), p. 186;
*Guillaume:* Lot, *Etudes,* p. 242; *Raoul:* Paul Meyer and Ernest Longnon,
*Raoul de Cambrai,* pp. lxx–lxxi; *Couronnement:* Frappier, *Cycle de Guil-
laume,* II, 59; *Prise d'Orange: ibid.,* II, 258.

but this is a task which, because of the expense it would entail
and the difficulty of correlating the disparate orthographies and
dialectal traits of the texts,[16] I am not prepared to undertake. It
would, in addition, be a more artificial approach to the problem
of formulaic language, since one would be considering resem-
blances between minute segments of texts composed as much
as two centuries apart in widely separated geographical areas.[17]
By confining the examination of each poem's formulas to those
which can be distinguished through a scrutiny of the poem itself,
we are at least assured of working with phrases which possessed
an identity as formulas in the mind of the poet who uttered them.
The possible objection that the material is incomplete, since it
does not include formulas which occur only once in a given
work but would be recognizable as formulas if other *chansons*
were searched for them, is, in a sense, valid, but completeness is
unattainable without a living oral tradition to provide the context
within which the poet's formula-generating abilities develop and
within which they can be judged as a totality. Students of medi-
eval French literature consider themselves fortunate if they can
date a text within ten or twenty years of its actual time of com-
position. It is asking too much, in all but a few cases, to attempt

[16] In practical terms this would require the preparation of a standardized
line, in, say, the *francien* dialect, for each of the thirty-three thousand lines
in question. While admittedly a formidable undertaking, its achievement is
not impossible: an analogous project has been begun for the relatively
limited corpus of Anglo-Saxon verse by Francis P. Magoun and Jess B. Bes-
singer. See Bessinger's *Short Dictionary of Anglo-Saxon Poetry in a Nor-
malized Early West-Saxon Orthography* (Toronto: University of Toronto
Press, 1960). A computer-generated concordance could then be compiled
based on the standardized lines, but printing out the original text. A suitable
program, called DISCON, has been developed by Sidney M. Lamb and
Laura Gould, who describe it in *Type-Lists, Indexes and Concordances
from Computers* (New Haven: Yale University Linguistics Automation
Project, 1967).

[17] "Not only the quantity but also the provenance of the material is of
importance for formula analysis. One must work with material of a single
singer at a given time, and then outwards by concentric circles to his group,
district, and so forth. Otherwise one uses material which is irrelevant to
the song and singer under scrutiny."—Lord, *Singer of Tales*, p. 289, note 11.

to find poems which we can be sure were sung in temporal and geographical proximity to those now extant in manuscript. The overriding consideration in a comparative study such as this is that the same criteria be applied rigorously to each poem. As long as this requirement is adhered to, analogies are valid. The formulas which are undistinguishable are undistinguishable in all the poems without discrepancy, and on this basis the data may be validly compared.

What conclusions can be drawn from them? There is no correlation between the percentage of formulas and either the dates or the lengths of poems. Thus it would be gratuitous to assume without further evidence that a gradual watering-down of the traditional style of *chansons de geste* took place through the course of the twelfth century. The most formulaic poem, *La Prise d'Orange*, is customarily dated around the middle of the century, while the early *Pèlerinage de Charlemagne* is near the lower limit of *chansons de geste*.[18] Neither does the type of

---

[18] To date poems on internal evidence is always hazardous. As a check on the relationship of formula density to dating, here is another set of dates taken from Raphael Levy, *Chronologie approximative de la littérature française du moyen âge* (Beihefte zur *Zeitschrift für romanische Philologie*, XCVIII; Tübingen: Niemeyer, 1957):

| poem | date | percentage of formulas |
|---|---|---|
| *Gormont* | 1125 | 29 |
| *Couronnement* | 1131 | 37 |
| *Guillaume* | 1140 | 31 |
| *Charroi* | 1144 | 29 |
| *Prise d'Orange* | 1148 | 39 |
| *Pèlerinage* | 1149 | 23 |
| *Alexandre* | ca. 1160 | 17 |
| *Enéas* | 1160 | 16 |
| *Raoul* | 1180 | 33 |
| *Moniage Guillaume* | 1185 | 24 |
| *Siège de Barbastre* | 1150–1200 | 23 |
| *Buevon* | 1275 | 15 |

Although Levy follows other authorities, there is no more correlation between formula density and date in his chronology than in the one I have adopted.

versification appear to be significant, since the octosyllabic *Gormont et Isembart* is near the middle of the grouping, far from *Enéas*; the alexandrine *Siège de Barbastre* and *Pèlerinage de Charlemagne* both rank higher than *Alexandre* and *Enéas*, which separate them from *Buevon de Conmarchis*, also in alexandrines.

Only one consistent explanation for the rankings is plausible: there is a marked distinction between the *chansons de geste* and the *romans courtois Enéas* and *Alexandre*. *Buevon de Conmarchis*, which contains a lower proportion of repeated hemistichs than any other poem treated, would seem to invalidate this distinction. But *Buevon*, authored by the unquestionably literate Adenet le Roi, who is known to have written the courtly romance *Cléomades*, is as much a product of the written art as *Enéas* or *Alexandre*, since it is the creation of a learned author and reflects courtly conventions in many of its aspects.[19] *Buevon*, *Enéas* and *Alexandre*, taken together, have an average 16 percent density of repeated hemistichs, while the mean percentage for the nine *chansons de geste* is 29.8.

The three romances present a strikingly uniform profile. It has always been recognized that writers repeat themselves, and the cliché or *cheville* or filler has never been accorded more than universal disapproval in the annals of literary criticism. Although the repetitions are not here under qualitative judgment but rather under quantitative estimation, the two aspects are relevant to each other. A filler (functional aspect) is cliché (valuational aspect) because of its statistical characteristics, since frequent oc-

---

[19] Thus Albert Henry, Adenet's editor, compares *Buevon* to the *Siège de Barbastre*: "Avec le *Siège de Barbastre* nous avons affaire à un tout homogène: matière de chanson de geste, style de chanson de geste, style un peu mécanisé déjà, mais s'adaptant parfaitement à la matière qu'il revêt. Style carré, dominé par le vers dont l'indépendance, sinon l'absolue souveraineté, se marque, presque partout, par la fixité de la césure et l'ignorance de l'enjambement, style précis, brutal, dur et limité comme une cuirasse. L'adaptation d'Adenet a quelque chose d'hybride et de trouble: sa démarche manque de décision."—*Les Œuvres d'Adenet le Roi*, II, 28. For a detailed treatment of Adenet's versification and formulas, see my dissertation cited above, note 12.

currence diminishes its value in the reader's eye. There is a continuum along which clichés can be ranged: the less rare the occurrence, the less the semantic weight and literary value. The data for repeated hemistichs in the romances suggest, however, that in the overall view the proportion of repetitions in written poetry is relatively constant. Since only eleventh, twelfth and thirteenth-century texts are in question, this conclusion should be regarded as tentative until it has been tested against factual analyses of works composed in other periods and other languages, and by writers of differing stature as well.

The *chansons de geste,* on the other hand, differ widely in proportion of formulas. Another technique is evident behind this phenomenon, a technique in which recourse to formulas is permissible and even desirable. The scribes who took down the cyclical manuscripts in which so many works of the *geste de Guillaume* have survived—among them the *Siège de Barbastre,* the *Moniage Guillaume,* the *Charroi de Nîmes,* the *Couronnement de Louis,* the *Prise d'Orange*—presumably imposed a selectivity of their own. At the very least we cannot assume that they chose the worst versions of these poems for the *manuscrits de luxe* destined to be read to noble patrons. And yet the *Couronnement de Louis* and the *Prise d'Orange* are the most repetitious of our eleventh, twelfth and thirteenth-century narratives. The terms cliché and stereotype, with their pejorative connotations, are applied with no regard to medieval taste when they are used to describe the formulaic style of these poems in which such a wide latitude of repetition was accepted.

The poems analysed here were not picked at random. Their choice reflected a desire to test the hypothesis whose formulation has colored Old French epic criticism for the last fifteen years: the conclusions to Jean Rychner's *La Chanson de geste: essai sur l'art épique des jongleurs.*[20] It may be put as follows: the early *chanson de geste* is the manuscript reflection of a genre which lived and flourished in the state of improvised performance be-

[20] Geneva: Droz, 1955.

fore an audience; evidence for this oral existence is found in the highly stylized narrative on all its levels, but most of all on that of the standard scene (motif) and the standard phrase (formula), the very means through which improvisational performance was made possible. To check the hypothesis on the basic, formulaic, level, I chose to scrutinize the formula content of the nine *chansons de geste* which Professor Rychner had analysed in his book,[21] and I added the *Siège de Barbastre* so as to be able to compare differing realizations of the same narrative material, that poem being a close relative to the source of Adenet le Roi's *Buevon de Conmarchis*. As a test I applied the same criteria to the *Roman d'Alexandre*, an early romance in a versification with the same syllable count as that of the *chansons de geste*; the *Roman d'Enéas*, a typical octosyllabic romance; and *Buevon de Conmarchis*, a fairly late reworking of an epic legend, as representatives of a genre which, if Professor Rychner's hypothesis turned out to be true, would not be expected to have been composed through the medium of formulas. If they had encompassed as many repetitions as the *chansons de geste*, or even approached the same degree of repetitiveness, his theory would have been gravely weakened. Any repeated half-verse in the romances, allowing as always for paradigmatic variations, inversions, lexical changes involving function words, and, in these poems, rhyme, was considered to be analogous to the epic formula and counted in the tally.

The results tend to confirm the hypothesis. They indicate a quantitative difference of 16 percent against 29.8 percent between the number of repetitions in the works known to have been composed in writing and those deemed by Rychner to have been improvised orally and only later committed to writing. This fundamental difference is basic to any understanding of the nature of formulaic language. It is perceived not primarily through the comparison of one work to another, but above all through

[21] Results of the analysis of the *Chanson de Roland* are given below, p. 34.

the analysis of works representative enough to stand, collectively, for the two genres. Henceforth these quantitative differences and all they imply should be taken into account in any definition of the *chanson de geste* in contradistinction to the romance.

Albert B. Lord has given his estimate of the threshold of formula density between oral and written works: "So far, I believe, we can conclude that a pattern of 50 or 60 percent formula or formulaic, with 10 to perhaps 25 percent straight formula, indicates clearly literary or written composition."[22] My quantitative examination of Old French narrative verse does not include figures for what Lord terms "formulaic expressions" and what I call "syntactic formulas," some examples of which will be treated in Chapter 5. But that part of Lord's statement which is directly relevant here, namely his estimate of "straight formula" density, closely parallels my own, in spite of the varying criteria by which his base statistics were collected. I would be more specific about the threshold and say that, in general, if an Old French narrative poem is less than 20 percent straight repetition, it probably derives from literary, or written, creation. When the formula density exceeds 20 percent, it is strong evidence of oral composition, and the probability rises as the figure increases over 20 percent. Conversely, as the formula density approaches the threshold of 20 percent, other factors, such as the presence of unrefined popular legends, formulas of oral narration, statements that the work is being sung, and so on, should be accorded more and more weight in the decision about the orality of the work in question. These general remarks apply to tests of individual poems. But taken as a whole, the set of figures reveals a distinction on the level of diction, between the two medieval modes of narration, *chanson de geste* and romance, long recognized as discrete in the tradition of scholarship and criticism. They differ not just in subject matter, versification, psychological content and thematic aspects, but in the most fundamental characteristic of all, the art of combining words. The 23 and 24 percent densities for the

[22] "Homer as Oral Poet," p. 24.

*Pèlerinage de Charlemagne,* the *Siège de Barbastre* and the *Moniage Guillaume* must be viewed with this in mind. One might not find 23 or 24 percent a convincing figure in itself, but it gathers credulity when one recalls that all the works traditionally called *chansons de geste* fall on one side of the threshold while those known as *romans* fall on the other. This combination of considerations convinces me personally of the oral nature of these three poems, which do not differ significantly from the more obviously formulaic *chansons de geste* in their qualitative aspects either. I invite comments on this interpretation, however, for I recognize that it is a delicate question, not to be settled lightly. Certainly for *Gormont et Isembart,* the *Charroi de Nîmes,* the *Chanson de Guillaume, Raoul de Cambrai,* the *Couronnement de Louis* and the *Prise d'Orange,* the case is clear. These six, and, I believe, the three less formulaic *chansons de geste,* provide convincing evidence that formulaic style and oral composition are inseparably linked.

The mourning over the demise of the theory of oral composition which greeted publication of Larry D. Benson's 1966 article, "The Literary Character of Anglo-Saxon Formulaic Poetry,"[23] was, then, to say the least, premature. Lionel J. Friedman claimed that Benson's work "disprov[ed] the second half of the Parry-Lord axiom that 'oral poetry is composed entirely of formulas . . . while lettered poetry is never formulaic'" since "if formulaic diction characterizes both kinds of poetry, it is no touchstone."[24] Morton W. Bloomfield more cautiously called for a reexamination of the theory, remarking that the optimism of those convinced that it is being accepted more and more widely as it applies to Old English poetry "perhaps . . . reflects the climate of four years ago" [1965].[25] But Benson's evaluation, circumspect in other re-

[23] *PMLA,* LXXXI (1966), 334–341.

[24] In his review of Renate Hitze's *Studien zu Sprache und Stil der Kampf-schilderungen in den "chansons de geste"* in *Romance Philology,* XXII (1969), 334–336.

[25] Review of Robert Creed, *Old English Poetry, Fifteen Essays,* in *Comparative Literature,* XXI (1969), 285–286.

spects, is unfortunately based upon a formulaic analysis which does not hold up under scrutiny.

A large portion of his evidence comes from two studies by Robert E. Diamond, "The Diction of the Signed Poems of Cynewulf,"[26] and *The Diction of the Anglo-Saxon Metrical Psalms*.[27] In the first of these Diamond examined every line of Cynewulf's four poems, matching them up against the totality of the poems and against the entire Anglo-Saxon poetic corpus; in the second, he chose, at random, about fifteen lines every fifteen pages, eleven passages totaling 153 lines, and compared them to the Anglo-Saxon Poetic Records. The sampling method employed for the *Metrical Psalms* is superior to previous attempts in that the samples are gathered from throughout the work and together constitute a sizable body of poetic material. Cynewulf's formulas were examined not on the basis of samples at all, but on entire poems. The two studies are, then, statistically valid and much more homogeneous than any comparisons made previous to Diamond's work.

Benson also added two studies of his own, one of the *Phoenix* poem, the other of the *Meters of Boethius*, both based on samples checked against the Anglo-Saxon Poetic Records, and, as samples, of doubtful reliability.

But the crux of the matter is this: when Benson begins to draw conclusions from Diamond's statistically reliable material and his own counts, technical vocabulary obscures the true significance of his results. Thus he finds that "a full analysis of the 3500 verses (1750 lines) of the *Meters* [*of Boethius*] shows that they contain about 250 whole-verse formulas used around 700 times; one such formula, '*ealla gesceafta,*' is used at least twenty-two times. Diamond . . . found that this sort of 'whole-verse' formula accounts for 19.9 percent of Cynewulf's verses, 1037 out of 5194 (2598 lines)."[28] Obviously the term "verse" is being used here, as it commonly is in the discussion of Old English poetry, to mean

---

[26] *Philological Quarterly*, XXXVIII (1959), 228–241.
[27] The Hague: Mouton, 1963.     [28] P. 229, note 19.

the "A" or the "B" part of the line, equivalent to what I have
termed, following usage, a "hemistich,"[29] and not to the Old
French verse, which is a whole poetic line. The term "whole-verse
formula" may be misleading when it is employed in the context
of the theory of oral poetry, especially since the problem of whole
formulaic verses, that is formulas which run from the beginning
of the poetic line to the end, has already drawn the attention of
scholars concerned with formulaic language.[30]

Therefore since Benson and Diamond found that 19.9 percent
of Cynewulf's lines and approximately 20 percent of the *Meters
of Boethius* are "whole-verse" formulas, these are the figures
which should have been compared with the results of previous
samplings and which should now be compared with the formulaic
analyses of Old French narrative poetry—although obviously a
truly accurate estimation would result only from a comparison of
hypothetically oral Old English verse with learned Old English
works—since what they call a "whole-verse" formula is what
Lord and Parry termed simply a "formula."[31] The higher figures
for their analyses, 43 percent for Cynewulf (restricting the evi-
dence to Cynewulf's works themselves) and 60 percent for the
sample of the *Meters*, really encompass what Lord calls "formu-
las and formulaic expressions"—my "semantic and syntactic
formulas"—and are consequently not to be compared with my
figures or with those cited from previous researchers. In con-
clusion, if the *Meters* and Cynewulf were counted in with the

[29] Strictly speaking, a poetic unit in the Old French decasyllabic epic,
either 4 or 6 syllables, is either not quite or just more than half a line.
This is often the case with Old English "verses", which are based on stress
counting rather than on syllable count.

[30] See, for example, Milman Parry, "Whole Formulaic Verses in Greek
and Southslavic Heroic Songs," *TAPA*, LXIV (1933), 179–197.

[31] Thus Lord, "Homer as Oral Poet," p. 26: "It is important to work from
line break to line break rather than with simple repetition of words and
phrases by themselves, because it is in terms of parts of a line, I believe,
rather than words in themselves, that the singer thinks. A formula extends
from one break to another. . . . I think that the repeated words or groups of
words are significant only when they stretch from break to break."

Old English narrative poems, they would represent marginal cases at 20 percent and slightly below, and could not be called oral from internal evidence. Even in the context of previous samplings, Cynewulf's poems and the *Meters* would be relatively thin in formulaic content, that is, close to the bottom of the list.

Benson's work shows not that the Anglo-Saxon poets in question, certainly learned and literate men, composed in the medium of formulaic language employed by oral poets, but merely that they had formulas in their poems, which is quite another state of affairs. There is nothing to prevent a learned author from using formulas, but as far as is now known no learned author has ever made formulaic language the ordinary medium of his writings. Only a strictly methodical approach to this problem will yield results. The question of whether or not a "transitional" text is possible is not yet closed by any means. But far from disproving the connection between formulaic language and orally improvised composition, Benson merely raises some interesting possibilities about the influence of traditional language on learned poetry which should be pursued with more rigorous method by scholars in the Old English area.

I have until this point omitted any account of the *Chanson de Roland*'s formula density, since this poem has, because of its literary excellence, been accorded a place apart from the body of *chansons de geste* in the critical literature.[32] It seemed desirable to establish the connection between formulaic language and oral composition without the *Roland* material so as to provide a context against which the formulaic aspects of the poem could be placed in perspective.

[32] Maurice Delbouille saw Rychner's exception of the *Roland* from the orally composed genre as a weakness in his theory: "Que voilà une belle et grande exception aux règles du jeu et du genre! Et qui constitue, contre l'idée du jongleur-improvisateur et du poème oral, la plus redoutable des objections!" "Les Chansons de geste et le livre," *La Technique littéraire des Chansons de geste: Actes du Colloque de Liège (septembre 1957)* (Bibliothèque de la Faculté de Philosophie et Lettres de l'Université de Liège, CL; Paris: "Les Belles Lettres," 1959), p. 307n.

Using the guidelines set out above, one can verify 2814 for-
mulas in the Oxford *Roland*,[33] or 35.2 percent of the 8004 hemi-
stichs in the poem.[34] This figure was arrived at through a pains-
taking process of counting, recounting, and testing which leaves
little room for error. Certainly if there is an error—that is by no
means impossible—it has been on the conservative side, for
certain hemistichs, although employed as formulas by the jong-
leur, may contain orthographic variations so diverse that they are
not perceived in the concordance as formulas. If the possibility of
error is set at 1 percent of the total number of hemistichs, this
would allow for my overlooking 80 formulas, which I consider
extremely unlikely, since that would amount to nearly 3 percent
of the actual number of formulas uncovered. Most probably,
then, the *Chanson de Roland* is formulaic to a degree of 35.2 per-
cent, with the possible addition of one percent as an allowance
for error.

Some critics, willing to concede oral composition for the earliest
stages of the Old French epic (Menéndez Pidal's *état latent*) but
reluctant to admit that its masterpiece could result from this
process, have assumed that the *Roland* poet took previously
existing poetic legends handed down by oral tradition and, pen in
hand, reworked them into the predecessor of the Oxford version,
ordering the material in such a way as to create a consummate
work of art. But there is no reason to place the *Roland* in a differ-

[33] The edition was that of Raoul Mortier, *Les Textes de la Chanson de
Roland*: vol. I, *Le Manuscrit d'Oxford* (Paris: Editions de la Geste Francor,
1940), which follows Oxford closely. The reader is invited to check my
figures through the use of the *Concordance to the Chanson de Roland*
(Columbus: Ohio State University Press, 1970).

[34] In his *Formulaic Diction and Thematic Composition in the Chanson de
Roland* (University of North Carolina Studies in the Romance Languages
and Literatures, XXXVI; Chapel Hill: University of North Carolina Press,
1961), Stephen G. Nichols' conclusions on the formulaic density of *Roland*
are curiously incomplete, as they concern only the first hemistichs of vv.
1–2000. He found 1157 "formulas" but it is obvious from the examples in
the schematic appendix that he was counting syntactic as well as semantic
patterns.

ent category from the other *chansons de geste* on the basis of formula density. Indeed *Roland* is one of the more formulaic works examined, its nearest neighbors in this respect being *Raoul de Cambrai*, slightly less formulaic at 33 percent, and the *Couronnement de Louis*, 37 percent. It contains proportionally more formulas than the *Chanson de Guillaume*, the *Charroi de Nîmes*, *Gormont et Isembart*, the *Moniage Guillaume II*, the *Siège de Barbastre* and the *Pèlerinage de Charlemagne*. Only the *Couronnement de Louis* and the *Prise d'Orange*, the latter occupying the maximum position, a mere two percentage points higher than the *Couronnement de Louis*—which Jean Rychner estimated, in a remarkably accurate intuitive judgment, to be the most formulaic of the twelfth-century works he treated[35]—surpass it in the relative abundance of repeated hemistichs. Since a high formula content is evidence of oral composition, the *Chanson de Roland* which we have in the Oxford version must be regarded as having descended in some way from the oral tradition, formulaic analysis having shown it to possess a typical formulaic profile.

We are now in a better position to consider the three alternatives for the *Roland's* mode of creation. The method will consist, again, of taking each alternative as a hypothesis to be measured against quantitative evidence for formulaic composition.

If several hypotheses are available to explain the existence of a given phenomenon, then the one which exhibits the greatest simplicity is preferred. The supposition that *Roland* was created in writing does not have the advantage of simplicity, as it necessitates a double assumption which has never been proven and may well be unprovable: that a literate poet would and could author a poem by means of formulas. Parry argued that it would be more difficult to construct a formula system than to write a poem without formulas because of the complexity of possible metric patterns in the Greek hexameter and what he saw as the economy (one formula for every idea in a given metrical context) of the Homeric formula system. But this argument applies as well to

[35] *La Chanson de geste*, p. 149.

other bodies of poetry: there is no reason to assume that a literate poet would wish to employ the same phrases many times over in his poem to the extent that fully one-third of his diction is repeated. The oral poet, we know from Lord's study of the Yugoslavian milieu, has a good motive for repeating himself with stylized phrases, namely the need to sing verses before a demanding audience at the rate of ten to twenty decasyllabic lines per minute,[36] a pace far too rapid to permit the constant generation of unique word combinations. The proponent of a hypothesis of written composition for *Roland*, then, merely substitutes one difficulty for another: having assumed that the poem derives from a process of composition in writing, he must show that extensive use of formulas is desirable and possible for a poet whose means of creating is the written word. His adversaries, on the other hand, have been provided by Lord and Parry with compelling proof that formulaic composition is the ordinary medium of contemporary Yugoslavian and ancient Greek oral poets, and that they use no other means of composing.

The second alternative, that the *Roland* is a composite creation, the result of a writer of genius coming into contact with the oral tradition and transforming a more or less primitive poem about Roncevaux into the magnificent version which comes down to us in the Oxford manuscript, deserves weighty consideration, all the more so now that concrete evidence for *Roland*'s formulas is available. For the skeletal hypothesis can now be fleshed out with additional information about the poem's style.

One is forced to speculate about the exact nature of the linguistic, stylistic, and esthetic changes the *remanieur de génie* would have made in the poem during the course of his intervention. If he did not himself possess formulaic skill, the formulas found in Oxford would derive from the preexisting oral tradition into the course of which the literate poet is presumed to have intervened. A further look at the formulaic density of *Roland*

[36] *Singer of Tales*, p. 17.

would, in this case, allow one to pick out those parts of the poem where the late *remanieur* reworked the formulaic text with literate, that is nonformulaic, additions of his own.

Distribution of formulas over the body of the poem is shown in the following set of figures. The Oxford manuscript has been broken down into groups of 100 verses, and the number and proportion of formulas within each group is noted.

| verses | formulas | per-centage | verses | formulas | per-centage |
|---|---|---|---|---|---|
| 1– 100 | 78 | 39 | 2001–2100 | 56 | 28 |
| 101– 200 | 94 | 47 | 2101–2200 | 70 | 35 |
| 201– 300 | 63 | 31.5 | 2201–2300 | 62 | 31 |
| 301– 400 | 48 | 24 | 2301–2400 | 69 | 34.5 |
| 401– 500 | 55 | 27.5 | 2401–2500 | 63 | 31.5 |
| 501– 600 | 91 | 45.5 | 2501–2600 | 44 | 22 |
| 601– 700 | 66 | 33 | 2601–2700 | 56 | 28 |
| 701– 800 | 75 | 37.5 | 2701–2800 | 72 | 36 |
| 801– 900 | 67 | 33.5 | 2801–2900 | 67 | 33.5 |
| 901–1000 | 74 | 37 | 2901–3000 | 64 | 32 |
| 1001–1100 | 75 | 37.5 | 3001–3100 | 76 | 38 |
| 1101–1200 | 78 | 39 | 3101–3200 | 54 | 27 |
| 1201–1300 | 104 | 52 | 3201–3300 | 79 | 39.5 |
| 1301–1400 | 70 | 35 | 3301–3400 | 86 | 43 |
| 1401–1500 | 64 | 32 | 3401–3500 | 80 | 40 |
| 1501–1600 | 83 | 41.5 | 3501–3600 | 68 | 34 |
| 1601–1700 | 76 | 38 | 3601–3700 | 51 | 25.5 |
| 1701–1800 | 67 | 33.5 | 3701–3800 | 60 | 30 |
| 1801–1900 | 73 | 36.5 | 3801–3900 | 52 | 26 |
| 1901–2000 | 77 | 38.5 | 3901–4002 | 63 | 30.9 |

No group of one hundred lines is less than 22 percent nor more than 52 percent formulas. While these extremes are far enough apart that, if viewed in isolation, they would appear to constitute a significant difference, when taken in the context of all 40 hundred-line segments, they merely illustrate that the *Roland* is not sporadically, but uniformly, formulaic. All the segments are more formulaic than the 807 decasyllabic verses of the *Roman d'Alexandre*, the most repetitious of the romances tested at 17 percent.

Which passages are most likely to have been inserted or reworked by an intervening literate poet? For a clue to the percentage below which one might consider nonformulaic composition to be at work, let us turn to the table of relative formulaic density for Old French narrative poems. There it appears that the most repetitive romance is 17 percent repeated hemistichs, while the least formulaic epic is 23 percent. The mean percentage for all the *chansons de geste* is 29.7.[37] The *Pèlerinage de Charlemagne*, the *Siège de Barbastre* and the *Moniage Guillaume*, lowest among the epics on the list, are all within one percentage point of each other, at 23 to 24 percent formulaic. Since only one *Roland* passage is less than 23 percent formulas, one can identify little as the possible intervention of a literate poet in the text on this basis. All hundred-line segments except verses 2501 to 2600 are more formulaic than the least formulaic *chanson de geste*; none are as little repetitive as the most repetitive romance, as we might have expected if the hypothesis of a learned use of previously existing oral materials were correct.

The one passage most likely to be literate, verses 2501 to 2600, tells of the evening following the French army's defeat of the pagan forces responsible for the destruction of Charlemagne's rearguard at Roncevaux. Of the 70 verses dedicated to this narration, 45 are given over to the emperor's two dreams of foreboding, one concerning his duel with Baligant, the other the trial of Ganelon. The remaining thirty verses show Bramimunde's lamentations before the ineffective pagan idols, which she helps to destroy, and her regrets over the mortally wounded Marsile. As interesting as these two scenes are, few would claim that they

[37] I am not eliminating the possibility of individual verses added to the poem sporadically. The statistical method which I employ could not detect such verses, and each instance alleged would have to be judged on its merits. But obviously the poem was not transformed into a masterpiece by the addition of a few verses here and there.

are on a literary level with the best *Roland* passages. It is difficult to conceive of them as improving the poem to any significant degree except that the two dreams, prefiguring the two remaining major episodes, contribute to cohesiveness of structure. But similar anticipations are scattered throughout the poem in more formulaic passages; nothing about this function of the two dreams strikes one as unique. Charlemagne, in fact, has two other dreams which fill an identical anticipatory role in verses 717 to 736, but the hundred-line segment which includes this passage is 37.5 percent formulaic, slightly above the figure of 35.2 percent for the poem as a whole.

On the basis of this examination of the hundred-line segments, then, there is no reason to suppose the intervention of a learned poet between the oral tradition and the archetype of Oxford.

Considerable doubt may still subsist, however, about whether the *Roland* is an orally composed text or a literary transformation of previously existing oral materials. Those who posit the necessity for the intervention of a learned poet do so upon the often unarticulated assumption that such an intervention was required to improve the poetic form of the legend, for the normal workings of the oral tradition could not produce such a masterpiece. The basis for these premises is not at all clear, and even though they are widely held, *Roland* criticism has never attempted to support them with carefully reasoned argumentation.

Let us try to formulate more clearly the circumstances which would attend a composite creation. Epic singers are, to judge from what we know of twentieth-century oral poets, nearly always illiterate.[38] Literacy would have made amelioration of the raw product feasible, allowing the poet the advantages of hindsight so that he could carry out revisions in a way analogous to the literary labor of any modern writer. An intervention between the oral tradition and the archetype of Oxford might have taken place in one of two ways. Either a literate man, not just one capable of reading and writing but a person with an aptitude for

[38] *Singer of Tales*, p. 20.

composing in writing, heard a jongleur sing a primitive version
of *Roland* and—whether he thought thereby to gain some ma-
terial advantage for himself (or his monastery), or was simply
inspired by artistic motives—taking these materials, transformed
them, adding passages here, eliminating others there, subtracting
or creating whole scenes perhaps, and reworked them into the
great archetype of Oxford; or else a jongleur, skilled at his trade
after experience at itinerant performing, and perhaps wishing to
devote his life to monastic service, learned how to write and
committed his song to parchment with extensive modifications
made possible by his literacy. The reworking must have entailed
rather elaborate changes, or there would be no reason to suppose
it at all. Although the *remanieur* would probably have changed
individual lines, he could not have done this for more than a
minimal number of cases, for Oxford does not differ significantly
from other *chansons de geste* in the proportion of its formulas,
even when it is divided into hundred-line groups. As a result,
the search for evidence should be transferred to a scrutiny of
entire scenes.[39] One does not create a great work of art by taking
an uninspired one and altering a few of its phrases.

For the most likely supposition is that the poet substantially
changed or perhaps even introduced entirely the great scenes
which lift *Roland* above the level of the entertaining but not
transcendently great epics more or less contemporary with it.
It follows, then, that an examination of the best scenes from Ox-
ford should reveal the nature of that work. If they show little or
no trace of the oral-formulaic style, then the poem is very likely
an amalgamation, a transformation, perhaps a collaboration be-
tween clerk and jongleur. In this case the collaboration envisaged
would not be the type imagined by Bédier, but the opposite: in-
stead of the clerk extracting legendary material from his archives

---

[39] This step is not redundant. Uniformity of formulaic traits in the
hundred-line segments lessens but does not preclude the possibility that
certain scenes were interposed: they could be contiguous with laisses of
exceptionally high formulaic density so as not to stand out in the analysis
of the segments.

or chronicles for the jongleur to rework into a form suitable for literary dissemination, the jongleur would have furnished the substance of the *chanson* to the clerk, who would be responsible for the most impressive artistic elements in the finished work. On the other hand, if these scenes resemble the rest of the text in their formulaic content, then presumably they are not the work of a *remanieur* whose mode of creation was the written word.

In choosing the episodes which convey upon the poem a great deal of its particular excellence, I do not wish to imply that the effect of great narrative poetry can be accounted for by its "great scenes" or that an appreciation of these scenes is an adequate substitute for intimate knowledge of the whole work. I am merely following to its logical conclusion a line of reasoning which dictates that, if the Oxford *Roland* results from a sudden mutation at the hands of a learned poet, then if he refined and perfected anything, it would be the scenes which he considered most important, and which modern critics have deemed most worthy of careful study. The *Roland* poet's way of emphasizing an episode is to repeat it in a series of similar laisses. Appropriately enough, the series of three—maximum number in any series of similar laisses—is most frequent at the decisive moments of the battle of Roncevaux: the two horn scenes and Roland's death. The latter includes two series: the hero first attempts to shatter his sword Durendal against a boulder and then begs pardon for his sins before the angels Michael and Gabriel transport his soul to paradise. Psychological finesse appears most clearly in the French council scene, so justly admired by Bédier. To these universally acclaimed episodes, I add another laisse which appeals to me particularly as not only poignant but also well-constructed: the scene in which Oliver, his vision obscured by loss of blood, strikes Roland on the helmet. This leads to a touching and ironic leave-taking, as Roland pardons Oliver, and the two bow to each other: *par tel amur as les vus desevred* (2009).

I have examined each of these scenes closely, using the same method and criteria as for the formula analysis of the whole poem. They are quoted in full below, the hemistichs which occur elsewhere in the poem being italicized. The formulas in small capitals are those whose other occurrences are confined to the scene in question.

*French council scene: the decision and the naming of the envoy*[40]
   XII  Li emper[er]es s'en vait desuz un pin.
        *Ses baruns mandet* pur sun cunseill fenir:
        Le duc Oger, (e) *l'arcvesque Turpin*,          170
        *Richard li Velz* e sun nev[old] Henri,

[40] Evidence: 168a: 137, 139, and 52 others *li empereres;* 169a: 166 *ses baruns mandet;* 169b: 62 *out sun cunseill finet,* 166 *pur sun cunseill finer;* 170b: 1124, 1243 *li arcevesques Turpin,* 2130 *l'arcevesque Turpin;* 171a: 3050, 3470 *Richard li velz;* 173a: 2433, 3058 *Tedbald de Reins;* 174a: 107 *e si i furent;* 174b: 107 *e Gerin e Gerers;* 175a: 1896, 2395, 3196, 3461 *ensembl'od els;* 176a: 576, 586, and 11 others *e Oliver;* 176b: 576, 3755 *li proz e li curteis,* 3186 *li proz e li vaillanz;* 178a: 674 *Guenes i vint;* 178b: 3748 *ki traïsun ad faite;* 179a: 3707, 3747, 3946 *desor cumencet;* 180a: 70, 244 and 10 others *seignurs barons;* 180b: 274, 740 *dist li emperere Carles;* 181a: 7, 10 and 17 others *li reis Marsilie;* 182a: 127 *de sun aveir,* 651 *de mun aveir;* 182b: 651 *vos voeill duner grant masse;* 183a: 128 *urs e leuns;* 183b: 128 *veltres enchaignez;* 184a: 31, 129, 645 *set cenz cameilz;* 184b: 31, 129 *e mil hosturs muers;* 185a: 32 [*d'or e d'argent*] *quatre cenz muls cargez* (transposition of the entire verse); 185b: see previous item; 186a: 694 *qu'il vos siurat,* 37 *vos le siurez;* 188b: 52 *ad Ais a sa capele,* 726 *a sa capele ad Ais,* 744 *ad Ais a la capele;* 189a: 695, 2620 *si recevrat;* 189b: 126 *la lei de salvetet;* 190b: 3716 *et si tendrat mes marches;* 191a: 735 *mais il ne sevent;* 191b: 375 *itels est sis curages;* 192a: 47, 243, and 13 others *dient Franceis;* 193a: 137, 139 and 52 others *li empereres;* 194a: 355, 663 and 31 others *li quens Rollant;* 194b: 3897 *se jo mie l'otrei;* 195a: 218 *en piez se drecet,* 2234 *sur piez se drecet;* 196a: 27, 123, and 11 others *e dist al rei;* 197a: 2, 2610 *set anz tuz pleins;* 198a: 2322, 2324, 2327, 2331 *jo l'en cunquis;* 201a: 7, 10 and 17 others *li reis Marsilie;* 202a: 568, 588 *de voz paiens;* 206b: 513 *alques de legerie;* 209a: 491 *dunt pris les chefs;* 209b: 491 *as puis de Haltoie;* 211a: 245, 299, 310, 476, 852, 2617 *en Sarraguce;* 212b: 595 *en tute vostre vie;* 214a: 137, 139 and 52 others *li empereres;* 214b: 139 *en tint sun chef enclin,* 771 *en tint sun chef enbrunc;* 215a: 772 *si duist sa barbe;* 217a: 263 *Franceis se taisent;* 218a: 195 *en piez se drecet,* 2234 *sur piez se drecet;* 219a: 2984, 3316, 3536 *mult fierement;* 220a: 27, 123 and 11 others *e dist al rei;* 222a: 239 *quant il vos mandet;* 222b: 7, 10, and 17 others *li reis Marsilies;* 224a: 869 *de tute*

*Espaigne; 2660 par tute Espaigne;* 225a: 189, 695, 2620 *si recevrat;* 225b: 695
*la lei que vos tenez;* 230a: 774 *anpres iço;* 230b; 774 *i est Neimes venud;* 231a:
775, 3377, 3532 *meillor vassal,* 1857 *meillors vassals;* 231b: 775 *n'out en la
curt de lui;* 232a: 27, 123 and 11 others *e dist al rei;* 232b: 776 *ben l'avez en-
tendut;* 233a: 342, 668, 721, 3792 *Guenes li cuens;* 235a: 618, 1563, 2700 *le rei
Marsiliun,* 880, 1214, 1905, 3773 *al rei Marsiliun;* 237a: 98 *od ses cadables;*
239a: 222 *quant ço vos mandet;* 239b: 82 *qu'il ait mercit de mei;* 243a: 47, 192
and 13 others *dient Franceis;* 244a: 70, 180 and 11 others *seignurs barons;*
244b; 252 *qui i purruns enveier;* 245a: 211, 299, 310, 476, 852, 2617 *en Sarra-
guce;* 245b: 235, 618, 1563, 2700 *le rei Marsiliun,* 880, 1214, 1905, 3773 *al rei
Marsiliun;* 264a: 1790, 3013 *respont dux Neimes;* 247b: 268, 320 *le bastun e
le guant,* 2727 *sun bastun e sun guant;* 248a: 259 *respunt li reis;* 249a: 261,
3954 *par ceste barbe;* 251a: 272 *alez sedeir;* 252a: 70, 180, and 11 others *seig-
nurs barons;* 252b: 244 *qui i enveieruns;* 254a: 292, 1008, and 10 others *res-
punt Rollant;* 254b: 258 *jo i puis aler ben;* 258a: 295 *se li reis voelt;* 258b: 254
*jo i puis aler mult ben;* 259a: 248 *respunt li reis;* 261a: 249, 3954 *par ceste bar-
be;* 262a: 325, 547 and 12 others *li doze per;* 263a: 217 *Franceis se taisent;*
264a: 2083 *Turpins de Reins:* 265a: 27, 123 and 11 others *e dist al rei;* 266a:
17, 134, 2800 *en cest pais;* 266b: 2736 *ad estet ja set anz;* 267b: 864 *e peines e
ahans;* 1761 *par peine e par ahans;* 268b: 247 *le guant e le bastun,* 320 *le bas-
tun e lu guant,* 2727 *sun bastun e sun guant;* 269b: 1083 *les Sarrazins d'Es-
paigne,* 1847 *as Sarrazins d'Espaigne;* 270a: 2853 *si vunt vedeir;* 271a: 137,
139, and 52 others *li empereres;* 272a: 251 *alez sedeir;* 273b: 2659 *se jo ne li
cumant;* 274b: 180, 740 *dist li emperere Carles;* 277a: 1288, 1360, and 8 others
*ço dist Rollant;* 278a: 47, 192, and 13 others *dient Franceis;* 280a: 332, 425
*mais li quens Guenes;* 280b: 3444 *tant par est anguissables;* 281b: 3940 *od ses
granz pels de martre;* 282a: 1914 *remes i est;* 283b: 142 *mult par out fier le
vis;* 284a: 118, 3115 *gent ad le cors;* 284b: 3158 *e larges les costez;* 287a:
293 *ço set hom ben;* 288b: 299 *en irai a Marsilie;* 292a: 254, 1008, and 10
others *respunt Rollant;* 293a: 287 *ço set hom ben;* 295a: 258 *se li reis voelt;*
296a: 375, 381, 396, and 10 others *Guenes respunt;* 299a: 211, 245, 310, 476,
852, 2617 *en Sarraguce;* 299b: 288 *qu'a Marsilium en alge;* 302a: 761 *quant ot
Rollant,* 1196 *quant l'ot Rollant;* 304a: 2223 *dunc ad tel doel;* 308a: 766,
2441 *dreiz emperere;* 310a: 211, 245, 299, 476, 852, 2617 *en Sarraguce;* 315b:
820 *des fius e des honurs;* 317a: 156, 833, 3595 *Carles respunt;* 319a: 327,
339, and 12 others *ço dist li reis;* 320a: 38 *si recevrez,* 85 *si recevrai,* 225,
695, 2620 *si recevrat;* 320b: 247 *le guant e le bastun,* 268 *le bastun e le
guant,* 2727 *sun bastun e sun guant;* 322a: 337, 456 "*sire,*" *dist Guenes;*
323b: 2662 *en trestut mun vivant;* 324a: 936, 964 *ne Oliver;* 325a: 262, 547,
and 12 others *li doze per;* 327a: 319, 339, and 12 others *ço dist li reis;* 329b:
1303 *ja n'i avrez guarant;* 331a: 137, 139 and 52 others *li empereres;* 332a:
280 *e li quens Guenes,* 425 *mais li quens Guenes;* 334a: 47, 192, and 13 others
*dient Franceis;* 337a: 322, 456, "*sire,*" *dist Guenes;* 337b: 2177 *car me dunez
cunget;* 339a: 319, 327, and 12 others *ço dist li reis;* 340a: 770 *de sa main
destre;* 340b: 2205 *l'ad asols e seignet,* 3859 *e asols e seignez.*

E de Gascuigne li proz quens Acelin,
*Tedbald de Reins* e Milun, sun cusin;
*E si i furent e Gerers e Gerin;*
*Ensembl'od els* li quens Rollant i vint,
*E Oliver, li proz e li gentilz;*
Des Francs de France en i ad plus de mil.
*Guenes i vint, ki la traïsun fist.*
*Des ore cumencet* le cunseill que mal prist. AOI.

XIII  *"Seignurs barons,"* dist li emperere Carles,                     180
*"Li reis Marsilie* m'ad tramis ses messages;
*De sun aveir me voelt duner grant masse,*
*Urs e leuns e veltres caeignables,*
*Set cenz cameilz e mil hosturs muables,*
*Quatre cenz mulz cargez del or d'Arabe,*
Avoec iço plus de cinquante care;
Mais il me mandet que en France m'en alge:
*Il me sivrat ad Ais, a mun estage,*
*Si recevrat la nostre lei plus salve;*
Crestiens ert, *de mei tendrat ses marches;*                          190
*Mais jo ne sai quels en est sis curages."*
*Dient Franceis:* "Il nus i cuvent guarde!" AOI.

XIV  *Li empereres* out sa raisun fenie.
*Li quens Rollant, ki ne l'otriet mie,*
*En piez se drecet,* si li vint cuntredire.
*Il dist al rei:* "Ja mar crerez Marsilie!
*Set anz [ad] pleins* que en Espaigne venimes;
*Jo vos cunquis* e Noples e Commibles,
Pris ai Valterne e la tere de Pine,
E Balasgued e Tuele e Sezilie.                                        200
*Li reis Marsilie* i fist mult que traïtre:
*De ses pai[ens il vus]* enveiat quinze,
Cha(n)cuns portout une branche d'olive;
Nuncerent vos cez paroles meïsme.
A vos Franceis un cunseill en presistes:
Loerent vos *alques de legerie.*

Dous de voz cuntes al paien tramesistes,
L'un fut Basan e li altres Basilies;
*Les chef en prist es puis desuz Haltilie.*
Faites la guer[re] cum vos l'avez enprise:     210
*En Sarraguce* menez vostre ost banie,
Metez le sege *a tute vostre vie,*
Si vengez cels que li fels fist ocire!" AOI.

XV  *Li emper[er]e en tint sun chef enbrunc,*
*Si duist sa barbe,* afaitad sun gernun,
Ne ben ne mal ne respunt sun nevuld.
FRANCEIS SE TAISENT, ne mais que Guenelun:
*En piez se drecet,* si vint devant Carlun,
*Mult fierement* cumencet sa raisun,
*E dist al rei:* "Ja mar crerez bricun,     220
Ne mei ne altre, se de vostre prod nun.
QUANT ÇO VOS MANDET *li reis Marsiliun,*
Qu'il devendrat jointes ses mains tis hom,
*E tute Espaigne* tendrat par vostre dun,
*Puis recevrat la lei que nus tenum,*
Ki ço vos lodet que cest plait degetuns,
Ne li chalt, sire, de quel mort nus muriuns.
Cunseill d'orguill n'est dreiz que a plus munt.
Laissun les fols, as sages nus tenuns." AOI.

XVI  *Apres iço i est Neimes venud;*     230
*Meillor vassal n'aveit en la curt nul,*
*E dist al rei:* "Ben l'avez entendud,
Guenes li quens ço vus ad respondud;
Saveir i ad, mais qu'il seit entendud.
*Li reis Marsilie* est de guere vencud:
Vos li avez tuz ses castels toluz,
*Od voz caables* avez fruiset ses murs,
Ses citez arses e ses humes vencuz;
QUANT IL VOS MANDET *qu'aiez mercit de lui,*
Pecchet fereit ki dunc li fesist plus,     240
U par ostage vos (en) voelt faire soürs;

Ceste grant guerre ne deit munter a plus."
*Dient Franceis*: "Ben ad parlet li dux." AOI.

XVII —"*Seignurs baruns*, QUI I ENVEIERUNS
*En Saraguce, al rei Marsiliuns?*"
*Respunt dux Neimes*: "Jo irai, par vostre dun!
Livrez m'en ore *le guant e le bastun.*"
RESPUNT LI REIS: "Vos estes saives hom;
*Par ceste barbe* e par cest men gernun,
Vos n'irez pas uan de mei si luign.                              250
ALEZ SEDEIR, quant nuls ne vos sumunt!"

XVIII —"*Seignurs, baruns*, QUI I PURRUNS ENVEIER
*Al Sarrazin ki Sarraguce tient?*"
*Respunt Rollant*: "JO I PUIS ALER MULT BEN!"
—"Nu ferez certes!" dist li quens Oliver;
"Vostre curages est mult pesmes e fiers:
Jo me crendreie que vos vos meslisez.
SE LI REIS VOELT, JO I PUIS ALER BEN."
RESPUNT LI REIS: "Ambdui vos en taisez!
Ne vos ne il n'i porterez les piez.                              260
*Par ceste barbe* que veez [blancheier],
*Li duze per* mar i serunt jugez!"
FRANCEIS SE TAISENT: as les vus aquisez.

XIX *Turpins de Reins* en est levet del renc,
*E dist al rei*: "Laisez ester voz Francs!
*En cest païs avez estet set anz;*
Mult unt oüd *e peines e ahans.*
Dunez m'en, sire, *le bastun e le guant,*
E jo irai *al Sarazin en Espaigne,*
*Sin vois vedeir* alques de sun semblant."       270
*Li empereres* respunt par maltalant:
"ALEZ SEDEIR desur cel palie blanc!
N'en parlez mais, *se jo nel vos cumant!*" AOI.

XX —"Francs chevalers," *dist li emperere Carles,*
"Car m'eslisez un barun de ma marche,
Qu'a Marsiliun me portast mun message."

*Ço dist Rollant*: "Ço ert Guenes, mis parastre."
*Dient Franceis*: "Car il le poet ben faire;
Se lui lessez, n'i trametrez plus saive."
*E li quens Guenes en fut mult anguisables*:     280
De sun col getet *ses grandes pels de martre*,
*E est remes* en sun blialt de palie.
Vairs out [les oilz] *e mult fier lu visage*,
*Gent out le cors e les costez out larges*:
Tant par fut bels tuit si per l'en esguardent.
Dist a Rollant: "Tut fol, pur quei t'esrages?
ÇO SET HOM BEN que jo sui tis parastres;
Si as juget QU'A MARSILIUM EN ALGE!
Se Deus ço dunet que jo de la repaire,
Jo t'en muvra[i] un si grant contr[a]ire     290
Ki durerat a trestut tun edage."
*Respunt Rollant*: "Orgoill oi e folage.
ÇO SET HOM BEN, n'ai cure de manace;
Mai[s] saives hom, il deit faire message:
SI LI REIS VOELT, prez sui por vus le face."
XXI   *Guenes respunt*: "Pur mei n'iras tu mie! AOI.
Tu n'ies mes hom ne jo ne sui tis sire.
Carles comandet que face sun servise:
*En Sarraguce* EN IRAI A MARSILIE;
Einz i f[e]rai un poi de [le]gerie,     300
Que jo n'esclair ceste meie grant ire."
*Quant l'ot Rollant*, si cumençat a rire. AOI.
XXII   Quant ço veit Guenes que ore s'en rit Rollant,
*Dunc ad tel doel* pur poi d'ire ne fent,
A ben petit que il ne pert le sens;
E dit al cunte: "Jo ne vus aim nient;
Sur mei avez turnet fals jugement.
*Dreiz emperere*, veiz me ci en present,
Ademplir voeill vostre comandement."
XXIII  —"*En Sarraguce* sai ben [qu']aler m'estoet. AOI.  310
Hom ki la vait repairer ne s'en poet.

Ensurquetut si ai jo vostre soer,
Sin ai un filz, ja plus bels n'en estoet:
Ço est Baldewin," ço dit, "ki ert prozdoem.
A lui lais jo *mes honurs e mes fieus*.
Gua[r]dez le ben, ja nel verrai des oilz."
*Carles respunt*: "Tro avez tendre coer.
Puisquel comant, aler vus en estoet."

XXIV  *Ço dist li reis*: "Guenes, venez avant, AOI.
    *Si recevez le bastun e lu guant.*                320
    Oït l'avez, sur vos le jugent Franc."
    —"*Sire*," *dist Guenes*, "ço ad tut fait Rollant!
    Ne l'amerai *a trestut mun vivant*,
    *Ne Oliver*, por ço qu'il est si cumpainz;
    *Li duze per*, por [ço] qu'il l'aiment tant,
    Desfi les ci, sire, vostre veiant."
    *Ço dist li reis*: "Trop avez maltalant.
    Or irez vos certes, quant jol cumant."
    —"Jo i puis aler, *mais n'i avrai guarant*: AOI.
    Nu l'out Basilies ne sis freres Basant."       330

XXV  *Li empereres* li tent sun guant, le destre;
    *Mais li quens Guenes* iloec ne volsist estre:
    Quant le dut prendre, si li caït a tere.
    *Dient Franceis*: "Deus! que purrat ço estre?
    De cest message nos avendrat grant perte."
    —"Seignurs," dist Guenes, "vos en orrez noveles!"

XXVI  —"*Sire*," *dist Guenes*, "*dunez mei le cungied*;
    Quant aler dei, n'i ai plus que targer."
    *Ço dist li reis*: "Al Jhesu e al mien!"
    *De sa main destre l'ad asols e seignet*,          340
    Puis li livrat le bastun e le bref.

*First horn scene: Roland refuses to sound for help*[41]
LXXXIII  *Dist Oliver*: "Paien unt grant esforz:
    *De noz Franceis m'i semblet aveir mult poi.*    1050

---

[41] Evidence: 1049a: 1006, 1039, and 10 others *dist Oliver*; 1050a: 1190 *de*

CUMPAIGN ROLLANT, *kar sunez vostre corn,*
*Si l'orrat Carles,* SI RETURNERAT L'OST!"
*Respunt Rollant:* "Jo fereie que fols!
*En dulce France* en perdreie mun los.
Sempres ferrai DE DURENDAL GRANZ COLPS;
Saglant en ert li branz entresqu'a l'or.
FELUN PAIEN mar i vindrent as porz;
*Jo vos plevis,* tuz sunt jugez a mort." AOI.

---

*noz Franceis;* 1051a: 1059 *l'olifan car sunez,* 1070 *sunez vostre olifan,* 2950 *sunez en vostre corn;* 1052a: 1060, 1071, 1703 *si l'orrat Carles,* 1714 *si l'orrat li reis Karles;* 1052b: 1060 *ferat l'ost returner;* 1053a: 254, 292, *and 10 others respunt Rollant;* 1054a: 360 *en dulce France,* 109, 2379 *de dulce France;* 1055b: 1065 *de Durendal asez;* 1057a: 1068, 1098 *felun paien;* 1058a: 968, 1069, 1072, 1704 *jo vos plevis;* 1058b: 937 *tuit sunt jugez a perdre,* 1069 *tuz sunt a mort livrez;* 1059a: 1051 *kar sunez vostre corn,* 1070 *sunez vostre olifan,* 2950 *sunez en vostre corn;* 1060a: 1052, 1071, 1703 *si l'orrat Carles,* 1714 *si l'orrat li reis Karles;* 1060: 1052 *si returnerat l'ost;* 1061a: 3378 *succurrez le;* 1062a: 254, 292, *and 10 others respunt Rollant,* 1073 *ço li respunt Rollant;* 1062b: 358, 3906 *ne placet Damnedeu;* 1064a: 2661, 3673 *en France dulce,* 2431 *de France dulce;* 1065b: 1055 *de Durendal granz colps;* 1066a: 1121 *ma bone espee;* 1068a: 1057, 1098 *felun paien;* 1069a: 968, 1058, 1072, 1704 *jo vos plevis;* 1069b: 937 *tuit sunt jugez a perdre,* 1058 *tuz sunt jugez a mort;* 1070a: 1051, 1059 *cumpaign (cumpainz) Rollant;* 1070b: 1051 *kar sunez vostre corn,* 1059 *l'olifan car sunez,* 2950 *sunez en vostre corn;* 1071a: 1052, 1060, 1703 *si l'orrat Carles,* 1714 *si l'orrat li reis Karles;* 1071b: 1703, 1766 *ki est as porz passant;* 1072a: 968, 1058, 1069, 1704 *jo vos plevis;* 1072b: 1704 *ja returnerunt Franc;* 1073a: 1089, 3718 *ne place(t) Deu;* 1073b: 254, 292, *and 10 other occurrences respunt Rollant;* 1074b: 3908 *par nul home mortel;* 1077a: 2910, 2917 *cum jo serai;* 1078a: 1462 *jo i ferrai;* 1079a: 2780 *de Durendal;* 1081a: 1745 *ja cil d'Espaigne;* 1081b: 948 *n'avrunt de mort guarant,* 1418 *de mort n'i ad guarant;* 1082a: 1006, 1039, *and 10 others dist Oliver;* 1083a: 3132 *veüd avum;* 1083b: 1847 *as Sarrazins d'Espaigne;* 1084b: 856, 2434, 3695 *e les vals e les munz;* 1086a: 2630, 2980, 3263, 3291, 3383 *granz sunt les oz;* 1086b: 2630 *de cele gent averse,* cf. also 2922, 3295; 1088a: 254, 292, *and 10 others respunt Rollant,* 1073 *ço li respunt Rollant;* 1089a: 1073, 3718 *ne place(t) Deu;* 1089b: 3718 *ne ses sainz ne ses angles;* 1091a: 536, 1485, 1701, 2336, 2738, 3909 *mielz voeill murir;* 1095a: 896 *puis que il est,* 3858 *puis que il sunt;* 1095b: 2986 *as chevals e as armes;* 1096a: 1048, 1909, 3048, 3812 *ja pur murir;* 1098a: 1057, 1068 *felun paien;* 1099a: 1006, 1039, *and 10 others dist Oliver;* 1101a: 1171 *vostre olifan;* 1101b: 1171 *ne deignastes suner;* 1102a: 1717 *s'i fust li reis;* 1102b: 1717 *n'i oüsum damage;* 1104a: 2426 *vedeir puez;* 1106a: 254, 292, *and 10 others respunt Rollant,* 1073 *ço li respunt Rollant.*

LXXXIV CUMPAINZ ROLLANT, *l'olifan car sunez:*
*Si l'orrat Carles,* FERAT L'OST RETURNER,                    1060
*Succurat nos li reis od tut sun barnet."*
*Respont Rollant: "Ne placet Damnedeu*
Que mi parent pur mei seient blasmet
*Ne France dulce ja cheet en viltet!*
Einz i ferrai DE DURENDAL ASEZ,
*Ma bone espee que ai ceint al costet:*
Tut en verrez le brant ensanglentet.
FELUN PAIEN mar i sunt asemblez:
*Jo vos plevis, tuz sunt a mort livrez."* AOI.

LXXXV —"CUMPAINZ ROLLANT, *sunez vostre olifan:*          1070
*Si l'orrat Carles, ki est as porz passant.*
*Je vos plevis, ja returnerunt Franc."*
—"*Ne placet Deu,"* ço li respunt Rollant,
"Que ço seit dit *de nul hume vivant,*
Ne pur paien, que ja seie cornant!
Ja n'en avrunt reproece mi parent!
*Quant jo serai* en la bataille grant
*E jo ferrai* e mil colps e .VII. cenz,
*De Durendal* verrez l'acer sanglent.
Franceis sunt bon, si ferrunt vassalment;          1080
*Ja cil d'Espaigne n'avrunt de mort guarant."*

LXXXVI *Dist Oliver: "D'*iço ne sai jo blasme.
*Jo ai veüt les Sarrazins d'Espaigne:*
Cuverz en sunt *li val e les muntaignes*
E li lariz e trestutes les plaignes.
*Granz sunt les oz de cele gent estrange;*
Nus i avum mult petite cumpaigne."
*Respunt Rollant:* "Mis talenz en est graigne.
*Ne placet Damnedeu ne ses angles*
Que ja pur mei perdet sa valur France!          1090
*Melz voeill murir* que huntage me venget.
Pur ben ferir l'emperere plus nos aimet."

LXXXVII Rollant est proz et Oliver est sage;

Ambedui unt me[r]veillus vasselage.
*Puis que il sunt as chevals e as armes,*
*Ja pur murir* n'eschiverunt bataille.
Bon sunt li cunte e lur paroles haltes.
FELUN PAIEN par grant irur chevalchent.
*Dist Oliver:* "Rollant, veez en alques!
Cist nus sunt pres, mais trop nus est loinz Carles. 1100
*Vostre olifan, suner vos nel deignastes;*
Fust i li reis, *n'i oüssum damage.*
Guardez amunt devers les porz d'Espaigne:
Veeir poez, dolente est la rereguarde;
Ki ceste fait, jamais n'en ferat altre."
*Respunt Rollant:* "Ne dites tel ultrage!
Mal seit del coer ki el piz se cuardet!
Nus remeindrum en estal en la place;
Par nos i ert e li colps e li caples." AOI.

*Second horn scene: Oliver accuses Roland of desmesure*[42]
CXXVIII *Li quens Rollant* des soens i veit grant perte. AOI.
*Sun cumpaignun Oliver en apelet:*

---

[42] Evidence: 1691a: 194, 355, 663, and 30 other examples *li quens Rollanz;* 1622a: 1160, 1994, 2201 *sun cumpaignun;* 1692b: 1545 *en apele Oliver;* 1693a: 1113, 1146, 1672, and 6 others *sire cumpainz* (the hemistich as it stands is hypersyllabic and is often emended to *sire cumpainz*); 1696a: 3037 *de tels barons;* 1696b: 2928 *cum remeines deserte;* 1698a: 1395, 1866 *Oliver frere;* 1699a: 581 *cumfaitement;* 1700a: 1006, 1039, and 10 other occurrences *dist Oliver;* 1701a: 536, 1091, 1485, 2336, 2738, 3909 *mielz voeill murir;* 1702a: 277, 1288, 1360, and 9 others *ço dist Rollant;* 1703a: 1052, 1060, 1071, 1714 *si l'orrat Carles;* 1703b: 1071, 1766 *ki est as porz passant;* 1704a: 968, 1058, 1069, 1072 *jo vos plevis;* 1704b: 1072 *ja returnerunt Franc;* 1705a: 1006, 1039, and 10 other examples *dist Oliver;* 1708a: 1716 *quant jel vos dis;* 1708b: 787 *jo n'en ferai nient;* 1711a: 3512 *ja avrum nos;* 1712a: 1548, 1676 *respont li quens;* 1713a: 277, 1288, 1360, and 9 other occurrences *ço dist Rollant;* 1714b: 1052, 1060, 1071, 1703 *si l'orrat Carles;* 1715a: 1006, 1039, and 10 others *dist Oliver;* 1716a: 1708 *quant jel vos dis;* 1717a: 1102 *fust i li reis;* 1717b: 1102 *n'i oüssum damage;* 1718a: 1174 *cil ki la sunt;* 1718b: 1346 *n'en deivent aveir blasme;* 1719a: 1006, 1039, and 10 other occurrences *dist Oliver;* 1719b: 249, 261, 3954 *par ceste barbe;* 1722a: 277, 1288, 1360, and 9 other examples *ço dist Rollant;* 1723a: 644, 2835, 3209,

"Bel *sire,* chers *cumpainz,* pur Deu, que vos enhaitet?
Tanz bons vassals veez gesir par tere?
Pleindre poüms France dulce, la bele:
*De tels barons cum or remeint deserte!*
E! reis, amis, que vos ici nen estes!
*Oliver, frere,* cumment le purrum nus faire?
*Cum faitement* li manderum nuveles?"
*Dist Oliver:* "Jo nel sai cument quere.                    1700
*Mielz voeill murir* que hunte nus seit retraite." AOI

CXXIX Ço *dist Rollant:* "Cornerai l'olifant,
*Si l'orrat Carles, ki est as porz passant.*
*Jo vos plevis ja returnerunt Franc."*
*Dist Oliver:* "Vergoigne sereit grant
E reprover a trestuz voz parenz;
Iceste hunte dureit al lur vivant!
QUANT JEL VOS DIS, *n'en feïstes nient;*
Mais nel ferez par le men loement.
Se vos cornez, n'ert mie hardement.                        1710
*Ja avez vos* ambsdous les braz sanglanz!"
*Respont li quens:* "Colps i ai fait mult genz!" AOI.

CXXX Ço *dit Rollant:* "Forz est nostre bataille;
Jo cornerai, *si l'orrat li reis Karles."*
*Dist Oliver:* "Ne sereit vasselage!
QUANT JEL VOS DIS, cumpainz, vos ne deignastes.
*Si fust li reis, n'i oüsum damage.*
*Cil ki la sunt n'en deivent aveir blasme."*
*Dist Oliver:* "Par ceste meie barbe,
Se puis veeir ma gente sorur Alde,                         1720
Ne jerrei(e)z ja mais entre sa brace!" AOI.

CXXXI Ço *dist Rollant:* "Por quei me portez ire?"
*E il respont:* "Cumpainz, vos le feïstes,
Kar vasselage par sens nen est folie;

---

3513 *e cil respunt;* 1726a: 2038 *morz sunt Franceis;* 1729a: 882, 3278, 3577,
3587 *ceste bataille;* 1732a: 703, 841, 905, 1195, 1404, 1949, 3329 *Carles li*
*magnes;* 1734b: 969 *e France en ert hunie.*

Mielz valt mesure que ne fait estultie.
*Franceis sunt morz* par vostre legerie.
Jamais Karlon de nus n'avrat servise.
Sem creïsez, venuz i fust mi sire;
*Ceste bataille* oüsum faite u prise;
U pris u mort i fust li reis Marsilie.     1730
Vostre proecce, Rollant, mar la ve[ï]mes!
*Karles li Magnes* de nos n'avrat aïe.
N'ert mais tel home des qu'a Deu juïse.
Vos i murrez *e France en ert hunie.*
Oi nus defalt la leial cumpaignie:
Einz le vespre mult ert gref la departie." AOI.

*Oliver unknowingly strikes Roland; they take leave of each other*[43]

CXLIX   As vus Rollant *sur sun cheval pasmet,*
        *E Oliver ki est a mort nasfret:*     1990
        Tant ad seinet li oil li sunt trublet;
        Ne loinz ne pres ne poet vedeir si cler
        Que rec[on]oistre poisset nuls hom mortel.
        *Sun cumpaignun,* cum il l'at encontret,
        Sil fiert amunt *sur l'elme a or gemet:*
        *Tut li detrenchet* d'ici qu'al nasel;
        Mais en la teste *ne l'ad mie adeset.*
        *A icel colp l'ad Rollant reguardet,*
        *Si li demandet* dulcement e suef:
        *"Sire cumpain,* faites le vos de gred?     2000
        Ja est ço Rollant, *ki tant vos soelt amer!*

[43] Evidence: 1989b: 1988 *sur sun cheval pasmet;* 1990a: 176, 576, and 11 other examples *e Oliver;* 1990b: 1965 *qu'il est a mort nasfret,* 2771 *il est a mort naffret;* 1994a: 1160 *sun cumpaignun;* 1995b: 1954 *sur l'elme a or agut;* 1996a: 2172 *li ad tut detrenchet,* 1299 *que tut li trenchet,* 1600 *tut li trenchat;* 1997b: 2159 *ne l'unt mie adeset;* 1998a: 3530, 3930 *a icest colp;* 1998b: 1851, 1978, 2086 *Rollant reguardet;* 1999a: 3611 *si li demandet;* 2000a: 1113, 1146, and 7 others *sire cumpainz;* 2001b: 2782 *qu'il tant suleit amer;* 2003a: 1006, 1039, and 10 other occurrences *dist Oliver;* 2006a: 254, 292, and 10 others *respunt Rollant;* 2008a: 2054, 2457 *a icel mot.*

Par nule guise ne m'aviez desfiet!"
*Dist Oliver*: "Or vos oi jo parler;
Jo ne vos vei, veied vus Damnedeu!
Ferut vos ai, car le me pardunez!"
*Rollant respunt*: "Jo n'ai nient de mal.
Jol vos parduins ici e devant Deu."
*A icel mot* l'un a l'altre ad clinet.
Par tel amur as les vus desevred!

*Roland attempts to destroy his sword Durendal*[44]
CLXXI  *Ço sent Rollant* la veue ad perdue;
        *Met sei sur piez*, quanqu'il poet s'esvertuet;

[44] Evidence: 2297a: 2259, 2284, 2355, 2366 *ço sent Rollant*; 2298a: 2277
*met sei en piez*; 2299a: 2218 *en sun visage*; 2299b: 2895 *perdue ad sa culur*;
2300a: 2576 *dedevant lui*; 2300b: 2338 *en une perre bise*; 2301a: 3380 *durs
colps i fierent* (see also 2090 *mil colps i fiert et plus*); 2302a: 2313 *cruist li
acers*; 2302b: 2313 *ne briset ne n'esgrunie*, 2340 *ne fruisset ne ne brise*;
2303a: 787, 1935 *ço dist li quens*; 2304a: 2316, 2344 *e! Durendal*; 2304b:
350, 2221 *tant mare fustes, ber*; 2306a: 1465, 3336, 3407 *tantes batailles*;
2306b: 865 *e vencues en champ*; 2307a: 525, 540, 553 *par tantes teres*, 2378
*de tantes teres*; 2308a: 2334, 2353 *que Carles tient*; 2308b: 2353 *ki la barbe
ad flurie*, 2334 *ki ad la barbe blanche*, 3618 *tresqu'en la barbe blanche*, 3173,
3503 *blanche ad la barbe*; 2309a: 2351 *ne vos ait hume*; 2311a: 1733 *n'ert
mais tel hume*; 2312a: 2338 *Rollant ferit*; 2313a: 2302 *cruist li acers*; 2313b:
2302 *ne freint ne ne s'esgruignet*, 2340 *ne fruisset ne ne brise*; 2314a: 959
*quant el le veit*, 3640 *quant ele vit*, 1110, 1932 *quant Rollant veit*; 2314b:
2342 *que ne la freindrat mie*; 2315a: 1483, 2343 *a sei meïsme*; 2316a: 2304,
2344 *e! Durendal*; 2317a: 1808 *cuntre soleil*; 2322a: 2324, 2327, 2331 *jo l'en
cunquis*, 198 *jo vos cunquis*, 2323, 2325 *si l'en cunquis*; 2323a: same; 2324a:
same; 2325a: same; 2331a: same; 2333a: 2751 *cunquis l'avrat*; 2334a: 2308a
*que Carles tient*; 2334b: 3173, 3503 *blanche ad la barbe*, 3618 *tresqu'en la
barbe blanche*, 2308 *ki la barbe ad canue*, 2353 *ki la barbe ad flurie*; 2335a:
3835 *a ceste espee*; 2335b: 3711 *e dulor e pesance*; 2336a: 1485, 1701, 3909
*mielz voeill murir*; 2338a: 2312 *Rollant ferit*; 2338b: 2300 *ad une perre byse*;
2339b: 2730 *ne vos sai dire quanz*; 2340b: 2302 *ne freint ne ne s'esgruignet*,
2313 *ne briset ne n'esgrunie*; 2341a: 1156, 1596, 2015, 2240, 3912 *cuntre le
ciel*; 2342b: 2314 *que n'en pout mie freindre*; 2343a: 2026, 2716 *mult dulce-
ment*; 2344a: 2304, 2316 *e! Durendal*; 2345a: 2506 *en l'oret punt*; 2349a: 2561
*il nen est dreiz*; 2351a: 2309 *ne vos ait hume*; 2351b: 2602 *i ferat cuardie*;
2353a: 2308, 2334 *que Carles tient*; 2353b: 2334 *ki ad la barbe blanche*, 2308
*ki la barbe ad canue*, 3618 *tresqu'en la barbe blanche*, 3173, 3503 *blanche ad
la barbe*; 2354a: 16, 96, 103, and 51 other examples *li empereres*.

En sun visage sa culur ad perdue.
Dedevant lui ad une perre byse:                    2300
.X. colps i fiert par doel e par rancune.
CRUIST LI ACERS, NE FREINT [NE] N'ESGRUIGNET.
"E!" dist li quens, "sainte Marie, aiue!
E! DURENDAL, bone, si mare fustes!
Quant jo mei perd, de vos n'en ai mais cure.
Tantes batailles en camp en ai vencues,
E tantes teres larges escumbatues,
QUE CARLES TIENT, ki la barbe ad canue!
NE VOS AIT HUME ki pur altre fuiet!
Mult bon vassal vos ad lung tens tenue:                    2310
Jamais n'ert tel en France l'asolue."

CLXXII  ROLLANT FERIT el perrun de sardonie.
CRUIST LI ACERS, NE BRISET NE N'ESGRUNIE.
Quant il ço vit QUE N'EN POUT MIE FREINDRE,
A sei meïsme la cumencet a pleindre:
"E! DURENDAL, cum es bele, e clere, e blanche!
Cuntre soleill si luises e reflambes!
Carles esteit es vals de Moriane,
Quant Deus del cel li mandat par sun a[n]gle
Qu'il te dunast a un cunte cataignie:                    2320
Dunc la me ceinst li gentilz reis, li magnes.
Jo l'en cunquis Namon e Bretaigne,
Si l'en cunquis e Peitou e le Maine;
Jo l'en cunquis Normendie la franche,
Si l'en cunquis Provence e Equitaigne
E Lumbardie e trestute Romaine;
Jo l'en cunquis Baiver e tute Flandres,
E Burguigne e trestute Puillanie,
Costentinnoble, dunt il out la fiance,
E en Saisonie fait il ço qu'il demandet;                    2330
Jo l'en cunquis e Escoce e Vales Islonde,
E Engletere, que il teneit sa cambre;
Cunquis l'en ai païs e teres tantes,

QUE CARLES TIENT, *ki ad la barbe blanche.*
*Pur ceste espee ai dulor e pesance:*
*Mielz voeill murir* qu'entre paiens remaigne.
Deus! Perre, n'en laiset hunir France!"

CLXXIII ROLLANT FERIT EN UNE PERRE BISE:
Plus en abat *que jo ne vos sai dire.*
L'espee cruist, NE FRUISSET NE NE BRISE,                    2340
*Cuntre ciel* amunt est resortie.
Quant veit li quens QUE NE LA FREINDRAT MIE,
*Mult dulcement* la pleinst a sei meïsme:
"E! *Durendal,* cum es bele e seintisme!
*En l'oriet punt* asez i ad reliques:
La dent seint Perre e del sanc seint Basilie,
E des chevels mun seignor seint Denise,
Del vestement i ad seinte Marie.
*Il nen est dreiz* que paiens te baillisent;
De chrestiens devez estre servie.                           2350
NE VOS AIT HUME *ki facet cuardie!*
Mult larges teres de vus avrai cunquises,
QUE CARLES TENT, *ki la barbe ad flurie.*
*E li empereres* en est ber e riches."

## Roland's death[45]

CLXXIV *Ço sent Rollant* que la mort le tresprent,
*Devers la teste* sur le quer li descent.

---

[45] 2355a: 2259, 2284, 2297, 2366 *ço sent Rollant;* 2356a: 3604 *desur la teste;* 2357a: 114, 165 *desuz un pin;* 2358a: 671, 1665, 2175, and 10 others *sur l'erbe verte;* 2358b: 3097 *si se est culchet adenz;* 2360b: 3367 *vers la gent paienie;* 2362b: 614 *a trestute sa gent,* 2834 *e trestute ma gent;* 2363a: 2045 *e! gentilz quens;* 2364a: 2239, 2383 *cleimet sa culpe;* 2364b: 1426 *e menut e suvent;* 2365a: 2370 *de mes pecchez,* 2388 *pur les pecchez;* 2365b: 2389 [*sun destre guant*] *a Deu en puroffrit;* 2366a: 2259, 2284, 2297, 2355 *ço sent Rollant;* 2366b: 1603 *de sun tens n'i ad plus,* 3840 *de sun tens n'i ad mais;* 2367a: 1021, 2266, 3128 *devers Espaigne;* 2367b: 2869 *est en un pui muntet;* 2370a: 2365 *pur ses pecchez,* 2388 *pur les pecchez;* 2373a: 2389, 3851 *sun destre guant;* 2375a: 194, 355, 663, and 30 other examples *li quens Rollant;* 2376a: 2165 *envers Espaigne;* 2376b: 3098 *turnet sun vis;* 2378a: 2307 *e*

> *Desuz un pin* i est alet curant,
> *Sur l'erbe verte s'i est culchet adenz,*
> Desuz lui met s'espee e l'olifan;
> Turnat sa teste *vers la paiene gent;*                    2360
> Pur ço l'at fait que il voelt veirement
> Que Carles diet *e trestute sa gent,*
> *Li gentilz quens,* qu'il fut mort cunquerant.
> *Cleimet sa culpe e menut e suvent;*
> PUR SES PECCHEZ DEU EN PUROFFRID LO GUANT. AOI.

CLXXV  *Ço sent Rollant de sun tens n'i ad plus.*
> *Devers Espaigne est en un pui agut;*
> A l'une main si ad sun piz batud:
> "Deus, meie culpe vers les tues vertuz
> DE MES PECCHEZ, des granz e des menuz                    2370
> Que jo ai fait des l'ure que nez fui
> Tresqu'a cest jur que ci sui consoüt!"
> *Sun destre guant* en ad vers Deu tendut:
> Angles del ciel i descendent a lui. AOI.

CLXXVI  *Li quens Rollant se jut desuz un pin;*
> *Envers Espaigne en ad turnet sun vis.*
> De plusurs choses a remembrer li prist:
> *De tantes teres* cum li bers cunquist,
> *De dulce France,* des humes de sun lign,
> *De Carlemagne,* sun seignor, kil nurrit.                2380
> *Ne poet muer n'en plurt e ne suspirt.*

---

*tantes teres*, 525, 540, 553 *par tantes teres;* 2379a: 109 *de dulce France,* 360, 573 *en dulce France;* 2380a: 538, 551 *de Carlemagne;* 2381a: 773 *ne pot muer,* 1642, 2381, 2517 *ne poet muer;* 2381b: 1836 *n'i plurt et se dement,* 2517 *n'en plurt et nes dement;* 2382a: 1036 *a lui meïsme;* 2382b: 1973 *n'i volt mie ublier;* 2383a: 2239, 2364 *cleimet sa culpe;* 2383b: 1132 *si preiez Deu mercit;* 2384a: 3100 *veire paterne;* 2384b: 1865 *ki unkes ne mentit;* 2386a: 3104 *e Daniël;* 2388a: 2365 *pur ses pecchez;* 2370 *de mes pecchez;* 2389a: 2373, 3851 *sun destre guant;* 2389b: 2365 *Deu puroffrid lo guant;* 2390a: 2526, 2847, 3610, 3993 *seint Gabriel;* 2391b: 139 *en tint sun chef enclin,* 214, 771 *en tint sun chef enbrunc;* 2392a: 696 *jointes ses mains;* 2392b: 3723 *est a sa fin alee;* 2394a: 53 *a seint Michel;* 2395a: 175, 1896, 3196, 3461 *ensembl'od els.*

*Mais lui meïsme ne volt mettre en ubli,*
*Cleimet sa culpe, si priet Deu mercit:*
*"Veire Paterne, ki unkes ne mentis,*
Seint Lazaron de mort resurrexis,
*E Daniel* des leons guaresis,
Guaris de mei l'anme de tuz perilz
PUR LES PECCHEZ que en ma vie fis!"
*Sun destre guant* A DEU EN PUROFFRIT;
*Seint Gabriel* de sa main l'ad pris.                            2390
Desur sun braz *teneit le chef enclin;*
*Juntes ses mains est alet a sa fin.*
Deus tramist sun angle Cherubin,
*E seint Michel* del Peril;
*Ensembl'od els* sent Gabriel i vint.
L'anme del cunte portent en pareis.

Formula density for these scenes is outlined in the following
table:

| scene | hemistichs | formulas | percentage formulas | verified outside scene | percentage verified outside scene |
|---|---|---|---|---|---|
| French council | 348 | 142 | 40.8 | 124 | 35.6 |
| first horn | 122 | 57 | 46.7 | 47 | 38.5 |
| second horn | 92 | 36 | 39.1 | 34 | 37.0 |
| leavetaking | 42 | 15 | 35.7 | 15 | 35.7 |
| Durendal | 116 | 54 | 46.6 | 36 | 31.0 |
| Roland's death | 84 | 42 | 50.0 | 37 | 44.0 |
| *totals* | 804 | 346 | 43.0 | 293 | 36.4 |

All six scenes taken together are more formulaic than the poem
as a whole by 7.8 percentage points. Each scene individually,
moreover, is proportionally more formulaic than the entire *Ro-
land*. Even when, to forestall the objection that some phrases
are being repeated for lyrical effect, formulas which are only
verifiable within the individual scene are subtracted from the
total, five of the six passages are seen to contain a higher pro-

portion of formulas than the poem as a whole, and the Durendal laisses are only three and one-half points less formulaic than the whole.

If the literate poet whom we are hypothetically assuming intervened late in the *Roland* tradition added any passages to the poem, the best scenes, considered here, are plainly not among them, for they bear the hallmarks of the oral tradition. There is no need to assume that a learned poet had to intervene in Oxford or its archetype in order to improve the literary quality of the legend unless he were a singer versed in the oral-formulaic style who had learned to write, since those passages which, in the estimation of literary critics, assure the *Roland*'s right to a place among the world's great epics, reveal an oral technique at work. If a *remanieur* who composed in the style of writers rather than in the oral-formulaic language had a role in the formation of these scenes, his intervention must have dated from a period considerably before the archetype was committed to parchment—long enough before that event to allow oral tradition to efface stylistic traces of his craft. It is difficult to conceive how a *Roland* already endowed with these scenes would have required any substantial "improvement" from the hands of a late literate poet. The comparison of *Roland* with the twelfth and thirteenth-century *chansons de geste* and romances showed the Oxford text fitting perfectly into the formulaic spectrum while differing radically from the poems known to have been created in writing. A truly learned poet would have to be supposed to have endowed his work with a formulaic profile which is, in its extent and its uniformity, just what one would expect from an oral poet. The hypothesis of a significant learned intervention between the jongleurs and Oxford does not stand up under factual analysis.

One is at liberty to speculate about the early stages of the legend, during which a learned man, perhaps even several, may have had some hand in its formation and transformation. There is, however, no stylistic evidence for this in the text which has come down to us.

We are left with but one cogent possibility supported by con-
crete evidence: the *Roland* which we possess must be a very nearly
unadulterated product of oral tradition, little changed, except
for its orthography, from the form in which it was first taken
down from the lips of a singer or written down by a singer who
had acquired literacy. If verses were added by eleventh or twelfth-
century scribes, they were not of such a nature as to have changed
the poem significantly for the better. While entertaining the pos-
sibility of the archetype of Oxford having been created by a
singer who learned how to write, one must bear in mind that the
uniformity of formulaic density found throughout the poem and
the highly formulaic character of its best scenes show that such a
singer's style was that of oral poetry and not that of poets who
create in writing.[46] It seems therefore more likely that the
*Roland* is an oral-dictated text, taken down by a scribe, or per-
haps by several scribes working in tandem, from the lips of a
singing poet. This would best account for the fact that the prime
method of poets who compose in writing, namely revision by
afterthought, is nowhere in evidence.

The presence of so many formulas in *Roland*'s key scenes poses
an unexpected problem for the critic. Should we suppose a causal
connection between the higher formula density of these passages
and their literary excellence? The six key scenes I have examined
contain on the average one-fourth more formulas than the poem
as a whole. But I doubt that such a conclusion would be warranted
were it based solely on the evidence I have presented. I do believe,
however, that the figures point up the desirability of a new critical

[46] Italo Siciliano's attempt, in *Les Chansons de geste et l'épopée*, Biblioteca
di Studi Francesi, III (Turin: Società Editrice Internazionale, 1968), pp. 132–
133, to prove the contrary is woefully insufficient. A few repetitions quoted
at random from Virgil, the *Enéas*, and other poems do not prove anything.
Beginning with Parry, researchers in this field have always admitted that
repetitions are a fact of literary life. Orally composed poems are dis-
tinguishable not because they contain repetitions, but because semantic
and syntactic repetitions are fundamental to their style.

orientation. For too long it has been assumed that lasting poetry could only be created in one way, that is by poets working with the methods of literate creators. The extent to which the *Roland* poet used traditional, formulaic language does not differ significantly from that of other poets who came after him: it is what he made out of that traditional language that sets him apart from them. Obviously his genius does not lie in a capacity for juxtaposing individual words in striking combinations, but rather in an ability to combine whole blocks of words with other blocks, while employing the methods of oral improvisation. In his greatest moments he relied upon the formulaic language not less, but more. It is time for medievalists to cease treating formulas like the repetitions or clichés of the written language. Literary works can be composed in a highly stylised diction: the *Roland* alone is proof of that. Instead of admitting grudgingly that it is a worthy piece of literature *in spite of* its formulas, we should take our cue from the poet himself and recognize that formulas are the basic matter of his creation and that it is the effective use of formulas that generates effective scenes.

Critics of medieval French literature have shown an obvious reluctance to admit that an unlettered, improvising poet is capable of composing, in the act of singing, a work of high artistic quality. Not only is this assumption gratuitous: it is ultimately based upon a circular reasoning which might not at first be apparent. The establishment of a critical tradition involves evaluation of thousands of literary works, of which some attract more admiration than others. The very idea we hold of perfection in the epic is eventually the result of a filtering of epic production through the fine mesh of thousands of accumulated critical reactions. But if one goes to the most ancient epic models, those most admired by the first systematic literary critic but still revered above all others in this age of criticism, one finds, as Parry proved, two orally-composed poems, the *Iliad* and the *Odyssey*. To hold that the *Chanson de Roland* is too well organized to be an orally-composed poem is ultimately to say that it is better constructed than Homer's masterpieces, and no critic has yet ventured this proposition. Further progress in medieval French epic criticism depends upon recognition that the assumption of the inferiority of oral poetry to written poetry is invalid.

# 3: The Episode of Baligant: Theme and Technique

THE STRUCTURE of the *Chanson de Roland* has been looked upon as three-fold, four-fold or five-fold. Those who regard the episode of Baligant as an intrusion upon the original framework of treason-betrayal-revenge and therefore eliminate it from the construction share the tripartite view. Fern Farnham, in an article entitled "Romanesque Design in the *Chanson de Roland*,"[1] imaginatively compares the poem's structure to the five-part recessed panel arrangement of the tympanum at Moissac and other similar Romanesque sculptural representations. The death of Roland holds the central position in her scheme, flanked symmetrically by, on the one hand, the battle of Roncevaux and Ganelon's plotting, and, on the other, "Baligant" (including Charlemagne's initial defeat of Marsile's forces) and Ganelon's trial. Pierre Le Gentil sees Roland's death as an integral part of the battle of Roncevaux, and agrees with Jean Rychner in giving the poem a four-part framework.[2] Rychner is intent on uncovering explicit signs of a partition into sittings (*séances*), divisions of the poem which would have been sung as continuous performances, but admits that he has found none unless one counts the recapitulated message scene at the beginning of "Baligant," which may have

---

[1] *Romance Philology*, XVIII (1964), 143–164.
[2] Pierre Le Gentil, *La Chanson de Roland* (Paris: Hatier-Boivin, 1955), p. 90; Jean Rychner, *La Chanson de geste: essai sur l'art épique des jongleurs* (Geneva: Droz, 1955), pp. 38–39.

been composed in order to bring the audience up to date at the start of a new sitting.[3]

There is, however, internal evidence of the poem's larger divisions. The first clue is in the episode of Baligant, which begins with verses which recall the poem's first laisse, telling how the emperor had been in Spain for seven years and laying out anew, as if the audience were unaware of it, the background of the entire war. This recapitulation would be unnecessary in a narrative of written creation. Its position at the head of a new turn in the plot suggests, however, that it marks the beginning of a major division in the performance, the poet having taken his rest after singing of the pagans' dispersal in the previous laisse. The textual repetition of phrases from the poem's inception can hardly be fortuitous:

| | |
|---|---|
| Carles li reis, nostre emperere magnes, | Li emperere par sa grant poestét, |
| **Set anz tuz pleins ad estéd** en Espaigne: | .VII. anz tuz plens ad en Espaigne estét; |
| Tresqu'en la mer cunquist la tere altaigne. | |
| N'i ad castel ki devant lui remaigne; | Prent i chastels e alquantes citez. |
| Mur ne citét n'i est remés a fraindre, | |
| Fors Sarraguce, ki est en une muntaigne. | |
| Li reis Marsilie la tient, ki Deu nen aimet (vv. 1–7). | Li reis Marsilie s'en purcacet asez (vv. 2609–2612). |

The flashback technique is worthy of note, but it is a device which occurs in oral and written literature with equal frequency. More interesting from the point of view of oral technique is the language used in the transition. Four elements are mentioned in the

[3] Rychner, pp. 49, 61–62.

juxtaposed passages, and in the same order: the emperor, his presence in Spain, his success in taking castles and towns (spread over two verses in laisse I, but there too couched in the words *castels* and *citez*), and finally the enmity of King Marsile. The first text takes seven verses to express what the second says in four, but the main difference is that laisse I gives a more precise account of the extent of Charlemagne's victories. The similarities far outweigh the differences: note especially the textual repetition of verse 2, with only a slight modification of word order for conformity to the new assonance. The episode of Baligant is, then, formally similar, in its inception, to the first verses of the poem, and to an extent that justifies our designating this type of beginning as an "articulation motif."

The later passage is obviously a *jongleresque* way of bringing an uninformed, or ill-informed, segment of his audience up to date at the beginning of a block of narrative. It occurs in spite of the fact that Marsile was himself the subject of the previous laisse and in spite of the fact that those present from the start of the performance would know this background information. But not having mentioned Baligant up to this point in his tale (and this is highly unusual with a poet who almost systematically inserts into his narrative anticipations of the other major developments, no doubt so as to persuade the audience to hear him out), the poet is now obliged to flash back to a point seven years before the narrative action began:

> Al premer an fist ses brefs seieler,
> En Babilonie Baligant ad mandet (vv. 2613–2614).

This admittedly abrupt, almost clumsy expansion of the poem's scope, is introduced in a formulaic way through the utilization of the inception motif. While the intrusion of Baligant may well cause surprise, the manner in which he makes his entry conforms to the style of *Roland*'s first laisse, and is in no way atypical of the jongleur's technique.

The second theme, the battle of Roncevaux, should logically

start after the bulk of Charles' army begins its homeward journey, that is subsequent to v. 702: *Vers dulce France tuit sunt achiminez*. And, in fact, an abbreviated but nonetheless clearly recognizable form of the articulation motif follows immediately, at the start of laisse 55:

> Carles li magnes ad Espaigne guastede,
> Les castels pris, les citez violees.
> Ço dit li reis que sa guere out finee.
> Vers dulce France chevalchet l'emperere (vv. 703–706).

Of the four elements found in the inception motifs of laisses 1 and 188 ("Baligant"), three are present here: the naming of the emperor, his presence in Spain and his capture of castles and towns. The fourth, Marsile's enmity, has its equivalent in the pagan army's lurking presence at the end of laisse 55:

> Paien chevalchent par cez greignurs valees, . . .
> En un bruill parsum les puis remestrent;
> Quatre cent milie atendent l'ajurnee.
> Deus! quel dulur que li Franceis nel sevent! AOI (vv. 710; 714–716).

The final great division of the poem is Ganelon's trial, preceded by the brief and poignant episode of *Alde la bele*, Roland's betrothed. The formal announcement *Desor cumencet le plait de Guenelun*[4] (v. 3704) ending laisse 266, precedes the fourth occurrence of the articulation motif, briefer still this time because, with the whole of Spain subdued, neither the vanquished castles and towns nor Marsile himself need be mentioned.

> Li empereres est repairét d'Espaigne,
> E vient a Ais, al meillor siéd de France (vv. 3705–3706).

---

[4] Ramón Menéndez Pidal, *La Chanson de Roland et la Tradition épique des Francs* (Paris: A. et J. Picard, 1960), p. 500, recognized the *reprise* of this verse in vv. 3747–3748, *Des ore cumencet le plait et les noveles/De Guenelun ki traisun ad faite*, as signalling the start of a seance.

The intervention of Alde's death scene necessitates a restatement of this inception two laisses farther on: *Li emperere est repairét ad Ais* (v. 3734).

In considering the architectonic significance of this articulation of the *Roland*'s four divisions, let us recall that we are dealing with two distinct modes of structure. On the narrative plane, the four large movements of the plot are each composed of a series of actions termed motifs, themselves composed of formulas. In actual performance, the largest division is the sitting, a segment of the poem sung before an audience as a continuous presentation, divided into laisses, groups of verses linked by a common assonance and bordered on either side by groups of differing assonances, of which the atomistic metrical unit is the hemistich. To the analytic sequence of narrative levels, theme-motif-formula, corresponds the sequence of performance, sitting-laisse-hemistich. Each element of the latter triad would, in actual performance, be defined by the shorter or longer pauses which surround it: the sitting by the intermissions in presentation which necessitate the inception motif, the laisse by the short hiatus between assonating series, filled perhaps with a musical interlude, and the hemistich by two brief pauses, the one occasioned by the paratactic movement of the phrase, the other by the obligatory "caesura" after the fourth syllable of each verse. Jean Rychner has shown conclusively[5] that in the *Chanson de Roland* more than in any other French epic, the middle element of each of these triads, namely motif and laisse, correspond to each other, the motif being generally coterminous with the laisse. One can verify upon simple observation that the formula corresponds to the hemistich. This leaves only the relationship between the third element of each triad, theme and sitting, to be elucidated.

Returning to the articulation motif, we find that its four occurrences are each at the threshold of a major *narrative* division, or theme. Their function, however, is not thematic but presentational. This can be seen most clearly at the beginnings of the

[5] As far as I know, this element of his analysis has never been questioned.

episode of Baligant and the battle of Roncevaux, where, on the
level of narration alone, the articulatory clusters of formulas are
most obviously redundant. But it is also discernible in the trial of
Ganelon, for here it follows immediately upon the articulatory
closing of the previous theme, "Baligant," with the announce-
ment of Ganelon's trial at the end of laisse 266: *Desore cumencet
le plait de Guenelun.* The articulation motif begins each segment
of the *performance*, and that is its primary function. That it also
introduces each theme illuminates the relationship between theme
and sitting in the poem: like the pairs hemistich-formula and
laisse-motif, the sitting and the theme are also coterminous. This
links the two triads in a functional cycle: on all three levels, nar-
rative and performance are almost perfectly matched in the
*Chanson de Roland.*

What of the question of a fifth division in the poem? Fern
Farnham would set the death of Roland aside as a pivotal episode
around which the other themes rest symmetrically. If Roland's
death were a possible *séance* of performance, then it would be
the only one which does not begin with an inception motif. Be-
cause of the remarkable conformity between sitting and theme,
and because no articulations of *séance* are present in the poem
except the four I have mentioned, I conclude that for the eleventh-
century tradition itself, the *Roland* was divided into four themes.
This does not prevent Professor Farnham and others from pro-
posing fruitful interpretations of the poem's structure from a
modern point of view; but for the tradition of singers whose
elaboration culminated in the archetype of Oxford, the four-
fold division must have been a reality of both performance and
narrative.

The four large divisions of the poem are, then, as follow:

| | |
|---|---|
| Vv. 1–702 | The plotting of the treason |
| vv. 703–2608 | The battle of Roncevaux (including Roland's death and the pursuit of Marsile's forces) |
| vv. 2609–3704 | The episode of Baligant |
| vv. 3705–4001 | The trial of Ganelon |

The third theme, the episode of Baligant hereinafter called simply "Baligant," has long been a subject of controversy, drawing the attention of almost every major *Roland* scholar. Although it comprises over one quarter of the Oxford version, many have found it an anomaly within the poem, often viewed as a late addition to the tradition, if not an interpolation. Jules Horrent considers it the key to a correct view of the manuscript filiation.[6] The rest of this chapter is devoted to the place of "Baligant" within the tradition. As in the previous chapter, I will base my conclusions largely upon the evidence of the poem itself and upon analogies with other oral literatures rather than upon external historical facts which have been taken up by many previous commentators. But since so much ink has been expended upon the question of "Baligant's" authenticity, it will be necessary to review previous findings[7] before going on to see what light can be shed on the episode by an examination of technique.

The episode of Baligant is absent from many of the *Roland* versions which have come down to us. Of the Latin texts, the

---

[6] *La Chanson de Roland dans les littératures française et espagnole au moyen âge* (Paris: Société d'Edition "Les Belles Lettres," 1951), p. 242.

[7] An exhaustive bibliography of "Baligant" would include virtually every important critical work which has ever been devoted to the *Roland*. The following items contain substantial commentary on the main problems: Fr. Scholle, "Die Baligantepisode, ein Einschub in das Oxforder Rolandslied," *Zeitschrift für romanische Philologie*, I (1877), 26–40; E. Dönges, *Die Baligantepisode im Rolandslied* (Marburg dissertation; Heilbronn, 1880); Charles A. Knudson, "Etudes sur la composition de la *Chanson de Roland*," *Romania*, LXIII (1937), 48–92; Paul Aebischer, "Pour la défense et l'illustration de l'épisode de Baligant," *Mélanges Ernest Hoepffner* (Paris: Société d'Edition "Les Belles Lettres," 1949), pp. 173–82; Jules Horrent, *La Chanson de Roland dans les littératures française et espagnole au moyen âge*, Bibliothèque de la Faculté de Philosophie et Lettres de l'Université de Liège, CXX (Paris: Société d'Edition "Les Belles Lettres," 1951), pp. 120–134; Ruggero M. Ruggieri, "Valore, tradizione e diffusione dell' episodio di Baligante'," *Cultura Neolatina*, XIII (1953), 57–85; Maurice Delbouille, *Sur la genèse de la Chanson de Roland (Travaux récents—propositions nouvelles)* (Brussels: Palais des Académies, 1954), pp. 32–61; Ramon Menéndez Pidal, *La Chanson de Roland et la tradition épique des Francs* (Paris: Picard, 1960), esp. pp. 123–129.

*Nota Emilianense*, the *Pseudo-Turpin Chronicle* and the *Carmen de prodicione Guenonis* do not include it. Branch VIII of the *Karlamagnús saga*, an account of Charlemagne's life based upon legendary French sources and compiled and translated into Old Norse for King Hákon Hákonarson around the middle of the thirteenth century, consists of a version of the *Chanson de Roland* which differs from all known manuscripts and excludes "Baligant."[8] Of the rhymed versions, Lyon omits the episode, as do the prose *Garin de Monglane* and the prose *Galien*. There are vestiges of "Baligant" in most of these versions, however: mentions of the emir's name, dreams which prefigure the episode, elements of plot which are inexplicable without it.[9] One cannot, therefore, conclude, on the basis of these seven texts, that there existed a primitive version of *Roland* without "Baligant." Still, six medieval authors or compilers, all working independently of each other, saw fit actively to exclude this important sequence of narrative from their accounts of Charlemagne's Spanish adventure. Did the historical improbabilities of the episode lead them to reject it, or was their literary sense outraged by the transformation "Baligant" works upon the tale of Roland's defeat?

The problem of the episode's relationship to the rest of *Roland* is best considered with the narrative events in mind, especially because many of the arguments both for and against it are based on elements of plot. The battle of Roncevaux, a Pyrrhic victory for the French rearguard, sets the stage for Baligant's advent. Charlemagne arrives at Roncevaux at the head of his troops immediately after his nephew's demise. Wishing to pursue the

---

[8] See Paul Aebischer, *Rolandiana Borealia. La Saga af Runzivals bardaga et ses dérivés scandinaves comparés à la Chanson de Roland. Essai de restauration du manuscrit français utilisé par le traducteur norrois*, Publications de la Faculté des Lettres de l'Université de Lausanne, XI (Lausanne, 1954) and "Les différents états de la *Karlamagnús saga*" in *Fragen und Forschungen, Festgabe für Theodor Frings*, Veröffentlichungen des Instituts für deutsche Sprache und Literatur, VIII (Berlin, 1956); also E. F. Halvorsen, *The Norse Version of the Chanson de Roland*, Bibliotheca Arnamagnaeana, XIX (Copenhagen: Munksgaard, 1959), esp. pp. 221–222.

[9] Horrent, *Roland dans les littératures française et espagnole*, pp. 120–134.

fleeing Saracens, he appoints four French knights to protect the bodies of his fallen rearguard. He then leads his men on the chase, but seeing that night is approaching, stops in a meadow to pray that God arrest the sun's movement so as to provide enough light and time for him to carry out his vengeance. An angel appears to announce that God has granted the emperor's wish:

> Pur Karlemagne fist Deus vertuz mult granz,
> Car li soleilz est remes en estant (vv. 2458–2459).

The pursuit is successful. The French overtake their enemies and begin to kill them; the bulk of the Saracen forces, leaping into the waters of the river Sebre after a prayer to their god Tervagant, are drowned. Since it is too late now to return to Roncevaux, the horses are let out to pasture, and the army passes the night on the banks of the Sebre. Worn out with grief and physical exertion, Charles falls asleep and is sent two dreams by God, through the intermediary of the angel Gabriel. Amid thunder, wind, frost, storms and fire falling from the heavens, he sees bears and leopards, dragons, and other fantastic beasts attacking his men, who call out to him for assistance. He is prevented from helping them by a fierce lion which attacks him; the two struggle, but the outcome hangs in doubt when the first dream ends. A second dream shows Charlemagne at Aix, where a bear is held in chains. From the direction of the Ardennes thirty bears approach to ask that their relative be freed, but a hound comes running out of the imperial palace to attack the largest of the thirty. The result of this battle is likewise left obscure, and Charlemagne sleeps on until the day.

In the meanwhile, Marsile has just returned to Saragossa, mortally wounded by Roland, who had cut off his right hand at Roncevaux. Twenty thousand of his men gather about to insult and destroy the idols of their gods Apolin, Tervagant and Mahumet. Amid this tumult, Marsile's wife Bramimunde mourns over Saragossa and her husband, expressing her fervent wish that the *amiralt* join battle with Charles to avenge the defeat of Roncevaux (vv. 2602–2604). This reference placed in the mouth of Bramimunde is the first mention in the poem of the emir of Babylon (Cairo), Baligant, who is named a few verses further on, at the beginning of the third *séance*:

> Li emperere par sa grant poestet,
> .VII. anz tuz plens ad en Espaigne estet;
> Prent i chastels e alquantes citez.
> Li reis Marsilie s'en purcacet asez:
> Al premer an fist ses brefs seieler,
> En Babilonie Baligant ad mandet,
> Ço est l'amiraill, le viel d'antiquitet,
> Tut survesquiet e Virgilie e Omer,
> En Sarraguce alt sucurre li ber;
> E, s'il nel fait, il guerpirat ses deus,
> E tuz ses ydeles que il soelt adorer,
> Si recevrat sainte chrestientet,
> A Charlemagne se vuldrat acorder.
> E cil est loinz, si ad mult demuret (vv. 2609–2622).

Baligant arrives with an impressive fleet and sends envoys to Marsile, asking him to submit to his sovereignty, which he does, remitting to Baligant the key to Saragossa. The emir arrives in the city shortly thereafter to receive from Marsile a glove symbolizing transfer of the fief.

At this point the scene moves back to the Sebre, where Charlemagne is just awakening from his night of troubled dreams. The French army returns to Roncevaux where, having pronounced a dirge over Roland's corpse, Charles orders that the fallen knights be buried in a common grave and the bodies of Roland, Oliver and Turpin be prepared for the trans-Pyrenean journey. He is making ready to turn northward: *Venir s'en volt li emperere Carles* (v. 2974), when two Saracen messengers ride up to announce the coming battle with Baligant's forces. The emperor summons his most trustworthy followers:

Si'n apelat Jozeran de Provence,
Naimon li duc, Antelme de Maience:
"En tels vassals deit hom aveir fiance.
Asez est fols ki entr'els se demente" (vv. 3007–3010).

He gives Rabel and Guineman Oliver's sword and the olifant and commands them to ride in the front rank, in place of the two dead heroes, with fifteen thousand men. Naimes and Jozeran de Provence form the rest of the Christians into divisions, ten in all. The Saracens are making similar preparations: Baligant, granting to his son Malprimes the right of first blow, forms thirty divisions. Battle is joined, with Rabel and Guineman winning the first combats, while Malprimes wreaks terror among the French ranks until he is killed by Naimes. Charlemagne has to come to the aid of his wise counselor and rescues him from Canabeus, whom the emperor kills. Baligant in the meantime has overcome Guineman. After some scenes of general combat, Charles and Baligant, the emperors of Christendom and Islam, come together on the field of battle to fight a cataclysmic duel. The French leader falters under his enemy's sword stroke, but God comes to his aid:

Mais Deus ne volt qu'il seit mort ne vencut:
Seint Gabriel est repairet a lui,
Si li demandet: "Reis magnes, que fais tu?" (vv. 3609–3611).

This intervention brings Charlemagne to his senses, enabling him to split Baligant's skull. When Marsile, on his deathbed in Saragossa, learns that his pagan ally has been stopped and the army put to flight, he turns toward the wall and dies. Saragossa is taken, its inhabitants given the choice between conversion to Christianity or death (except Bramimunde who will be converted later *par amur*), and the French return to Aix, leaving the olifant at Saint Seurin de Bordeaux along the way and burying the bodies of Roland, Oliver and Turpin at Saint Romain de Blaye. Upon his arrival at the seat of empire, Charlemagne summons his judges: *Desore cumencet le plait de Guenelun* (v. 3704).

This, in brief, is the tale told in the episode of Baligant. I have purposely telescoped certain parts of the narrative, providing greater detail at those points where previous scholars have thought they found evidence for "Baligant's" inauthenticity. I have considered the episode proper to comprise verses 2609 to 3704, but the events recounted just after Charlemagne's first dream, namely the second dream prefiguring the great battle between the emir and himself, the destruction of the pagan trinity of idols, and, finally, Bramimonde's regrets, all lead up to the episode. If some poet or poets transformed the *Roland* by integrating the episode of Baligant into a previously existing epic whose climax occurred with the battle of Roncevaux, then these three laisses must have been inserted at the same time. Likewise there are passages after verse 2609 which, continuing for a moment with the same hypothesis, certainly would subsist from a previous version, to wit laisses 202–212 (vv. 2845–2973), telling of Charles' return to Roncevaux, his funeral regrets, and the preparation of the bodies, as well as the bulk of laisse 266, the army's return to Aix. Although the *séance* of Baligant extends from verse 2609 to verse 3704, then, I regard the possible interpolation of scenes as running from verse 2555 to verse 2844, and from verse 2974 to verse 3682.

What would the *Chanson de Roland* be like without the episode of Baligant? The duel between Charlemagne, emperor of Western Europe, and Baligant, supreme lord of the Arab world, transforms the poem from the account of a battle in the Pyrenees between French and Saracen fighting men, brought about by the personal resentment of one Christian chief for another, into an almost cosmic struggle of good and evil wherein right triumphs over all that is culturally and religiously strange. Roncevaux alone, or the clash between two worlds? "Il est certain," writes Maurice Delbouille,[10] "que la première conception est plausible, mais il est non moins certain que la seconde, plus ambitieuse et plus noble, la dépasse de cent coudées en donnant au poème la sig-

[10] *Sur la genèse*, p. 36.

nification politique et religieuse qui en fait l'épopée d'un monde et d'une époque." To limit it to the story of Roland's death, he continues, would reduce immeasurably the deep significance of its poetic conception. But granting the effect of "Baligant's" inclusion upon the *Roland*'s scope, and granting too that it raises the subject from what might be called a somewhat parochial level to a zenith where two cultures confront each other in real and symbolic combat, it is difficult to see what conclusions to draw concerning the relative lateness or "inauthenticity" of the theme. Could an eleventh-century singer not have conferred this vast cultural and religious significance upon the song by adding a thousand verses or so to a previous version? That is a possibility unaffected by our realization of the grandeur of *Roland* with "Baligant." But why deny the merit of having created "Baligant" to the singer responsible for the balanced construction of the rest of the Oxford text? Simply because we know that the normal way for narrative songs to grow from simple *chants d'actualité* to true epics, in both proportion and scope, is precisely through a process of slow, multisecular accretion. The question of "Baligant's" relationship to other parts of *Roland* will not be solved, in either direction, by appeals to the broader scope of the poem's final conception.

The same argument does not apply, however, to the problem of whether Charles' defeat of Baligant is a more fitting revenge for Roland's death than the death of Marsile alone would have been. Although "Baligant" confers cosmic scope exclusively in the Charlemagne-Baligant duel and its outcome, the question of revenge involves an examination of organic relationships, or how the episode fulfills latent expectations set up in the earlier part of *Roland*. Martín de Riquer observes that Marsile's retreat to Saragossa does not constitute a true vengeance for Roncevaux and Roland's death, since it leaves Marsile in possession of the same town he held at the beginning of the poem's action.[11] What-

[11] *Les Chansons de geste françaises* (2nd, revised edition, translated by I.-M. Cluzel; Paris: Nizet, 1957), p. 90.

ever version "Baligant" was added to would have contained the taking of Saragossa, and perhaps this event was present in an earlier state of the poem in much the same form as has come down to us in Oxford. Menéndez Pidal's explanation is closer to reality:

> La deuxième vengeance, exercée sur Baligant, éclipse la vengeance obtenue grâce au miracle renouvelé de Josué. Voilà ce qu'on peut regarder comme un exemple de mauvais goût: faire d'abord intervenir Dieu lui-même, avec un stupéfiant miracle astronomique [the stopping of the sun's movement], pour rendre possible une vengeance complète; ensuite, comme si le Tout-Puissant n'avait pas assez fait, on pense qu'une nouvelle bataille est nécessaire; et celle-là reçoit du Ciel un secours beaucoup plus insignifiant, manifesté seulement par l'apparition de l'ange qui donne du courage à Charlemagne, au cours du duel qui l'oppose à Baligant.[12]

While I would not go so far as to proffer the accusation of *mauvais goût* to the singer responsible for "Baligant," Menéndez Pidal's perception of the overblown quality of Charles' revenge in "Baligant" is well conceived. Revenge is effective only if it is inflicted upon the party responsible for the original misfortune, in this case Marsile. There is no necessity for the poet to bring in a distant scapegoat in order to expiate Roland's death. Marsile's death and the taking of Saragossa, goals of Roland's original advice in the French council scene, are adequate to avenge his martyrdom. "Baligant" may appeal to some tastes, but it is by no means a *necessary* addition. What is more, it distracts from the unity of the total work. It breaks into Roland's"[13] restrained structural balance, where the punishment of the criminal fits the crime committed, with an ill-suited type of medieval "overkill." Even the manner of Marsile's death counterweighs Roland's exemplary end. Roland falls a glorious con-

---

[12] *La Chanson de Roland*, p. 125.

[13] In this chapter the designation "Roland" denotes those lines which remain when the episode of Baligant is removed (vv. 2555–2844 and 2974–3682), as distinct from *Roland*, which is the entire poem including "Baligant."

queror, attended by angels; Marsile dies in misery and renders his soul to the devils:

> Quant l'ot Marsilie, vers sa pareit se turnet,
> Pluret des oilz, tute sa chere enbrunchet:
> Morz est de doel si cum pecchét l'encumbret;
> L'anme de lui as vifs diables dunet. AOI (vv. 3644–3647).

Léon Gautier's enthusiastic declaration concerning the structure of *Roland* with "*Baligant*," ". . . il faut n'avoir pas l'esprit littéraire pour contester une aussi belle et aussi profonde unité," is today no more than a paradoxical curio.[14]

Paul Aebischer has expressed the opinion that the schematic parallelism between Charlemagne and Baligant proves the episode's authenticity. According to this point of view, the emperor could not measure himself against someone else's vassal, but only against a sovereign of the same stature as himself: the counterpart of Roland is Marsile, the counterpart of Charles is Baligant, and the episode is a logical development of these hierarchical correspondences.[15] But there is a fundamental weakness in this reasoning. The hierarchical parallel for Roland in the Saracen camp is not Marsile, but Marsile's nephew Aelroth, who requests from his uncle the right to attack Roland (laisse 69) and is killed by the French hero (laisse 93) in the first single combat of the battle of Roncevaux. The arrangement of combats stresses this correspondence: the French peers meet the pagan peers in the same order in which they have been named by Marsile, so that there can be little doubt the poet meant Aelroth, first among his peers, to be Roland's counterpart. As in the matter of vengeance, the creation of "Baligant" goes far beyond the needs of the tale of Roncevaux. The episode *creates* a new parallelism between Charles and Baligant, similar in kind, although radically different in its relationships, to that of Roland and Oliver. This type of

[14] *Les Epopées françaises* (2nd ed.; Paris: Palmé, 1878–1889), I, 426n.
[15] "Pour la défense," p. 177.

generation of new characters is a not unknown in oral tradition. Far from affirming the necessity of "Baligant" in the poem, the superimposed parallelism is an indication of late changes in the *Roland* tradition, changes which resulted in a different structure.

It is time we turn toward positive evidence of "Baligant's" lack of integration with the rest of *Roland*. The most obvious place to begin is at the episode's beginning, where Baligant is introduced abruptly, without any previous announcement from the poet of the arrival of this leader of all Islam. Charlemagne's first dream, obscure though it is, prefigures some titanic struggle between the emperor and a formidable adversary. But this kind of anticipatory clue, occurring shortly before the arrival of Baligant himself and really a part of the episode, is not what one looks for. The "Roland" poet's technique places low value upon suspense. Time and time again the audience is told of the major events long before they occur, sometimes even long before the groundwork has been laid for them. Thus already in verse 9 we are told, of Marsile: *Nes poet guarder que mals ne l'i ateignet.* Ganelon is *introduced* with an anticipation of his treachery: *Guenes i vint, ki la traïsun fist* (v. 178), and the verse which follows this one tells when the trouble will begin: *Des ore cumencet le cunseill que mal prist.* Ganelon drops the glove granting him authority to speak for Charles:

> Dient Franceis: "Deus! que purrat ço estre?
> De cest message nos avendrat grant perte."
> "Seignurs," dist Guenes, "vos en orrez noveles" (vv. 334–
> 336).

Before the main body of the French army leaves the rearguard behind, Charles has two dreams (laisses 56 and 57) prefiguring Ganelon's betrayal and his trial at Aix: not a word of Baligant. Long before Roland's death, but during the battle of Roncevaux, storms and an earthquake give premonitions of what is to come:

Dient plusor: "Ço est li definement,
La fin del secle, ki nus est en present."
Il nel sevent, ne dient veir nient:
Ço est li granz duels por la mort de Rollant (vv. 1434–1437).

And still nothing of Baligant. Maurice Delbouille remarks ingenuously: "Pourquoi donc le poète aurait-il dû—ou seulement pu—annoncer l'arrivée de Baligant avant ou pendant la bataille de Roncevaux? Il aurait, du coup, réduit d'autant l'intérêt de son récit et diminué la force de l'oeuvre."[16] The answer is simple: the poet *has* announced every other major development in the plot, including Ganelon's treason, Marsile's death, Roland's martyrdom and the final trial. He has announced all the key scenes which his audience can look forward to, except the battle between the two most powerful armies of his mythical world, a battle of which he says himself: *Ne fut si fort enceis ne puis cel tens* (3382). How can we maintain there is no anomaly here? Charles A. Knudson missed the point when he declared: "C'est ne pas se rendre compte que si Marsile croyait [l']arrivée [de Baligant] prochaine, tous ses calculs du début du poème seraient inutiles. Plus besoin de feindre une soumission et de laisser sacrifier les otages: il s'agirait de temporiser quelques jours avec Charlemagne, en attendant le secours de Baligant, et puis de livrer bataille. Le poète l'a bien compris, et il annonce Baligant quand il le faut, et pas avant."[17] Although it appears unlikely, there may be some as yet unexpressed reason why a poet keeps a scrupulous silence until verse 2613 and then reports that Baligant was sent for in the first year of the war. But Knudson obscures the basic distinction between the poet's announcement of the episode and Marsile's knowledge of the timing of the emir's arrival. The poet has taken pains to maintain this distinction on a previous occasion, when he offered his own knowledge in contrast to the opinion of his characters: *Il nel sevent, ne dient veir nient* (v. 1436). For the

[16] *Sur la genèse*, p. 43.          [17] "Etudes sur la composition," p. 58.

lack of anticipation of the duel between two emperors, there is no
cogent explanation except that the technique of anticipatory an-
nouncements entered the Roland tradition long before "Baligant"
was included in the plot, and later singers did not feel obliged to
make up the lack.

Certain discrepancies of *dramatis personae* also set "Baligant"
apart from "Roland." Ten characters appear for the first time in
the episode: Jozeran de Provence (v. 3007), Antelme de Maience
(3008), Rabel (3014), Guineman (3014), Herman de Trace (3042),
Nevelun (3057), Godselme (3067), Hamon de Galice (3073),
Rembalt (3073) and Tierri d'Argonne (3083).[18] Of these ten,
three play such an important role that their absence from the
earlier sections requires comment. Jozeran de Provence is intro-
duced in the company of Naimes and Antelme de Maience.
Charles remarks about the three:

> "En tels vassals deit hom aveir fiance.
> Asez est fols ki entr'els se demente" (vv. 3009–3010).

With Naimes, Jozeran draws the army up into divisions (vv.
3026–3095); he is shown at the beginning of the battle proper,
in the company of Tierri d'Argonne, Gefrei d'Anjou, Oger le
Daneis and Charlemagne, but is never seen or heard of again
in the poem. Who is this knight, so worthy of Charles' confidence
that he shares with the venerable Naimes the task of preparing
the battle formations? His presence is as mysterious as Baligant's
own arrival. Rabel and Guineman are likewise honored to an
astonishing degree for total newcomers: they take the place of
Roland and Oliver, one carrying the latter's sword and the other
the olifant, to lead the French into combat. Rabel kills Torleu,
King of Persia, in the first single combat of the battle; Guineman
kills *"un rei Leutice"* (v. 3360) but is later killed by Baligant
himself (v. 3468). Neither warrior is further mentioned: Guine-

---

[18] The latter personage, appearing in vv. 3083 and 3534, is distinct from
the Tierri, brother of Gefrei d'Anjou, who fights Pinabel in the judicial
combat over Ganelon's guilt.

man is unmourned, Rabel forgotten. The introduction of new names might lead one to suspect only that "Baligant" does not stem from the same tradition as "Roland," but that three characters fill such important roles only to fade into oblivion is strong evidence for the episode's lateness.

Jules Horrent notes a basic flaw in the poem's movement which places "Baligant" in contradiction with "Roland," but which is corrected if "Baligant" is omitted from the early *Chanson de Roland*.[19] Charlemagne has pursued the fleeing Saracens to the river Sebre, where they drown or are cut to pieces by his men. Rather than go on to take Saragossa and put an end to Marsile's resistence, the cause of the entire campaign which is the poem's subject, he returns to Roncevaux, buries the dead, prepares the bodies of Roland, Oliver and Turpin for the return journey into France, and makes ready to leave Spain. At this point Baligant's men appear:

> Venir s'en volt li emperere Carles,
> Quant de paiens li surdent les enguardes (vv. 2974–2975).

Roland's martyrdom is pointless if Charlemagne neglects to take Saragossa, the only city remaining in Saracen hands in all of Spain. But if the episode of Baligant is omitted, Charles simply proceeds to finish off his undertaking, capturing Saragossa and Queen Bramimonde. Other contradictions are the inclusion of the Hungres in both Charles' army (v. 2922) and Baligant's (v. 3254) and the fact that the olifant, although split at Roncevaux when Roland used it to kill the last Saracen (v. 2295), sounds out above the other horns in "Baligant" (vv. 3302, 3310). These two errors are minor, and one could argue that they might occur in any poem, oral or written, without affecting matters of attribution or interpolation, but to have Charlemagne ignore the opportunity of liquidating his Spanish enemies is an incredible blunder. The emperor who is thus refusing to force his will upon his worst enemy, refusing to complete the vengeance of his own nephew,

---

[19] *La Chanson de Roland*, pp. 250–251.

is then *constrained*, by the unexpected approach of Baligant's army rather than by any act of his own will, to subdue the chief of all Islam. This development, inexistent if we accept the episode of Baligant, is in complete contradiction with the tightly controlled motivation of *Roland* without "Baligant."

Contrary to the belief of "Baligant's" defenders, then, the episode is not logically or symbolically necessary to complete the sweep of actions set in motion early in the poem. On the contrary its many puzzling elements are best explained (and in some cases are *only* explicable) if we assume that "Baligant" and "Roland" did not undergo elaboration by the same singers in the period during which the basic movement of the *Chanson de Roland*'s plot was being formed in the oral tradition.

But what of the poem's language? Surely it has something to tell us about the relationship between "Baligant" and the remainder of the poem. It has been claimed that certain lexical differences separate "Baligant" from "Roland": the pagans are called *la contredite gent* in v. 1932, but *gent averse* in vv. 2630, 2922 and 3295; "Baligant" uses *confusion* to signify "ruin" (vv. 2699, 3276), and "Roland" employs *exill* (1862, 2935) in the same sense; *corn*, "horn," and *corner*, "to blow a horn," are omitted from "Baligant"; the episode does know the usage of *entre* as "and" (3073, 3075); the battle flag is called *enseigne* and *dragun* in "Roland" but *estandart* is added in "Baligant" (3267, 3330, 3552), where *targe* (3361, 3569) supplements *escut*; *Oger de Denemarche* (749, 3856, 3947) becomes *Oger li Daneis* (3033, 3544, 3546) in the episode.[20] Maurice Delbouille's reply to these instances is convincing: the variations of phrasing between *la contredite gent* and *gent averse* and between *Oger de Denemarche* and *Oger li Daneis* can be ascribed to differences of assonance, since in each case the phrases in question are in the second hemistich. Both *confusion* and *exill* also appear at the assonance. Finally, for *corner*, *corn*, *estandart* and *targe*, the occurrences

[20] Horrent, *La Chanson de Roland*, p. 254.

are too few and too limited to isolated passages to prove that the difference can be imputed to anything other than chance.[21]

The examination of some individual words and phrases, then, leads us to no new conclusion about the uniformity of the *Chanson de Roland*'s language. It reinforces, in fact, what one would consider the natural state of affairs were not "Baligant's" lateness evident from the analysis of narrative elements: a relative stability of lexicon throughout the poem. But in oral poetry, the fundamental index of technique is not the lexicon of isolated words but language viewed in its formulaic aspect. One is led, therefore, to a study of "Baligant's" formulas.

A tally of formulas found within the episode of Baligant (vv. 2555–2844; 2974–3682) reveals a total of 680. Thus 34.5 percent of the 1998 hemistichs of "Baligant" are formulaic. Since the total for the entire *Chanson de Roland* is 35.2 percent formulas, and the figure for all episodes except "Baligant" taken together is 2134 formulaic hemistichs out of 6006, or 35.5 percent, there is no significant difference between the relative density of formulas in the two parts of the work. But these figures show only that "Baligant" is a product of the oral tradition in the same way as the rest of *Roland*. We cannot conclude that it derives from the *same* tradition as the rest of "Roland" without examining the two repertories constituted by "Baligant's" and "Roland's" formulas and the relationship between them.

In the previous chapter[22] I stated that there are at least 2814 formulas in the entire *Chanson de Roland*. A distinction must now be drawn between two highly ambiguous and mutually confusing uses of the term "formula." When discussing to what extent the *Chanson de Roland* is formulaic, or what percentage of the episode of Baligant is made up of formulas, I used the word to signify all the examples of hemistichs which are repeated at least once within the poem itself, with the understanding, of course, that some phrases undoubtedly existed as formulas in the poet's

[21] Delbouille, *Sur la genèse*, pp. 46–49.     [22] Above, p. 34.

mind which were not used more than once simply because there
was no occasion for them to be useful. Thus the hemistich *Fran-
ceis murrunt* occurs six times in *Roland*, and, in the denotation
of "formula" which I have used until now, one can say that these
are six formulas. But in another sense they are one formula,
*Franceis murrunt*, which manifests itself six times. One is led to
adopt the terminology of statistical linguistics and call these two
entities "formula types" (*Franceis murrunt*) and "formula tokens"
(the six actualizations of the phrase found in the poem). The dis-
tinction is necessary at this point because if "Baligant" is the
elaboration of a different tradition of poets than the rest of *Roland*,
an elaboration integrated into the main *Roland* tradition shortly
before the archetype of Oxford was written down, then this
independent process of elaboration should be discernible through
the occurrence of different formula types in the two parts of the
poem.

The situation is this: of the 907 formula types found in the
entire poem, 526 are found exclusively in "Roland" (vv. 1–2554;
2845–2973; 3683–4002), 81 occur exclusively in "Baligant," and
300 are common to the two parts. More than three times as many
formula types have at least one occurrence in each of the poem's
two sections as are limited to "Baligant" alone. "Baligant" does
not, therefore, have a formulaic repertory of its own. On the
contrary, this overall view of the abstract formula types turns
up fewer formulas exclusively in "Baligant" than one might ex-
pect, for the episode constitutes just a shade under one quarter
of the whole poem but retains exclusive possession of only slight-
ly more than one-tenth of the types.

When we turn our attention to specific formulas, this judg-
ment is corroborated. The following formulas occurring only in
"Baligant" are arranged in descending order of frequency.

| | |
|---|---|
| *li amiralz* (24 examples) | *sis guierat* (3022, 3042, 3083) *les guierat* (3034), *els guierat* (3067), *les guierunt* (3074) |
| *dist Baligant* (2686, 2769, 3135, 3180, 3295, 3600) | |

*e Bramimunde* (2595), *e Brami-*
*donie* (2822, 3655, 3680)

*par tut le camp* (2947, 2999, 3525)

*e la disme est* (3230, 3246, 3260)

*ferez, baron* (3366, 3392, 3472)

*cil i ferrat* (3051), *cil i ferrunt*
(3199, 3320)

*cume flur en estet* (3162), *cume*
*flur en avrill* (3503), *cume flur*
*en espine* (3521)

*de cele gent averse* (2630), *e tante*
*gent averse* (2922), *la meie gent*
*averse* (3295)

*ço est une gent* (3231, 3247, 3261)

*e la quarte est* (3225, 3241, 3255)

*e la quinte est* (3226, 3242, 3256)

*e la siste est* (3227, 3243, 3257)

*e la sedme est* (3228, 3244, 3258)

*s'il troevent oi* (3004, 3025), *se jo*
*truis o* (2676)

*cil d'Ociant* (3286, 3526), *cels*
*d'Occiant* (3474)

*e Tervagan* (2589, 2712, 3491)

*avez faites en camps* (3336), *avez*
*faites pur mei* (3407)[23]

*de bachelers* (3020, 3197)

*ses filz Malpramis* (3176), *bels*
*filz Malpramis* (3184)

*puis brochet le cheval* (3341), *ben*
*brochet sun cheval* (3430)

*carbuncles e lanternes* (2633), *lan-*
*ternes e carbuncles* (2643)

*cher sire, si ferum* (2441, 2688)

*chevalers unt* (3070, 3218)

*jo vos cumant* (2673), *jo te cumant*
(2815)

*par les degrez* (2821, 2840)

*ço dient tuit li altre* (3039), *ço*
*dient tuit li Franc* (3046)[24]

*.x. escheles* (3192), *dis escheles*
(3237)

*dist Bramimunde* (2714, 2734)

*dist Clarien* (2771, 2790)

*e le dragon* (3330, 3550)

*li dui message* (2704, 2765)

*l'ad enchacet asez* (2785), *asez l'ad*
*enchalcet* (2796)

*li ad enz el cors mise* (3363), *li ad*
*enz el cors mis* (3356)

*eschiez e barges* (2625, 2729)

*des esperons* (3341, 3430)

*de lor espiez* (3475, 3569)

---

[23] These two phrases differ in their assonating words. One might conclude, despite their resemblance in other respects, that they are not two examples of the same formula type, were it not for the fact that they share the same first hemistich formula type: *tantes batailles.*

[24] Both preceded by *vint milie sunt.*

e l'estandart (3267, 3552)

en ad fait aprester (2624), i ad fait aprester (2627)

fait sun eslais (2997, 3166)

e galees curant (2729), e galies e nefs (2625)[25]

granz colps s'entredunerent (3568), mult granz colps s'entredunent (3582)

ja devers els (3030, 3071)

des jaianz de Malprese (3253), des jaianz de Malpreis (3285)

justees sunt (3347, 3384)

male confusiun (2699, 3276)

est mult de grant saveir (3279), est mult de grant vertut (3602)[26]

mult haltement (3270, 3300)

paien d'Arabe (2810, 3555)

que mi paien le sacent (3136), que si paien l'oirent (3524)[27]

e li paien (3385), e li paiens (3445)

paien respundent (2685, 3400)

li paien Baligant (2654), al paien Baligant (2725)

pent a sun col (2991, 3149)

plus de cent milie (3000, 3402)

el premer chef devant (3018, 3195)

la premere est (3238, 3253)

e li quens Jozerans (3023, 3044)

li quens Ogers (3033, 3531)

li quens Rabels (3348, 3352)

.xv. milie de Francs (3019, 3196)

quite li cleim (2748), quite vus cleimet (2787)

recleimet Deu (2998, 3099)

e la terce est (3224, 3285)

tient sun espiet (2992, 3152)

trestute Espaigne (2703, 2721)

veez paien (3337, 3537)

venez, paien (2844, 3326)

de venir ne se repentent (3011), de venir se demurent (3081)[28]

vint milie sunt (3039), .xx. milie sunt (3046)

si Arrabiz (3011, 3081)

Carles ad dreit (3359, 3367)

Karles de France (3234), Carles de France (3443)

ki Deu nen amat unkes (3261), que Deus nen amat unkes (3638)

---

[25] Both preceded by eschiez e barges.
[26] Both preceded by li amiralz.
[27] Preceded by sunez voz graisles (3136) and sunet la [i.e. une buisine] cler (3524).
[28] Both preceded by si Arrabiz.

| | |
|---|---|
| *en France irai* (2681), *en France*<br>    *irat* (2732) | *Tierris, li dux d'Argone* (3083),<br>    *Tierri le duc d'Argone* (3534) |
| *e Jozeran le cunte* (3075, 3535) | *Torleu, le rei persis* (3204, 3354) |
| *Marsiliun* (2674, 2726) | *cuntre Franceis* (2675, 3203) |

Several proper names of persons who do not appear in other parts of the song can be removed from the list of formulas whose exclusive presence in "Baligant" may be significant: *li amiralz, dist Baligant, cil d'Ociant, bels filz Malpramis, dist Clarien, des jaianz de Malprese, li paien Baligant, e li quens Jozerans, li quens Rabels, si Arrabiz, e Jozeran le cunte, Tierris li dux d'Argone* and *Torleu le rei persis*. Others are attached to situations only occurring in "Baligant" and cannot therefore be expected to turn up in "Roland." The most salient of these are the drawing up of the French and Saracen armies into divisions, which gives *la premere est, e la terce est, e la quarte est, e la quinte est, e la siste est, e la sedme est, e la disme est, dis escheles, sis guierat, de bachelers, chevalers unt, justees sunt, el premer chef devant, ja devers els, ço est une gent, .xv. milie de Francs, vint milie sunt* and *ço dient tuit li altre*, and the arrival of Baligant's fleet, with *carbuncles e lanternes, eschiez e barges* and *e galees curant*. These categories account for 34 of the 81 formula types confined to "Baligant."

Among the remaining 47 it would be informative if there were many phrases which duplicate the function of other formulas found exclusively in "Roland." In the case of second hemistichs, this duplication would have to encompass the assonance for the phrase to be considered a true alternative. A careful comparison of the formulas of both parts uncovers only five examples of phrases in "Roland" which are truly equivalent to "Baligant" formulas. They are: *parmi le cors li mist* (1248, 1306) equivalent to *li ad enz el cors mis* (3356), *e tute Espaigne* (224) equivalent to *trestute Espaigne* (2703, 2721), *nos avum dreit* (1212) functionally equivalent, if one wishes to stretch the point, to *Carles ad dreit* (3359, 3367), *Carles li reis* (1, 2658, 2892, 2982) equivalent to *Karles de France* (3234, 3443) and, with transformation of the first hemistich to allow for the difference in syntax, *Damesdeus mal te duinst* (1898) equivalent to [*de vos seit hoi*] *male confusiun* (2699). In only 5 cases out of 81, then, are there signs of two distinct formulaic repertories being present in "Roland" and "Baligant." Far from indicating an independent process of traditional elaboration for "Baligant," these alternative formulas show, by their paucity, the relative uniformity of formulas throughout the poem, albeit in a negative way.

If "Baligant" does not betray signs of having had a separate life in the years directly preceding the writing down of the Oxford manuscript, what positive relationship is revealed by formulas which the two episodes share? Maurice Delbouille has examined selected phrases of the *Chanson de Roland* in an effort to answer this question, comparing their uses in "Roland" and "Baligant" and contrasting them to the formulaic style of the *Chanson de Guillaume*.[29] He concludes that formulas for spurring, spearing, and mentions of the byrnie and the hauberk, the shield and the helmet, are uniform in "Roland" and "Baligant," and that two particular cases, *pleine sa hanste* and *sur l'erbe verte*, both used frequently in the poem, present no anomalies which would lead one to separate "Roland" from "Baligant." All of these actions and objects are, on the other hand, presented differently in the *Chanson de Guillaume*. Professor Delbouille goes on to study the distribution of assonances and the relative length of laisses in the two parts, concluding that the technique of both is consistent throughout the poem. My examination of formulas, of necessity encompassing some of the phrases already studied by Professor Delbouille, but not limited to cases chosen for their obviousness, will complement his findings. One advantage of beginning a stylistic study with a numerical inventory is that one is thus presented with those formulas which are most prominent in the poet's art. These are not always the most striking phrases, and certainly not the stylistically singular ones.

In order to minimize the effect of formulas which are so infre-

29 *Sur la genèse*, pp. 49–61.

quent and of such specific meaning as to be attached only to special plot situations and whose predominance in the inventory of formula types might distort our view of the relationship between "Roland's" style and that of "Baligant," I have singled out those types represented by at least four occurrences in the poem, and list them below according to semantic categories, together with the indication that they occur in "Roland" (R), in "Baligant" (B), or in both (RB).

Individual battle actions

*si vait ferir* (1282, 1291, 1537, 1574, 1618, 3354, 3464, 3548), *e vait ferir* (1353), *puis vait ferir* (1625), *il vait ferir* (1599), *si vunt ferir* (1185, 3351), *puis vunt ferir* (3601), *e vunt ferir* (1382), *si's vunt ferir* (3568)      16 R B

*sun cheval brochet* (1197, 1245, 1325, 1549), *sun cheval broche* (1125), *son cheval brochet* (1290), *sun ceval brochet* (1582, 1634), *le cheval brochet* (1225, 1313, 1738, 2055, 3165, 3353)      14 R B

*que mort l'abat* (1273, 1279, 1302, 1307, 1507, 1612, 1622, 1894, 3357, 3364, 3428, 3450, 3468, 3619)      14 R B

*l'escut li freinst* (1247, 1276, 1305), *l'escut li freint* (1199, 1227, 1270, 1283, 1314, 1354, 1575, 1893, 3448)      12 R B

*el cors li met* (1228, 1301, 1576, 1602, 1621, 3427), *el cors li mis* (3457)      7 R B

*de sun osberc* (1284, 1293, 1300, 1601, 3426, 3449, 3466)      7 R B

*e l'osberc li derumpt* (1227, 1575, 1893), *e l'osberc li desclot* (1199), *l'osberc li descumfist* (1247, 1305), *e l'osberc li desmailet* (1270)      7 R

*pleine sa hanste* (1204, 1229, 1250, 1287, 1295, 1541, 1577)      7 R

*vait le ferir* (1198, 1226, 1499, 1584, 1902, 3424, 3447)      7 R B

*brochent les bien* (3877), *brochet le bien* (1536, 1573, 2128), *brochet le ben* (1891, 1944)      6 R

*del cheval l'abat mort* (1204), *l'abat mort des arçuns* (1229, 1577), *l'abat mort de la sele* (1295), *l'abat mort el chemin* (1250)      5 R

*brochent ad ait* (1184, 1802), *brochent ad eit* (3541), *brochent a eit* (3350)      4 R B

*laschet la resne* (1617, 2996), *lascent les resnes* (3349),
   *laschent lor reisnes* (1381)                                            4 R B

*puis ad ocis* (1554, 1895, 3469), *pois ad ocis* (1358)                4 R B

General descriptions of battle or of armies

   *ceste bataille* (882, 1238, 1729, 3278, 3489, 3577, 3587,
   3902)                                                                        8 R B

   *la bataille est* (1320, 1396, 1412, 1653, 1661, 3381, 3393,
   3420)                                                                        8 R B

   *granz sunt les oz* (1086, 2630, 2980, 3263, 3291, 3383)        6 R B

   *e ferir e capler* (1681), *i fierent e si caplent* (1347), *n'i
   fierge o n'i capleit* (3462), *ben i fierent e caplent* (3475),
   fierent e caplent* (3888)                                           5 R B

   *as chevals e as armes* (1095, 2986), *e de chevals e d'armes*
   (3040), *lur chevals e lur armes* (3857)                           4 R B

   *tantes batailles* (1465, 2306, 3336, 3407)                        4 R B

Arming or description of knight before battle

   *siet el cheval* (1488, 1571, 1615, 1890, 2127), *siet el ceval*
   (1534, 1597)                                                             7 R

   *l'estreu li tint* (348, 3156), *l'estreu li tindrent* (3113), *l'estreu
   li unt tenut* (2820)                                                    4 R B

   *lacent lor elmes* (996), *laciet sun elme* (2500), *lacet sun
   helme* (2989), *lacet sun elme* (3142)                               4 R B

Designations of persons (by name, common or collective
noun)

   *li emperere* (214, 829, 1114, 1149, 1987, 2105, 2398, 2488,
   2496, 2554, 2605, 2609, 2737, 2772, 2785, 2962, 3060,
   3096, 3288, 3301, 3405, 3556, 3660, 3734, 3749, 3852,
   3999), *li empereres* (16, 96, 103, 137, 139, 163, 168, 193,
   271, 331, 661, 669, 718, 739, 771, 783, 1796, 1812, 1834,
   1860, 2354, 2443, 2881, 2987, 3190, 3454, 3501, 3705)         55 R B

   *li quens Rollant* (194, 355, 663, 707, 751, 777, 792, 803,
   1145, 1321, 1338, 1545, 1580, 1629, 1671, 1691, 1761,
   1785, 1869, 1897, 2066, 2099, 2124, 2134, 2152, 2163,
   2166, 2215, 2233, 2246, 2375, 2701, 2775)                         33 R B

   *li amiralz* (2602, 2647, 2731, 2813, 3140, 3172, 3232, 3252,
   3265, 3279, 3311, 3391, 3396, 3463, 3490, 3504, 3553,
   3564, 3580, 3602, 3643), *li amiraill* (2747, 3214, 3520)       24   B

*li reis Marsilie* (7, 10, 62, 78, 144, 181, 201, 235, 438, 441, 873, 908, 1150, 1448, 2570, 2612, 2778, 2795, 2808, 2827)                                                                                           20 R B

*li doze per* (560, 826, 937, 948, 965, 1346, 1415, 2410, 2793, 3187), *les doze pers* (1513, 3756), *li duze per* (262, 325), *les duze pers* (547)                                                              15 R B

*e Oliver* (176, 576, 586, 903, 1345, 1351, 1990, 2216, 2776, 2963, 3186, 3690, 3755, 3776)                                                                                                                     14 R B

*seignurs barons* (70, 180, 244, 254, 740, 1127, 1165, 3281), *seignors barons* (1176, 1515, 1854, 3406, 3750)                                                                                                 13 R B

*Naimes li dux* (673, 2417, 2423, 2882, 3023, 3036, 3044, 3061, 3423, 3444, 3544, 3937), *Naimon li duc* (3008)                                                                                                13 R B

*li arcevesque* (1414, 1481, 1487, 1497, 1673, 1682, 1737, 2068, 2193, 2222)                                                                                                                                    10 R

*sire cumpainz* (1113, 1146, 1546, 1693, 1868, 1983), *sire cumpaign* (1672, 1976, 2027), *sire cumpain* (2000)                                                                                                10 R

*de cels de France* (857, 1852, 2116, 2132, 2150, 2777, 3188, 3422, 3703)                                                                                                                                         9 R B

*Carles li magnes* (703, 841, 905, 1949, 3329), *Charles li magnes* (1195), *Karles li magnes* (1404, 1732)                                                                                                     8 R B

*Gefreid d'Anjou* (106, 2951, 3093, 3545), *Gefrei d'Anjou* (2883, 3535, 3938)                                                                                                                                    7 R B

*l'arcevesque Turpin* (170, 2963), *l'arcevesques Turpin* (2130), *li arcevesques Turpin* (1124, 1243), *Turpin li arcevesque* (1605)                                                                            6 R

*la rereguarde* (754, 778, 858, 883), *sa rereguarde* (574, 584)                                                                                                                                                  6 R

*ami Rollant* (2898, 2909, 2916, 2933), *amis Rollant* (2887)                                                                                                                                                     5 R

*al rei Marsiliun* (245, 880, 1214, 1905, 3773)                                                                                                                                                                   5 R

*seint Gabriel* (2390, 2395, 2526, 2847, 3993)                                                                                                                                                                    5 R B

*e li Franceis* (1347, 1416, 1813, 1835, 3476)                                                                                                                                                                    5 R B

*Guenes li quens* (233, 342, 668, 721, 3792)                                                                                                                                                                      5 R

*devant Marsilie* (891, 900, 911, 919, 933)                                                                                                                                                                       5 R

*barons Franceis* (1863, 2986, 3335), *baruns Franceis* (2509)                                                                                                                                                    4 R B

*cent milie Francs* (842, 2907, 2932, 3124)                                                                                                                                                                       4 R B

*sun cumpaignun* (1160, 1692, 1994, 2201)                                                                                                                                                                         4 R

le cunte Guenelun (415, 1816, 3809), del cunte Guenelun
(1569)                                                                          4 R

e Bramimunde (2595, 2822, 3655, 3680)                        4    B

de Carlemagne (522, 538, 551, 2380)                            4 R

Carles li reis (1, 2658, 2892, 2982)                                4 R B

de Guenelun (665, 3748, 3751, 3904)                            4 R

Oliver e Rollant (947, 1413, 1512, 3016)                        4 R B

### Epithets

sur l'erbe verte (671, 1665, 2175, 2236, 2269, 2273, 2358,
2448, 2565, 2652, 2876, 3097, 3453, 3972), sur la verte
herbe (2573), desure l'herbe verte (1612)                    16 R B

ki sunt a or gemez (3911), ki ad or sunt gemmez (1031), ki
a or est gemmee (1373), ki est gemmee ad or (1587), ki
gemmet fut ad or (1585), ki est a or gemmet (2500), ki
ad or est gemmet (3142) ki gemmet fut a or (2288)        8 R B

de bons espiez trenchanz (554), a mun espiet trenchant
(867), sun bon espiet trenchant (1301), de sun espiet
trenchant (3051), e sun espiet trenchant (3114), de lur
espiez trenchanz (3351), a voz espiez trenchant (3378)    7 R B

ki la barbe ad canue (2308), a la barbe canue (3654), ki la
barbe ad flurie (2353), a la barbe flurie (970), od la barbe
flurie (2605)                                                              5 R B

en France dulce (2661, 3673), ne France dulce (1064), de
France dulce (2431)                                                     4 R B

### Speech

dient Franceis (192, 243, 278, 334, 734, 1047, 1508, 1544,
1579, 1604, 1628, 1652, 3275, 3299, 3343, 3358)        16 R B

ço dist li reis (319, 327, 339, 508, 698, 1768, 1789, 2950,
3015, 3072, 3627, 3814, 3848), ço dit li reis (705, 1758)  15 R B

e dist al rei (27, 123, 220, 232, 265, 416, 428, 496, 676, 776,
962, 3841), et dit al rei (832), il dist al rei (196)          14 R B

Guenes respont (296, 375, 381, 396, 518, 529, 567, 582, 616,
659, 743, 749, 760, 1770)                                            14 R

dist Oliver (1006, 1039, 1049, 1082, 1099, 1170, 1274,
1700, 1705, 1715, 1719, 1938, 2003)                          13 R

respont Rollant (254, 292, 1008, 1053, 1062, 1073, 1088,
1106, 1394, 1591, 1752, 1883, 2006)     13 R

ço dist Rollant (1288, 1360, 1376, 1456, 1558, 1702, 1722,
1922), ço dist Rollanz (277), ço dit Rollant (1713, 2207)     11 R

dient paien (61, 77,   450, 467, 1590, 1666, 2060, 2115,
2146, 3303)     10 R B

a icest mot (1180, 1524, 1677, 1884, 1911, 1939, 1988, 2031,
3379, 3621)     10 R B

e cil respunt (644, 2835, 3209, 3513), e cil respont (1723),
e cil respundent (946, 2440, 2688, 2754)     9 R B

sin apelat (63, 1020, 3007, 3507, 3976), sin apela (2814),
si apelad (1237), si apelat (3534)     8 R B

dist l'arcevesque (799, 1280, 1349, 1441, 1876, 2144, 2182,
2221)     8 R

respundent Franc (2487, 3761, 3837, 3951), respondent
Franc (3414, 3630), respundent Francs (3558, 3779)     8 R B

si li ad dit (445, 469, 648, 746, 1231, 2823), si lur ad dit
(1164)     7 R B

dist l'un a l'altre (1910, 1942, 2131, 3798), dit l'un a l'altre
(2114, 2698)     6 R B

dist Baligant (2686, 2769, 3135, 3180, 3295, 3600)     6   B

dist Blancandrins (47, 88, 370, 377, 392, 506)     6 R

Munjoie! escriet (1234, 1260, 1350, 1378, 3620), Munjoie!
escrient (3092)     6 R B

apres li dist (1296, 1303, 1335, 2292), enpres li dient (357)     5 R

ço dist Marsilie (943, 2755, 2831), ço dist Marsilies (520,
603)     5 R B

jo vos plevis (968, 1058, 1069, 1704), je vos plevis (1072)     5 R

cleimet sa culpe (2239,   2364, 2383), clamez voz culpes
(1132)     4 R

a icel mot (2008, 2054, 2457), a icez moz (990)     4 R

paien escrient (1906, 3168, 3298, 3471)     4 R B

e prient Deu (1837), e priet Deu (2518), si priet Deu (2016,
2241)     4 R

Carles respunt (317, 833, 3595), Charles respunt (156)     4 R B

Commentary

*men escientre* (539, 756, 768, 2073, 2286), *mien escientre*
(552), *sun escientre* (1116), *men escient* (524)                    8 R

*de ço qui calt* (1405, 1806, 1840, 1913), *de ço qui chelt*
(2411), *d'iço, seignurs, qui calt* (3339)                            6 R B

*voeillet o nun* (2043, 2220, 3170), *voillet o nun* (1419),
*voelent u nun* (1659), *voellet o nun* (2168)                        6 R B

*desor cumencet* (179, 3704, 3747, 3946)                             4 R

Moral judgment

*mielz voeill murir* (1701, 2336, 3909), *melz voeill murir*
(1091), *mielz voeil murir* (1485), *meilz voelt murir* (536,
2738)                                                                 7 R B

*ja pur murir* (1048, 1096, 1909, 3048), *ja por murir* (3041,
3812)                                                                 6 R B

*ja mais n'ert hume* (376), *ja mais n'iert an* (653), *ja mais
n'iert home* (1873), *ja mais n'iert hume* (1984), *ja mais
n'erst hume* (2254)                                                  5 R

*ja mais n'ert jor* (915), *ja mais n'ert jurn* (971, 2901), *ja
mais n'ert jur* (2915, 3905)                                         5 R

*meillor vassal* (231, 775, 3377, 3532), *meillors vassals*
(1857)                                                               5 R B

*de vasselage* (25, 898, 1182, 3163, 3901)                          5 R B

*asez est melz* (44), *asez est mielz* (58, 1518), *si est il asez
melz* (1743)                                                         4 R

*en guise de baron* (1226, 1902), *en guise de barun* (1889),
*en guise de barons* (3054)                                          4 R B

*mult par est proz* (546, 559, 3546, 3915)                          4 R B

Emotions

*si grant doel ad* (1631, 2789, 3506), *si grant doel ai* (834,
2929, 2936), *si grant doel out* (2219)                              7 R B

*pluret des oilz* (3645, 3712, 4001), *ploret des oilz* (2943),
*plurent des oilz* (1446, 2415)                                      6 R B

*a grant dolur* (816, 1977, 2914, 3741)                             4 R

*ne poet muer* (1642, 2381, 2517), *ne pot muer* (773)              4 R

*ne poet muer n'en plurt* (825, 841, 2193, 2873)                    4 R

Movement

puis sunt muntez (1142, 2708, 2811, 3003, 3091, 3869),
    puis sunt muntet (2851), pois est munted (660), puis est
    muntez (2816)                                                         9 R B

car chevalcez (1783), kar chevalchez (1175), car chevalchez
    (2428, 3296), si chevalcez (3018), si chevalcherent
    (2812), si cevelcent (3195)                                          7 R B

paien s'en fuient (2162, 2164, 2460, 3625, 3634)                         5 R B

puis si chevalchet (1469, 2444, 3117), puis si chevalchent
    (855, 1183)                                                          5 R B

descendirent a pied (120), i descendrunt a pied (1746), i
    descendent a piet (2071), descendut est a piet (2479)                4 R

Franceis descendent (1136, 1797, 2489, 2952)                             4 R

Location

ensembl'od lui (104, 1805, 1839, 2130, 2817, 3936), en-
    sembl'od li (2578, 3637), ensembl'od els (175, 1896,
    2395, 3196, 3461)                                                   13 R B

en Rencesvals (901, 912, 923, 934, 944, 963, 985, 2225,
    2483, 2716, 2791, 2854, 2855)                                       13 R B

en Sarraguce (211, 245, 299, 310, 476, 852, 2617), de Sar-
    raguce (677, 2752, 2762, 2768, 3650, 3676)                          13 R B

d'altre part est (916, 931, 940, 975, 1124, 1562)                        6 R

cuntre le ciel (1156, 1596, 2015, 2240, 2341, 3912)                      6 R

en la grant presse (1967, 2057, 2070, 2090, 2129)                        5 R

apres icels (3021, 3198), apres iceste (725), apres iço
    (230), anpres iço (774)                                             5 R B

par tantes teres (525, 540, 553), de tantes teres (2378), e
    tantes teres (2307)                                                  5 R

Tere Maior (600, 952, 1532, 1667, 1784)                                  5 R

en cest pais (17, 134, 266, 2800)                                        4 R B

en ceste tere (35, 1908, 2736, 2797)                                     4 R B

devers Espaigne (1021, 2266, 2367, 3128)                                 4 R

Manner

par amur e par feid (86, 3460, 3801, 3893), par feid e par
    amur (2897, 3770), par feid e par amor (3810)                        7 R B

*isnelement* (2085, 2453, 2536, 2766, 2988, 3575, 3884)  7 R B

*par grant vertut* (1246, 1551, 1754, 2851, 3878)  5 R

*mult fierement* (219, 2984, 3316, 3536)  4 R B

Miscellaneous noun formulas which fit into none of the above categories

*un faldestoed* (115, 609, 2653), *un faldestoet* (407), *qu'el faldestoed* (452), *del faldestod* (2804)  6 R B

*l'anme de lui* (1268, 1553, 3647), *l'anme de tei* (2934)  4 R B

*le destre poign* (2719, 2781), *el destre poign* (484, 2678)  4 R B

*la lei de crestiens* (38, 471, 2683), *la crestiene lei* (85)  4 R B

*set cenz cameilz* (129, 184, 645), *set cenz camelz* (31)  4 R

*en ceste tere* (35, 1908, 2736, 2797)  4 R B

Miscellaneous verbal formulas

*n'i ad celoi* (411, 1803, 1814, 1836, 3462, 3805)  6 R B

*empeint le ben* (1249, 1540, 1756), *empeint le bien* (1272), *enpeint le ben* (1203), *empeinst le ben* (1286)  6 R

*sis guierat* (3022, 3042, 3083), *les guierat* (3034), *els guierat* (3067), *les guierunt* (3074)  6 B

*si recevrat* (189, 695, 2620), *si recevrai* (85), *si recevrez* (38), *si recevez* (320)  6 R B

*Franceis murrunt* (904, 928, 938, 951, 969, 989)  6 R

*jo l'en cunquis* (2322, 2324, 2327, 2331), *jo vos cunquis* (198)  5 R

*ne laisserat* (1252, 1498), *ne leserat* (1206), *ne lesserat* (859, 1931)  5 R

*si l'orrat Carles* (1052, 1060, 1071, 1703), *si l'orrat li reis Karles* (1714)  5 R

*perdut i ad* (2167), *perdut avum* (2700, 2148), *perdud avuns* (2119), *perdut avez* (3498)  5 R B

*ço sent Rollant* (2259, 2284, 2297, 2355, 2366)  5 R

*se truis Rollant* (893, 902), *se trois Rollant* (935, 986), *se trois Rolland* (914)  5 R

*Carles se dort* (718, 724, 736, 2569), *Karles se dort* (2525)  5 R B

| | |
|---|---|
| *out sun cunseill finet* (62), *out finet sun cunseill* (78), *pur sun cunseill finer* (166), *pur sun cunseill fenir* (169) | 4 R |
| *halt sunt li pui* (814, 1755, 1830, 2271) | 4 R |
| *quant Carles veit* (2476, 3006, 3728, 3815) | 4 R B |

There are 145 formula types in this list, 55 occurring in "Roland" alone, 86 shared by the two parts, and 4 confined to "Baligant." Many of the formulas found only in "Roland" or "Baligant" should be excluded as evidence for uniformity of style, however, since they contain the names of persons or groups who only appear in one of the two sections: *respont Rollant, ço dist Rollant, ço sent Rollant, se truis Rollant, ami Rollant, dist Oliver, sire cumpainz* (a form of address used only between Roland and Oliver), *sun cumpaignun, li arcevesque, l'arcevesque Turpin, dist l'arcevesque, Guenes li quens, le cunte Guenelun, de Guenelun, Guenes respont, la rereguarde, dist Blancandrins, li amiralz,* and *dist Baligant.*[30] Still others occur in unique situations: *out sun cunseill finet* and *set cenz cameilz* in the council scenes which open the poem, *Franceis murrunt* in the sequence of Saracen boasts preceding Roncevaux, *si l'orrat Karles* in the two horn scenes, and *sis guierat* in the ordering of the French army before the battle with Baligant's army. Limiting ourselves to the formulas whose occurrences may be indicative of differing styles in the two parts, we are left with 34 of the most frequent formulas occurring in "Roland" alone, and only one, *e Bramimunde,* in "Baligant," while 86 of these formulas are shared by both "Roland" and "Baligant." These figures corroborate the hypothesis that "Baligant" does not possess a formulaic repertory of its own.

Note too that the overwhelming majority of formulas at the opposite end of the semantic axis from those mentioned in the

[30] Most of these proper name formulas show the characters in action or are used in direct address. Formulas referring to Roland and Oliver in the third person are sometimes found in "Baligant" despite the fact that these personages die before the episode begins, thus *li quens Rollant, e Oliver,* etc.

previous paragraph, those most lacking in specific content, those
which may be inserted in almost any scene, are shared by "Bali-
gant" and "Roland": *sur l'erbe verte, a icest mot, e cil respont,
sin apelat, dist l'un a l'altre, si li ad dit, apres li dist, de ço qui
calt, voeillet o nun, ensembl'od lui, apres icels, en cest pais, en
ceste tere, isnelement,* and *n'i ad celoi.* Because of their versatility,
these phrases are, with the more specific formulas denoting in-
dividual battle actions, the introduction and content of speech,
and the proper names of characters, the most basic to the art of
epic storytelling. Only four highly versatile formulas found fre-
quently in "Roland" alone compare with these: *a icel mot* (which
should perhaps be treated as a variant of *a icest mot,* found in
both parts of the poem), *men escientre, d'altre part est,* and *ne
laisserat.*

In general, the formulas of "Baligant" differ little, then, from
those found in the remainder of the *Chanson de Roland.* No study
of technique would be complete, however, without consideration
of the poem's laisse structuration. Does the interrelation of
"Baligant's" laisses reflect the same workmanship as in encoun-
tered in the first, second, and fourth parts of the song?

In his study of the jongleurs' epic art, Jean Rychner outlined
five possible types of linkage between consecutive laisses, point-
ing out that each was to be seen in the *Chanson de Roland.*[31]
They are: 1) *enchaînement,* the repetition, at the beginning of a
laisse, of what was said at the end of the previous one; 2) the
*reprise bifurquée* or branched repetition, in which the repeated
element is found not at the end of the preceding laisses, but to-
ward the middle; 3) a second type of branching (we will call them
types one and two) where the corresponding passages are both
at the beginning of their respective laisses; 4) parallel laisses,
which recount actions that are not identical but are of the same
type (as, for example, a series of battles whose elaboration is
similar, but which each involve a different pair of protagonists);

[31] *La Chanson de geste: essai sur l'art épique des jongleurs* (Geneva:
Droz, 1955), chapter IV, "La Structure strophique des chansons."

and 5) similar laisses, in which the same action is taken up in two, or sometimes three, successive laisses, and recounted in a slightly different way each time.

Within the structuration of *Roland*'s laisse sequence the five types occur with unequal frequency. In "Roland" 31 laisses are linked through *enchaînement*, 6 through the first type of forked repetition, 8 through the second, 48 in parallel, and 26 in a relationship of similarity. In "Baligant" the figures are 7 in *enchaînement*, 2 for the first type of branching, and 15 in parallel. The totals are 24 laisses linked in some manner in "Baligant," constituting 34 percent of the laisses in the episode, and 119 in "Roland," or 54 percent.[32] There is, then, variation between the proportions of linked laisses in the two parts of the poem, but it is probably not wide enough, *in itself*, to justify conclusions about *Roland*'s unity.

To look at the *kinds* of sequential structuration found in "Baligant" is more informative. Neither the incidence of *laisses enchaînées* (10 percent of the total number of laisses in "Baligant," 14 percent in "Roland") nor that of parallel laisses (28 percent in "Roland" as against 21 percent in "Baligant") serves to differentiate the two parts, and the first type of branched repetition accounts for a meager 3 percent in each. Absence of the second type of branched repetition is surprising, but not in itself conclusive one way or the other, since only 8 laisses are found in this relationship in "Roland." But the significance of the fact that not a single set of similar laisses is to be seen in "Baligant" can hardly be overestimated, for the *Chanson de Roland*'s similar laisses are certainly among the poem's most striking devices. No less than 9 groupings of similar laisses, totaling 25 laisses in all (laisses 40–42, 43–44, 83–85, 133–135, 136–138, 171–173, 174–176, 206–207, 208–210) appear in "Roland," ranging from the preliminaries of Ganelon's plot to Charlemagne's regrets over his nephew's corpse. What is more, they almost invariably occur at key moments in the plot, the most important being the se-

[32] All percentage totals are rounded.

ries which climaxes the first horn scene and the two series of three laisses each leading up to and culminating in Roland's death. If any trait of the Oxford poet's style can be called striking, it is his use of similar laisses to illustrate the high points of his masterpiece. And yet there is not a trace of this practice in "Baligant," not even in the climactic duel between the emperors of East and West!

I do not believe that this finding is compatible with the theory of "Baligant's" primitiveness. Assuming for a moment that the series of poets responsible for the subtle development of Ganelon's treason, for the strong clash of characters in the two horn scenes, for the lyrical moments preceding Roland's death, for the powerful expression of grief in Charlemagne's regrets, are also responsible for the episode of Baligant, did they conceive of this thousand-verse portion of the work as unimportant to the point of failing to merit the most effective literary device at their disposal? The defenders of "Baligant's" genuineness do not consider the episode in this way. Maurice Delbouille claims that the poem with "Baligant" "est . . . plus ambitieuse et plus noble," that its inclusion "[donne] au poème la signification politique et religieuse qui en fait l'épopée d'un monde et d'une époque."[33] But both points of view cannot be valid. Either "Baligant" is, in spite of its poetic poverty, an essential and even dominant feature of the work, transforming it conceptually and structurally for the better and making it one of the world's great epics—and in this case the poets have revealed a lack of esthetic sense highly improbable in view of the fine artistic capabilities evident in the rest of the poem—or else "Baligant" is subordinate and supernumerary, an episode whose art does not come up to the earliest parts, which could easily have been omitted without impinging upon the Roland's unity, and which may well have come late to the tradition.

Can any order be salvaged from the chaos of these contradictory testimonies? We have seen that the lack of anticipatory

[33] Sur la genèse, p. 36.

announcement of "Baligant," certain discrepancies of *dramatis personae*, the defective logic of Charlemagne's attempt to return into France without taking Saragossa, as well as other less important but corroborating contradictions between the two parts,[34] lead to the conclusion that "Baligant" was not a part of the *Roland* tradition for very long. An examination of "Baligant's" laisse sequences reinforced this conclusion. The formulas, however, seem to tell a different story, for "Roland" and "Baligant" possess a uniformity of style which, in isolation from the other points we have considered, leads to the opposite deduction, that the poem's two major divisions must have passed, as a unity, through the same style-creating process, or, in the terminology of oral-formulaic studies, must have been elaborated in the same tradition of singers. But the opposition between these two conclusions is only apparent. As in the case of those historical problems of the *Roland* tradition treated by Menéndez Pidal, the solutions can be found if we treat the poem not as a monolith, but rather as a work which passed through a long process of continual creation before being written down in the Oxford manuscript. Justification for this view is founded upon the formulaic nature of *Roland*, for a formulaic technique can only result from a long, traditional elaboration. Just as the poem's subject reaches back through the opaque centuries to the battle of Roncevaux itself,[35] so its technique is the result of elaboration over those same centuries by hundreds, perhaps even thousands, of poets.

The technique of similar laisses must be very old. Their antiquity is attested by their presence in the "Fragment of the

---

[34] Menéndez Pidal points out, for example, that while there are four instances in "Roland" of the "coup épique" in which a warrior's blow is so strong as to split his adversary (and sometimes his adversary's horse too) in half, "l'auteur de l'épisode de Baligant n'emploie pas cette formule, qu'il juge sans doute archaïque. Charlemagne, même avec l'aide de l'archange Gabriel, ne fend pas en deux le corps de l'émir de Babylone, mais seulement sa tête jusqu'à la barbe blanche (O, l. 262)." *La Chanson de Roland*, p. 377, note 1.

[35] Menéndez Pidal, *La Chanson de Roland*, pp. 181–447.

Hague," which dates from the end of the tenth century.[36] Already
in the twelfth century, when some of the earliest texts were being
copied down by scribes, the technique of similar laisses was in
decline. At the end of his illuminating chapter on the *chanson de
geste's* strophic structure, Jean Rychner draws a distinction be-
tween songs in which the laisse is a functional, coherent entity,
and those in which the narrative tends to transcend the laisse
and distort its contours. At these two poles he places the *Chanson
de Roland*, a model of strophic coherence (but note that all his
examples are taken from "Roland" rather than "Baligant"), and
the *Moniage Guillaume II*, whose composite laisses are far more
narrative than lyrical in nature. It is no accident that the oldest
and most archaizing text is the most functionally strophic. I
would posit a gradual evolution from the lyrical structure of a
poem like *Roland* without "Baligant" toward a linear structure
like the *Moniage Guillaume*, the latest in date of the *chansons
de geste* treated by Rychner. But "Baligant" lacks any trace of
this archaic technique, even though it was sung together with
"Roland" by poets who knew the similar laisses of the poem
without "Baligant." It must certainly have been integrated into
the *Roland* tradition, or generated within it, no earlier than the
eleventh century.

The uniformity of formulaic language does not weigh against
this opinion. Fifty years of oral tradition would be a sufficiently
long period of time for the poem's style to become uniform. Each
singer in the oral tradition is at liberty to change any individual
verse, and even to modify larger portions of the received work
as he sees fit, as long as his audience does not prevent him from
doing so by its protestations. We know from Albert B. Lord's
testimony and analyses that a singer may alter every line of a
song he has just heard sung, and still produce what is, in effect,
the same song, for in the oral tradition the reproduction of a song
consists not in a phrase by phrase rendering of the previous ver-
sion, but in a re-creation, often with quite different phraseology,

[36] Menéndez Pidal, *La Chanson de Roland*, pp. 372–381.

of what is basically the same plot. Through this gradual process (gradual because, although the poem is in a constant state of flux, the traditional *connaissances* of both singer and audience exert a strongly conservative influence), the poem comes inevitably to change. But within the tradition of any given poem there is greater stability on the level of themes than on the formulaic level. Thus it may well be that the principal elements of *Roland*'s plot, including "Baligant," were constituted before the middle of the eleventh century, and that even some of the highly mythical themes had for hundreds of years been passed along in the same tradition as the central historical events, while others represent more recent innovations; this course of development would not necessarily be detectable as a *formulaic* variation between the different parts of the song, for the jongleurs who transmitted it during the latter part of the eleventh century would have substituted formulas of their own liking while remaining more or less faithful (to an extent verifiable in the other *Roland* manuscripts) to the basic plot. This process would eventually produce the uniformity of formulas we find in the Oxford *Roland* despite the composite nature of its narrative.

Is "Baligant" authentic? The question is badly posed. It has too much the smell of ink about it. One might call the late integration of the episode an "interpolation," but that term too has all the wrong connotations. It is too closely related, in scholarly parlance, to "scribal intervention," whereas "Baligant," a product of the oral tradition, was generated and elaborated in song rather than by the pen. Yes, "Baligant" is authentic, as authentic as Charlemagne's beard, Roland's sword Durendal, the personage of Oliver or Ganelon's treachery.[37] It is mythically authentic. No, it is not authentic, if by that term one means "present in the poem as it was first conceived." But its introduction into *Roland* transformed the previous state of the myth, although certainly not on a greater scale than the introduction of Oliver and the moral test, or of Ganelon and the idea of treachery. Oxford is the most es-

[37] Compare Martín de Riquer, *Les Chansons de geste françaises*, p. 88.

thetically pleasing and archaic version we have, and we have it with "Baligant"; it possesses mythical grandeur with "Baligant," despite the inconsistencies, and there is no alternate version which equals it in this respect. Whether "Baligant" improved the poem or not is a matter of taste and conjecture: we have no choice but to accept the episode as an example of the ordinary process of mythical expansion carried out by the oral tradition upon Roland's poetic legend.

# 4: *Roland's* Formulaic Repertory

THE FORMULAS DISCUSSED in this study are, as has been pointed out, limited to those which recur within the *Chanson de Roland* itself. This methodological restriction, as well as having permitted the tabulation of valid material for a quantitative comparison of *Roland* with other *chansons de geste*, carries with it the advantage of revealing a body of formulas defined by the poet's own criterion: those phrases which were of sufficient utility to have been repeated by him within his work. Through an inventory of the *Chanson de Roland's* formulaic repertory, I would now like to show how the formulas are distributed semantically within the work.

The movement of thought in the *Chanson de Roland* is highly paratactic. Each verse is added on to the one before, with few subordinating conjunctions to indicate the relationships between clauses or sentences. The lack of logical indicators allows the listener's (or reader's) mind to supply its own connective links; thus the syntax itself, by its lack of explicit connectives, tends to draw the audience into the logical texture of the verse movement. Parataxis results therefore in little ambiguity, despite a pronounced effect of laconism. No one perceived or expressed this basic intuition about *Roland's* style, and, we now know, about the style of oral poetry in general, better than Erich Auerbach,[1] whose analysis of *Roland's* paratactic phrase structure is a classic

[1] *Mimesis: The Representation of Reality in Western Literature,* translated from the German by Willard Trask (New York: Doubleday, 1957), Ch. V.

of literary criticism. But as if to counterbalance this paratactic movement on the verse level, a complementary and opposite hypotactic tendency is present on the motif/laisse level, where the *Roland* poet repeats certain scenes of capital importance in similar laisses, emphasizes analogous actions in parallel laisses, links motifs with echoing verses, and, probably in order to inform recent arrivals to his audience and at the same time persuade those already present to stay on, recapitulates and anticipates the thread of narrative. Parataxis between clauses and hypotaxis in the plot movement combine to produce a powerful stylistic tension. An acquaintance with the essential differences between oral and written poetry has permitted a reinterpretation of the phenomenon of parataxis in the *Chanson de Roland*.

The incremental or "adding-on" style is not only perfectly compatible with oral improvisation and traditional transmission, but, as has been amply demonstrated by Parry,[2] Notopoulos[3] and Lord,[4] is in itself indicative that a poem in which it dominates was composed orally. The oral poet constructs his song by means of formulas which have been filtered through a multisecular tradition of poets in such a way that they have become relatively autonomous units, endowed with syntactic adaptability precisely because they have been pruned of most of their logical indicators. The paratactic quality is directly related to flexibility of technique. As we shall see, formulas are not rigidly fixed word sequences: changeable features in their structure allow them to fit together easily within the metrical pattern so as to facilitate storytelling even under the pressure of rapid delivery.

Formulaic language is subject to grammatical analysis like any other utterance, but the language of written literature is regarded by the stylistician as individual words juxtaposed so as to achieve

---

[2] "The Distinctive Character of Enjambement in Homeric Verse," *TAPA*, LX (1929), 200–220.

[3] "Parataxis in Homer: A New Approach to Literary Criticism," *TAPA*, LXXX (1949), 1–23.

[4] "Homer and Huso III: Enjambement in Greek and Southslavic Heroic Song," *TAPA*, LXXIX (1948), 113–124.

the maximum effect of originality, while that of oral literature is most profitably viewed as the juxtaposition not of discrete words but rather of stylized metrical units.[5] Oral poetry does not work its effect through rare and unexpected word combinations: on this level it is relatively predictable and repetitious like any other traditional art (romanesque sculpture, Gregorian chant, Flamenco dancing). Nevertheless its beauty, although quite distinct in kind from that of nontraditional narrative, is undeniable. Viewing it functionally as an incremental combination of patterned hemistichs, semantic and syntactic formulas, rather than of words with a life apart from those patterns, is a step in the formulation of a set of critical principles through which oral poetry will be seen as what it is rather than distorted through the lens of critical and scholarly conventions developed with written poetry in mind. The reader of e.e. cummings might analyse into its component words an image such as "No one, not even the rain, has such small hands," whose effect comes from the unexpected, obliquely stated and unique metaphor. The critic of oral poetry must take Homer's metaphorical noun-epithet combination "rosy-fingered dawn" as a single unit, not rare because it is repeated time and time again, not unexpected because it is a standard phrase for narrating the coming of day. "Rosy-fingered dawn" is a substantival formula which the critic would be wrong to pick apart in search of subtle significance, just as he would err in attaching special value to the color green in any particular instance of *Roland*'s formula *sur l'erbe verte*, for the adjective *vert* occurs in the poem only in conjunction with *erbe* and therefore has no life apart from *erbe* in the poem's diction. Each element of the oral poetic language might be usefully viewed as functioning in

[5] Cf. Renate Hitze, *Studien zu Sprache und Stil der Kampfschilderungen in den Chansons de geste*, Kölner Romanistische Arbeiten, Neue Folge, XXXIII (Geneva: Droz, 1965): "An die Stelle der rein lexikologischen Studien . . . können jetzt systematische Zusammenstellungen der epischen Formeln treten, denn nicht vom einzelnen Wort ging die Komposition jedes Verses aus, sondern von einer syntaktisch festgefügten Wortfolge" (p. 30).

a manner analogous to the next smaller unit of written poetic language: hemistichs (syntactic/rhythmic groups) as words, laisses (complex, semantically patterned units) as sentences.

The repertory of the *Chanson de Roland*'s formulas, many of which will be examined in this chapter, should be regarded as constituting the habitual or received segment of the Oxford poet's semantic patterns, either received from his predecessors in the tradition or habitual in his own practice. While some of the formulas may be his personal creation, a large number were common to various branches of the *Roland* tradition, as can be seen by even a superficial comparison of Oxford with the other versions. Formulas were not restrictions upon the poet's creativity any more than, on the metrical and organizational levels, the sonnet form was a restriction upon DuBellay's or Shakespeare's imagination. They are a *datum*, conferring, if anything, a liberty to consecrate attention to the combination of hemistichs into laisses, to problems of organization on larger levels of composition, and to the music and gestures of performance which are forever lost to us.

*Roland*'s formulas may be divided into two broad groups: those which provide the essential actions of the plot, generally verbal in nature, some attached exclusively to certain motifs, such as "single combat," "boast before battle," "general battle" or particular message scenes, others still denoting specific actions but less restricted in context, such as those employed for the introduction of speech; and substantival, adjectival and adverbial phrases relatively unrestricted as to the type of motif in which they appear.[6] Many, but by no means all, of the second group are ornamental formulas, a category which will be treated more fully in Chapter V.

Among the predicate formulas—those which bear specifically

[6] I have chosen in most cases to classify the formulas in broad semantic categories and not according to traditional motifs because so many of them are not restricted to one motif but rather denote actions general enough to be useful within many different motifs. See "Formulas in the *Couronnement de Louis*," *Romania*, LXXXVII (1966), 334–335, and Hitze, *Studien zu Sprache und Stil*, p. 23.

the weight of narration—scholars have accorded most attention
to the phrases employed in battle scenes, since the single combat
motif in which they are found is an easily recognized configu-
ration of frequent use, constituting uninterrupted scenes of
up to sixteen consecutive laisses (as *Roland*, laisses 93 to 108).
When battle formulas do occur, they come in close succession
within the laisse. It would seem that if one type of formula pre-
dominates in the *Roland*, it is the battle formula. And yet this
is not the case. Another semantic category of predicate formula
plays just as important a role, is indispensible in almost every
scene, and is, in fact, found more frequently: the formula for
presentation of speech. Expressions consisting of the verbs of
speaking, *dire, respundre, demander, escrier, apeler, mander,
cumander,* and *reclamer,* in conjunction with a proper name or
designation of rank or position, invariably open dialogue, and
they introduce the utterances of each character each time he
speaks, even though this repeated identification of the speaker
might be superfluous to a reader of the poem. This stylistic char-
acteristic, shared by most *chansons de geste,* may be ascribed
directly to the exigencies of oral presentation, for an audience
with no written record to refer back to needs constantly to be
kept informed of the alternation of dialogue. Indeed one of the
stylistic innovations of the new twelfth-century narrative genre,
the romance, will be the depiction of a rapid, witty dialogue in
which only the content of each reply tells the reader or listener
who is speaking. In Chrétien de Troyes' *Chevalier au lion,* the
famous dialogue in which the lady of the fountain accepts Yvain's
love contains the following verses:

> — Dame, fet il, la force vient
> de mon cuer, qui a vos se tient;
> an ce voloir m'a mes cuers mis.
> — Et qui le cuer, biax dolz amis?
> — Dame, mi oel. — Et les ialz, qui?
> — La granz biautez que an vos vi.

— Et la biautez qu'i a forfet?
— Dame, tant que amer me fet.
— Amer? Et cui? — Vos, dame chiere.
— Moi? — Voire voir. — An quel meniere?
— An tel que graindre estre ne puet. . . .[7]

Such an exchange would not be possible within the conventions of the *Chanson de Roland,* where the paramount effect is retardation of the *répliques* rather than the acceleration necessary for such a sparkling interplay of minds as Chrétien has devised.

The formulas introducing speech are, because of their quantity and variety, an excellent example of how the jongleur adapts his formulaic language to the metrical, syntactic and semantic context. They usually occur in the first hemistich position, requiring four syllables, and if the character's name itself contains three syllables or can be expanded to three syllables by the addition of a noun in apposition or of a title, or by the substitution of a synonymous designation (*l'emperere* for *li reis,* for example), then the word *dire,* in present or past tense, suffices by itself to fill the hemistich: *dist Oliver* (13 occurrences),[8] *dist l'arcevesque* (8), *dist Baligant* (6), *dist Blanca[n]drins* (6), *dist al paien* (vv. 1608, 1632, 1898), *dist Pinabel* (3788, 3892, 3906), *dist Clarien* (2724, 2771), *dist Bramimunde* (2714, 2734), *dist li paien* (537, 550), *dist l'emperere[s]* (2482, 3846), *dist l'amiraill* (3508, 3589), *dist as messages* (143, 2742). For proper names of two syllables, the fillers *ço* or *e* are added, unless the plural verb form *dïent* can be employed to make up the fourth syllable: *dient Franceis* (16 occurrences), *e* [or *il*] *dist al rei* (14), *ço dist li reis* (15), *ço dist al rei* (vv. 920, 3709), *dient paien* (10 occurrences), *ço di[s]t Rollant* (11), *ço dist Marsilie[s]* (5), *dient alquanz* (vv. 983, 3746), and *ço dist li quens* (787, 1935). Combined with elements other than proper names or titles, *dire* appears in *di[s]t l'un a l'altre* (6 occurrences), *si li ad dit* (7), *apres* [or *enpres*] *li di[s]t* (5), *e di[s]t apres* (vv. 1948, 1958) and *e dist un mot* (2087, 2281). Less often it appears in a second hemistich formula: *dist li emperere Carles* (180, 274, 740), *dist Marsilies li reis* (563, 2741), *ço dient tuit li altre* (3039, 3046 [*li Franc*]), and "*ço n'iert*," *dist Guenes* (544, 557), which includes the beginning of Ganelon's utterance. Once the verb is in the future tense: *jo lur dirrai* (2913, 2919 [*jes lur*]).

The verb *respundre*, second to *dire* in speech formulas, is, because of its syllabic length, never combined in first hemistich formulas with names or titles of more than two syllables. Repeated within *Roland* we find: *Guenes respunt* (14 occurrences), *respunt Rollant* (13), *e cil respont* [or *respondent*] (9), *cil li respunt* (vv. 3956, 3982 [*respundent*]), *respundent Francs* (8 occurrences), *paien respundent* (vv. 2685, 3400), *C[h]arles respunt* (4 occurrences), *respont li quens* (vv. 1548, 1676, 1712), *respunt dux Neimes* (246, 1790, 1013), *respunt li reis* (248, 259) and *ço respunt Guenes* (358, 606), the last being the only phrase in which, because of the mute *e* occurring at the cesura, *ço* is required to supplement *respunt*. The two basic verbs *dire* and *respundre*, in combination with *e* and *ço*, can combine with just about any Old French name, title or personal designation. They form a simple but totally adequate system for introducing dialogue. *Demander* only introduces speech twice in the formula *si li demandet* (1999, 3611), both occurrences of which appear after a sword blow hits the hero who is about to speak, once Roland struck by the blood-blinded Oliver, and the other time Charles in danger of being defeated by Baligant. *Escrier*, on the other hand, is the normal verb for cries of encouragement, defiance, or rally in actual conditions of battle: *paien escrient* (4 occurrences), *Franceis escrient* (vv. 1112, 3475), *apres escriet* (1542, 2805), *puis si escrie[n]t* (1921, 2985) and *s'en escriet mult halt* (3334, 891 [*cil s'escriet*]). Of equal frequency is *apeler*, followed either immediately or in the second hemistich by the name of the person to whom the subject will speak: *sin apelat* (8 occurrences), *Carles apelet* (3014, 3947), [*li quens Rollant*] *apelet Oliver* (1145, 1671). Less frequent verbs are *mander: iço vus mandet* (125, 430, 470 [*quar ço vos*], 680 [*e si vos*]);[9] *cumander: li reis cumandet* (2432, 2970, 3952); and *reclamer: recleimet ses Franceis* (3405, 3556).

Most of *Roland*'s formulaic speech patterns depend, then, on the two verbs *dire* and *respundre*, nearly always in the first hemistich. Even when the verb *parler* occurs, nonformulaically, the jongleur often falls into the tautology of employing a first-hemistich introductory expression with *dire*, out of the deeply engrained habit of his formulaic style:

> Blancandrins ad tut premereins parléd,
> E dist al rei: "Salvet seiez de Deu" (vv. 122–123).

> Par grant saveir cumencet a parler
> Cume celui ki ben faire le set,
> E dist al rei: "Salvez seiez de Deu" (426–428).

> Apres parlat ses filz envers Marsilie,
> E dist al rei: "Guenes ad dit folie" (495–496).

> Par grant veisdie cumencet a parler,
> E dist al rei: "Salvez seiez de Deu!" (675–676).

> Cascun parolet altresi cume hum,
> Diseient li: "Sire, rendez le nus!" (2559–2560).

In the three verses which call for a formula of greeting, an identical second hemistich formula, *salvez seiez de Deu*, underscores the patterned nature of these combinations. This may be a particular stylistic habit of the Oxford jongleur, since the first four examples do not appear in corresponding verses of the Venice 4 or Châteauroux manuscripts. Oxford sometimes does use *parler* to introduce direct discourse, as in vv. 752, 762, 1206, 1252, 1803 and 2656.

It should not be surprising that phrases introducing speech

[9] *Mander* in *ses baruns mandet* (vv. 166, 169) denotes the process of calling an assembly rather than actual speech.

are so abundant in the poem, with approximately one in every twelve formulas employed for this purpose. The *Chanson de Roland* is as much a work of council scenes, legal proceedings and dialogue on the field of battle as a work of physical combat, and, at least for the modern reader, the interplay of personalities is its most interesting aspect. There are *chansons de geste* without battles, such as *Le Pélerinage de Charlemagne à Jérusalem et à Constantinople*, but one devoid of dialogue is inconceivable. Moreover, the first theme of *Roland*, consisting mainly of councils and the negotiation of the betrayal, without a single battle, is only one tenth of one percent less formulaic than the Roncevaux section, made up largely of single combat laisses. Battle formulas are absent from council scenes, but speech formulas are spread throughout the entire song and are, as will be seen, indispensable for describing a typical epic battle. The dramatic quality of the *Roland*, with its sharp contrast of conflicting personalities, Ganelon-Roland, Roland-Oliver, Charlemagne-Baligant, Tierry-Pinabel, would have been impossible for the singer to achieve, were he not endowed with a facility for manipulating dialogue through an abundance of speech formulas.

The Danish folklorist Axel Olrik formulated a series of "epic laws of folk narrative" one of which is instructive in this regard.[10] It posits that, in folktales and folk poetry alike, the maximum number of characters engaging in conversation at any one time is three, and normally two are actually speaking, in opposition to each other, in each exchange. The *Roland*'s speech formulas—and this is equally true of the other *chansons de geste*—are designed to facilitate the construction of conversations between two characters at a time, but hardly ever more than two. When a multitude of characters is participating in a council, or communicating with each other on the battlefield, a polarity is created between them and their leader by means of formulas such as

[10] "Epische Gesetze der Volksdichtung," *Zeitschrift für deutsches Altertum*, LI (1909), 1–12. An English translation is found in Alan Dundes, *The Study of Folklore* (Englewood Cliffs: Prentice-Hall, 1965), pp. 131–141.

*dient paien, dient Franceis, respundent Franc* or *e cil respundent.*
When literary critics speak of rigidity as a quality of epic style,
this relative inflexibility in the manner of communication between
characters is largely responsible. In the famous French council
scene which terminates with enmity between Roland and Ganelon,
the polarization is evident. When Charlemagne asks for advice
(laisse 13), Roland gives it to him directly, counselling against
accepting the Saracens' terms (l.14). Ganelon answers Roland,
but by speaking to Charlemagne rather than to his stepson, and
even his barely softened insult of Roland, *"Ja mar crerez bricum,/
Ne mei ne altre, se de vostre prod nun!"* (l.15) is couched in
words addressed to the emperor. Naimes clarifies Ganelon's
statement and supports him, but still speaks directly to the em-
peror. Finally the French nobles ratify Naime's qualification of
Ganelon's advice as the decision to be adopted, *"Ben ad parlét
li dux"* (l.16). This technique continues through the selection
of an ambassador, each character speaking to only one person at
a time, even though his words are meant for more than one. The
sole exception is the legal phrase of defiance pronounced by
Ganelon directly to Roland, before the emperor, as was required
by feudal law for the breaking of allegiance between two vassals:

> E dit al cunte: "Jo ne vus aim nient:
> Sur mei avez turnet fals jugement.
> Dreiz emperere, veiz me ci en present:
> Ademplir voeill vostre comandement" (laisse 22).

But the very conditions under which such a breaking of faith
had to be accomplished in order to render it legal (*"Desfi les ci,
sire, vostre veiant,"* v. 329, later taken up as a defense by Ganelon
when he declares, *"Jo desfiai Rollant, le poigneor,/ Et Oliver e
tuiz lur cumpaignun;/ Carles l'oid e si noble baron,"* in vv. 3775–
3777, and leading to his acquittal by the jury of his peers), ex-
plains this exception. The poet is underscoring Charlemagne's

participation in the scene of defiance, and the anomaly, with its obvious legalistic purpose, confirms the relevance of Olrik's law for the *Roland*. If the forms and use of introductory speech formulas conform to the basic polarization of character in the *Chanson de Roland*, the formulas characters employ to open a dialogue sometimes set a particular tone. In the relatively ceremonial atmosphere of epic where embassies are an important element in plot development, the reactions of subordinates—messengers, ambassadors, counselors—to their lords occur frequently enough to be expressed in stylized language. The formula of greeting, spoken by an approaching messenger, is *salvez seiez de Deu*, sometimes amplified by an appositive or balancing phrase in the following line. Thus Blancandrin greets Charlemagne:

> E dist al rei: Salvet seiez de Deu,
> Le glorius, que devuns aurer!
> Iço vus mandet reis Marsilies li bers (vv. 123–125).

But when Blancandrin reports back to Marsilie with Charlemagne's peace offer, the poet has him address his coreligionist in the name of the Saracen "gods" of the *chanson de geste*:

> E dist al rei: "Sals seiez de Mahum
> E d'Apolin qui seintes leis tenuns!
> Vostre message fesime a Charlun" (vv. 416–418).

Ganelon, who subsequently accompanies Blancandrin back to Marsile's camp as Charles' ambassador, is not nearly so diplomatic about his host's religious sentiments as Blancandrin had been toward the emperor of the Franks:

> E dist al rei: "Salvez seiez de Deu,
> Li glorius, qui devum aurer!
> Iço vos mandet Carlemagnes li ber . . ." (vv. 428–430).

He knows well the conventions of ambassadorial courtesy, says
the poet:

> Par grant saver cumencet a parler
> Cume celui ki ben faire le set,

but the insolent tone of his delivery, led off by his formulaic
greeting on the part of the Christian god, enrages Marsile. The
poet modifies the configuration of the greeting formulas when
Ganelon reports back to the French, omitting the whole-line ex-
tension of *Deu/Mahum* that was present in the first three ex-
amples, and beginning the message directly, perhaps to emphasize
Ganelon's proud tone after the apparently successful and loyal
accomplishment of the dangerous embassy:

> Par grant vesdie cumencet a parler
> E dist al rei: "Salvez seiez de Deu!
> De Sarraguce ci vos aport les clefs.
> Mult grant aveir vos en faz amener . . ." (vv. 675–678).

These examples show that formulaic style does not deprive the
*Roland* tradition of the ability to introduce subtle shadings of
character into the workings of its personages, for here, as in many
other recurring motifs, they are effected through the play of for-
mulas rather than the juxtaposition of individual words.

Another set of formulas associated with speeches, more exten-
sive than the group used in greetings, is that of the standard reply
of acquiescence, employed either for the acceptance of a counsel
or as agreement to a command.

| | |
|---|---|
| "Ben serat fait," li quens Guenes respunt. | v. 625 |
| "Ben serat fait," Guenes respundit. | 632 |
| E cil respundent: "Cher sire, si ferum." | 2688 |
| "Dreiz emperere, cher sire, si ferum." | 2441 |
| E cil respundent: "Sire, vus dites veir." | 2754 |
| Respondent Franc: "Sire, vos dites veir." | 3414 |
| Respunt Rollant: "Sire, mult dites bien." | 1752 |
| Respundent Franc: "Sire, vos dites bien." | 2487 |

> Paien respundent: "Sire, mult dites bien."           2685
> Respundent Franc: "Or avez vos bien dit."            3837
> Guenes respunt: "Ben seit vostre comant."            616
> E cil respundent: "(Sire,) a vostre comandement."    946

These phrases are usually found near the end of laisses, in accordance with the *Roland* tradition's convention of terminating council laisses by a chorus of agreement from the subordinate knights present. At times momentous decisions are taken through phrases of this kind, such as Thierry's offer to represent the emperor's interests in the judicial combat with Pinabel (accepted by the other nobles with *"Or avez vos ben dit,"* v. 3837), Roland's designation of Ganelon for the embassy (quickly ratified without so much as a comment from Charlemagne with *dient Franceis: "Car il le poet ben faire,"* v. 278), and the initial acceptance of the strategy of retreat, formulated by Ganelon and supported by Naimes (*dient Franceis: "Ben ad parlet li dux,"* v. 243). Although not all of these hemistichs are repeated verbatim within the *Roland,* together they obviously form a standard manner of expressing agreement in council scenes. The *Roland* tradition's formulas are not restricted to actions peripheral to the basic narration; I emphasize that the major plot developments, the turning points of the action, are themselves often made up of formulas.

Another standard pattern shows characters reacting to speech with formulas containing the words *oir* and *entendre: quant l'ot Marsilie* (vv. 601, 3644), *quant [l']ot Rollant* (302, 761, 1196), *quant l'oit Guenes* (499), *quant l'ot li reis* (745), *Karles l'oit* (1757, 1788, 3777), *Karles l'entent* (1766), *ben l'avez entendud* (232, 776). Perception of action rather than of speech is signaled by analogous formulas using the verb *veir: quant Carles veit* (2476, 3006, 3728, 3815), *quant Rollant veit* (1110, 1932), *quant Guenes veit* (3780), *quant Naimun veit* (3452), *quant ço veit Guenes* (303), *quant veit Tierri* (3850), *quant veit li quens* (2342), *quant veit li reis* (2447). Although some of these expressions are unique in the poem, they share a basic pattern for presenting reactions. The poet can alter them metrically as is needed, with the addition of particles or the inversion of words, or semantically with the substitution of metrically equivalent names. When a verbal formula will not fit, the substantival *a icel mot* (4 examples) or *a icest mot* (10) may sometimes suffice.

The actual content of speech is also studded with groups of formulas which render the common feelings of characters. Many of these formulas occur when battle is engaged, or when preparations are being made for the conflict, and illustrate that the typical epic battle consists as much of speech as it does of the patterned ritual of single combats.

The utterance which leads up to battle is the knightly *vantance* or boast, the serious counterpart of the delightful *gabs* of the *Pèlerinage de Charlemagne*. The most obvious example of the boast in *Roland* is in the series of parallel laisses in which the twelve Saracen peers, chosen on the spot at the request of Aelroth, Marsile's nephew, come forth one at a time to brag about the defeat they will impose on the French at Roncevaux. In the Oxford text the series of boasts is incomplete,[11] being limited to eight. Except in the case of laisse 76, where one of the essential elements of the motif is couched in the words of Marsile, I include here only a few relevant introductory verses and the peer's boast itself:

[11] The Venice 4 manuscript contains the *vantance* of Corsablis, reported only indirectly in Oxford:

> Rois Consabrin si est da l'altre part:
> Barbarin est e de molt males art;
> E il a parlé a lei de bon vasal:
> "Por tut l'or Deo non voio eser coart;
> Se trovo François, no laxaro ne asalt:
> Eo sum li terço, or se n'adreli el quart." (vv. 838–843)

Oxford's laisse 71 combines laisses 68 and 69 of Venice 4, and places the boast in *discours indirect libre*:

> Reis Corsalis, il est de l'altre part:
> Barbarins est e mult de males arz.
> Cil ad parlet a lei de bon vassal:
> Pur tut l'or Deu ne volt estre cuard.

71 "Jo cunduirai mun cors en
   Rencesvals;
   Se truis Rollant, ne lerrai que
   nel mat."
72 Uns amurafles i ad de Bala-
   guer. . . .
   Devant Marsilie cil en est
   escriet:
   "En Rencesvals irai mun cors
   guier.
   Se truis Rollant, de mort serat
   finet,
   E Oliver e tuz les doze pers:
   Franceis murrunt a doel e a
   viltet.
   Carles li magnes velz est e
   redotez,
   Recreanz ert de sa guerre
   mener:
   Remeindrat nus Espaigne en
   quitedet."
73 "En Rencesvals guierai ma
   cumpaigne,
   .XX. milie ad escuz e a
   lances.
   Se trois Rollant, de mort li
   duins fiance.
   Jamais n'ert jor que Carles ne
   se pleignet."
74 D'altre part est Turgis de
   Turteluse. . . .
   Devant Marsilie as altres si
   s'ajust,
   Ço dist al rei: "Ne vos esmaiez
   unches!
   Plus valt Mahum que seint
   Perre de Rume!
   Se lui servez, l'onur del camp
   ert nostre.
   En Rencesvals a Rollant irai
   juindre,

De mort n'avrat guarantisun
   pur hume.
Veez m'espee, ki est e bone e
   lunge:
A Durendal jo la metrai en-
   cuntre;
Asez orrez laquele irat desure.
Franceis murrunt, si a nus
   s'abandunent;
Carles li velz avrat e deol e
   hunte:
Jamais en tere ne portera
   curone."
75 De l'altre part est Escremiz de
   Valterne. . . .
   Devant Marsilie s'escriet en la
   presse:
   "En Rencesvals irai l'orgoill
   desfaire.
   Se trois Rollant, n'en porterat
   la teste,
   Ne Oliver, ki les altres cade-
   let;
   Li .XII. per tuit sunt jugez a
   perdre;
   Franceis murrunt e France en
   ert deserte.
   De bons vassals avrat Carles
   suffraite."
76 D'altre part est uns paiens,
   Esturganz;
   Estramariz i est, un soens
   cumpainz:
   Cil sunt felun, traitur sudui-
   ant.
   Ço dist Marsilie: "Seignurs,
   venez avant!
   En Rencesvals irez as porz
   passant,
   Si aiderez a conduire ma gent."
   E cil respundent: "(Sire,) a
   vostre comandement!

Nus asaldrum Oliver e Rol-
lant;
Li .XII. per n'avrunt de mort
guarant.
Noz espees sunt bones e tren-
chant;
Nus les feruns vermeilles de
chald sanc.
Franceis murrunt, Carles en
ert dolent.
Tere Majur vos metrum en
present.
Venez i, reis, sil verrez veire-
ment:
L'empereor vos metrum en
present."

77 Curant i vint Margariz de
Sibilie. . . .
Vint en la presse, sur les altres
s'escriet
Et dist al rei: "Ne vos esmaiez
mie!
En Rencesvals irai Rollant
ocire,
Ne Oliver n'en porterat la vie;
Li .XII. per sunt remes en
martirie.
Veez m'espee, ki d'or est en-
heldie:

Si la tramist li amiralz de
Primes.
Jo vos plevis qu'en vermeill
sanc ert mise.
Franceis murrunt e France en
ert hunie;
Carles li velz a la barbe flurie,
Jamais n'ert jurn qu'il n'en ait
doel e ire.
Jusqu'a un an avrum France
saisie;
Gesir porrum el burc de seint
Denise."

78 De l'altre part est Chernubles
de Munigre. . . .
Ce dist Chernubles: "Ma bone
espee ai ceinte;
En Rencesvals jo la teindrai
vermeille.
Se trois Rollant li proz enmi
ma veie,
Se ne l'asaill, dunc ne faz jo
que creire,
Si cunquerrai Durendal od la
meie.
Franceis murrunt e France en
ert deserte."

One can reconstruct a skeletal framework for the *vantance* motifs
by placing in series the first hemistich formulas and key words
found in more than one laisse. The logic of the statement thus
epitomized is represented in the right hand column:

*D'altre part est* (present          A Saracen appears
in 4 laisses)
*devant Marsilie* (5)                before Marsile:
*en Rencesvals* (6)                  "I will take my men to the

| | |
|---|---|
| *se trois Rollant* (5), with three additional mentions of Roland | battlefield and kill Roland, |
| *ne* [or *et*] *Oliver* (3), with one other mention of Oliver | and Oliver |
| *li .XII. per* (3) | and the peers; |
| *veez m'espee* (2), or other mention of Saracen's sword (2) | my weapon, |
| *vermeil* (3) | red with blood, |
| *Durendal* (2) | better than Durendal, |
| *Franceis murrunt* (6) | will bring death to the French; |
| *Carles li velz* [or *magnes*] (3) or other mention of Charles (3) | Charlemagne |
| *jamais n'ert jorn* (2) | will come to sorrow. |

To fill out each statement into a metrically and syntactically viable whole, of course, a second hemistich—or, in the case of the key words *vermeil* and *Durendal* which are not couched in formulas, a syntactic carrier—is added, but its form depends on the assonance of the particular laisse in which it occurs. Thus *Franceis murrunt* is followed by:

| | |
|---|---|
| *a doel e a viltiet* | assonance in é (<a) |
| *si a nus s'abandunent* | u.e, un.e |
| *e France en ert deserte* (2) | ę.e, ai.e |
| *Carles en ert dolent* | an, en |
| *e France en ert hunie* | i.e, in.e |

Seldom is an element of the archetypal series included in the second hemistich, as is the case in *Carles en ert dolent* of laisse 76. The first hemistichs thus contain the bulk of the narrative (and this is true not only of the *vantance* motif, but of most

others as well) while the second hemistichs are primarily orna-
mental. The tradition of this particular motif has evolved in such
a way that no one laisse in any extant manuscript contains all
the elements of the logical progression, and yet its identity as a
standard scene is unmistakable. Like formulas, the motifs are
flexible rather than rigid, but as Michael Holland observes,[12] the
order of elements is, except when two occupy the same verse,
invariable, even in laisse 76 where Marsile's order to his two
vassals contains part of the *vantance* material.

The *vantance* motif as seen in these eight laisses may appear
banal at best, although one must not rule out the effect of sus-
pense that the accumulation of threats may have had upon the
song's late-eleventh-century auditors. This same motif, however,
vested with dramatic tension, plays a central role in the narration
of Roland's choice not to call for help, for the three similar
laisses in which the hero refuses to sound his *olifant* contain
*vantances* which are fundamentally similar to those of the series
just discussed. The passage occurs just after Oliver has sighted
the pagan army. Like the French council scene which results in
Ganelon's being named ambassador, it sets up an opposition
between two strong-willed men, insistently emphasized through
reiteration, and may even be said to constitute the dramatic high
point of the *Chanson de Roland*.

laisse 83:   Dist Oliver: "Paien unt grant esforz;
             De noz Franceis m'i semblet aveir mult poi!
             Cumpaign Rollant, kar sunez vostre corn:
             Si l'orrat Carles, si returnerat l'ost."
             Respunt Rollant: "Jo fereie que fols!
             En dulce France en perdreie mun los.
             Sempres ferrai de Durendal granz colps;
             Sanglant en ert le branz entresqu'a l'or.

[12] *"Rolandus Resurrectus,"* in Pierre Gallais and Yves-Jean Riou, ed.,
*Mélanges offerts à René Crozet* (Poitiers: Société d'Etudes Médiévales,
1966), I, 400.

> Felun paien mar i vindrent as porz:
> Jo vos plevis, tuz sunt jugez a mort." AOI

84: "Cumpainz Rollant, l'olifan car sunez:
> Si l'orrat Carles, ferat l'ost returner,
> Succurrat nos li reis od tut sun barnet."
> Respont Rollant: "Ne placet Damnedeu
> Que mi parent pur mei seient blasmet
> Ne France dulce ja cheet en viltet!
> Einz i ferrai de Durendal asez,
> Ma bone espee que ai ceint al costet:
> Tut en verrez le brant ensanglentet.
> Felun paien mar i sunt asemblez:
> Jo vos plevis, tuz sunt a mort livrez." AOI

85: "Cumpainz Rollant, sunez vostre olifan:
> Si l'orrat Carles, ki est as porz passant.
> Je vos plevis, ja returnerunt Franc."
> "Ne placet Deu," ço li respunt Rollant,
> Que ço seit dit de nul hume vivant,
> Ne pur paien, que ja seie cornant!
> Ja n'en avrunt reproece mi parent!
> Quant jo serai en la bataille grant
> E jo ferrai e mil colps e .VII. cenz,
> De Durendal verrez l'acer sanglent.
> Franceis sunt bon, si ferrunt vassalment;
> Ja cil d'Espaigne n'avrunt de mort guarant."

Roland's negative reply to his companion's request consists of six essential elements:

1. Jo fereie que fols                          This would be wrong,
   Ne placet Damnedeu
   Ne placet Deu
2. En dulce France en perdreie     for my [my country's, my line-
   mun los                                        age's] reputation would suffer;
   Ne France dulce ja cheet en
   viltet

Ja n'en avrunt reproece mi
parent
3. Sempres ferrai                          but with blows of my sword
   Einz i ferrai
   E jo ferrai
4. de Durendal granz colps                Durendal,
   de Durendal asez
   de Durendal
5. sanglant en ert li branz en-           red with blood
   tresqu'a l'or
   tut en verrez le brant ensang-
   lentet
   verrez l'acer sanglent
6. jo vos plevis, tut sunt jugez a        I will bring death to the pagans.
   mort
   jo vos plevis, tuz sunt a mort
   livrez
   ja cil d'Espaigne n'avrunt de
   mort guarant

Of these six, the four which constitute the *vantance* proper are also present in the Saracen peers' laisses: power of the sword (*ferrai, veez m'espee*), covered with blood (*vermeil, sanglent*); mention of Durendal; and defeat of the enemy (*Franceis mur- runt, mort*). In both series, the reinforcing, but semantically slight, formula *jo vos plevis* is employed to introduce a threat (laisses 77, 83, 84).

The considerable difference in effectiveness between Roland's *vantance* and the boasts of the twelve Saracen peers is not in the make-up of the motif itself—the alterations are not terribly sig- nificant, and Roland's words contain no stylistically striking phrases—but in the balancing function of the three similar laisses as an expression of Roland's will against his friend's plea. Of itself the *vantance* constitutes the hero's reply to Oliver's request. Rather than have Roland oppose a direct "No" to his companion, the tradition simply shows him proceeding with the *vantance*, the speech which normally precedes combat, as if to say that he is going on immediately with preparations for battle despite the counsel of prudence he has just received. The contemporary audience, infinitely more familiar than we with the function and proper place of motifs, must have appreciated this fact, even though the paratactic style omits explanation for the procedure. As with formulas, the effectiveness of a motif does not depend upon the unique shape of any given example of that motif, but rather upon its skillful juxtaposition with other motifs—here with a dramatic result. The qualities of the motif—relative stability of the configuration of phrases which go to make it up, but variety of function depending on the context—are analogous to the characteristics of formulas, for these too vary in form to fit the context and take on particular effects, while retaining their basic identity.

A speech formula similar to the *vantance*, but directed toward encouraging the actions of a knight other than the speaker, is the exhortation to greater effort in battle, which normally takes the form of an imperative: *car chevalchez* (vv. 1175, 2428, 3296),[13] *venez, paien* (2844, 3326), *ferez i, Francs* (1211, 1233), *ferez, Franceis* (1258, 1937), *ferez, baron* (3366, 3392, 3472), *ferez, paien* (1543, 1578, 3397), *kar tres ben les veintrum* (1233, 1578). The French battle cry is also an exhortation to valor, though a more general one: *"Munjoie!" escriet* (6 occurrences); when referred to in the third person, it is *l'enseigne Carle* (1179, 1973), *ço est l'enseigne Carle* (1350, 1234 [*Carlun*]), with a Saracen counterpart, *l'enseigne paienor* (1221, 1921 [*paienie*]).

The public praise which was, to the society portrayed in *Roland*, the highest recompense for prowess and the counterpart of the *male cançun* (1014, 1466) with which Roland himself is preoccupied, is also conveyed in formulas spoken on the field of battle by combatants, or in quieter moments such as council scenes, or at times in the words of the poet-persona himself: *cist colp est de baron* (1280, 1288 [*produme*]), *mult par est proz* (4 occurrences), *est mult bon chevaler* (1673, 2067 [*bien bon*]), *n'ad tel vassal* (545, 558), *vasselage ad e mult grant estultie*

---

[13] See p. 95 above.

(1478, 2606), *de vasselage* (followed by *fut asez chevaler*, 25; *est il ben alosez*, 898; *li poust remembrer*, 1182; *est suvent esprovet*, 3163; *te conoissent ti per*, 3901), *e de grant vasselage* (2278, 3875), *de bon vassal* (*li poust remembrer*, 1972), *a lei de chevaler* (752, 1143), *ja mais n'iert home* ([*n'ert hume*] *ki encuntre lui vaille*, 376; *plus se voeillet venger*, 1873; *ki tun cors cuntrevaillet*, 1984; *plus volenters le serve*, 2254), *que oümes tanz chers* (2178, 2406 [*que jo aveie*]), *ja pur murir* (6 occurrences), *mielz voeill murir* (7 occurrences), *meillor vassal* (5 occurrences), *mult grant prod i avrez* (699, 3459 [*avreiz*]), *de tels barons* (1696, 3037), *suz cel n'ad gent* (*que Carles ait plus chere*, 3031; *ki plus poissent en camp*, 3049; *ki l'osast querre en champ*, 1782 as a comment of opprobrium), *suz ciel n'ad rei* (*plus en ait de meillors*, 1442; *qu'il prist a un enfant*, 2739), *est mult de grant saveir* (3279, 3602 [*vertut*]), *en guise de baron* (4 occurrences), *nen unt poür ne de murir dutance* (823, 3613). At the other extreme, the formula of disculpation, spoken by Oliver twice and once by the narrator to remove all blame from the French who will die at Roncevaux, is: *n'en deivent aveir blasme*, 1346, 1718, 1174 [*ne funt mie a blasmer*]). *Ben resemblet barun* (3172) and *ben resenblet marchis* (3502), both applied to Baligant, reflect the conditional variation of the formula of praise common in the *chansons de geste* where an unbeliever is commended to the highest extent consonant with his non-Christian state. In v. 3764, *s'il fust leials, ben resemblast barun*, Ganelon, as vallainous as ever was a Saracen, is seen from a point of view analogous with the narrator's qualified admiration of Baligant in v. 3164, *Deus! quel baron, s'oüst crestientét!*[14] It is only a step further to irony, and, as with the *vantance* motif, the transformation in function is brought about not by a change in the formula itself, but by

---

[14] Martín de Riquer, in "¡Dios, que buen vassallo, si oviesse buen señor!," *La Leyenda del graal y temas épicos medievales* (Madrid: Editorial Prensa Española, 1968), pp. 221–226, discussing the famous verse of the *Poema de mio Cid*, mentions an expression of the *Waltharii Poesis*, whose similarity to the formulas treated here indicates a possible parentage between the Germanic epic and the Romance: *est athleta bonus, fidei si jura servaret.*

contextual means. The seemingly praiseworthy *n'avez baron de si grant vasselage* (v. 744) and *n'avez baron ki mielz de lui la facet* (750), spoken by Ganelon who refers respectively to Roland and Oger de Denemarche, are an ironic means of persuading Charlemagne to reconstitute his army in such a way as to facilitate the success of Ganelon's treasonous plot, a manner, one might say, of damning Roland with strong praise. Only the context, that is the audience's knowledge of Ganelon's embassy, endows these phrases with a meaning other than what Charlemagne perceives in them. Shortly thereafter Naimes innocently echoes Ganelon's treacherous evaluation when he comments that, once Roland had been named, no man could succeed in persuading him to relinquish command of the rear-guard, so fierce is his pride: *n'avez barun ki ja mais la remut* (v. 779).

Blame as well as praise is meted out on the battlefield, but usually to the enemy: *unkes n'amat cuard* (v. 2134), with the whole-verse form *unches n'amai cuard ne cuardie* (1486); *ki Deu nen amat unkes* (3261, 3638 [*que Deus*]); *ço est une gent* (completed by *ki unches ben ne volt*, 3231; *ki Damnedeu ne sert*, 3247; *ki Deu nen amat unkes*, 3261), *de vos seit hoi grant perte* (3299) with its whole-verse variation *de vos seit hoi male confusion* (3276), and *Deus tut mal te tramette* (1608, 1632 [*consente*]). The verbal insults directed against the bodies of fallen Saracens by French knights are sometimes introduced by *apres li di[s]t* or *e di[s]t apres*, as in the following examples:

> Apres li dist: "Turnet estes a perdre!" (1296).
> Apres li dist: "Ja n'i avrez guarant!" (1303).
> Apres li dist: "Culvert, mar i moustes!" (1335).
> Apres li dit: "Culvert paien, cum fus unkes si os . . ." (2292).
> E dit apres: "Un col avez pris fort!" (1948).
> E dist apres: "Paien, mal aies tu!" (1958).

Another less widely used pattern, rather curious in that it employs indirect discourse as well as direct, is:

> Ne leserat, ço dit, que n'i parolt:
> "Ultre, culvert! . . ." (vv. 1206–07).

Ne laisserat que n'i parolt, ço dit:
"Culvert paien . . ." (1252–53).

These insults counterbalance and sometimes even echo[15] the
*vantance* which precedes the single combat formulas. The two
speech patterns thus serve as a frame for the duels of the *Chanson
de Roland.*

The expression of affectivity in the *Roland* is made up almost
exclusively of formulas denoting grief, dominated by the motif
of the *planctus,* a regret spoken over the body of a fallen hero,
which will be discussed in detail in the next chapter.

The only major type of short utterance remaining to be dis-
cussed from a formulaic point of view is the prayer. The last
words of Oliver and Turpin before their deaths are related in
similar formulaic terms:

Oliver:  *Cuntre le ciel ambesdous ses mains juintes,*
         *Si priet Deu que pareis li dunget* (vv. 2015–2016).
Turpin:  *Cuntre le ciel amsdous ses mains ad juinz,*
         *Si priet Deu que pareis li duinst* (2240–2241).

The French knights' prayer for Roland's protection and Charle-
magne's for the dead of Roncevaux, uttered after his pursuit of
the fleeing pagan army, are couched in the same first hemistich
formula: *et prient Deu* (1837, 2518 [*priet*]), and the emperor's
request for the sun to stop in the sky is the second hemistich
form, *si priet Damnedeu* (2449). The only prayers whose content
is given as direct discourse are in the form which has come to be
called the "epic *credo.*"[16] The wording of Turpin's counsel to the
French army to beg God's forgiveness for their sins, *clamez vos*

---

[15] Vv. 1209–1210, *Il fist que proz qu'il nus laisad as porz:/Oi n'en perdrat
France dulce sun los,* are a reply by Roland, in almost identical terms, to
the boast of Aelroth, whom he has just killed: *Fols est li reis ki vos laissat
as porz./Enquoi perdrat France dulce sun los,* vv. 1193–1194.

[16] See Edmond-René Labande, "Le *credo* épique: à propos des prières
dans les chansons de geste," *Recueil de travaux offert à M. Clovis Brunel*
(Paris: Société de l'Ecole des Chartes, 1955), II, 62–80.

*culpes, si preiez Deu mercit!* (1132) is taken up again to introduce Roland's *credo: cleimet sa culpe, si priet Deu mercit* (2384). Charlemagne's *credo* prior to the great battle with Baligant's army, announced and introduced by *recleimet Deu* (2998, 3099), shares only its opening phrase *veire paterne* (3100, 2385) and mention of the biblical Daniel, *et Daniel* (3104, 2387), with Roland's prayer.

The longer speech motif which occupies laisses of a higher formulaic proportion than all others save one (Ganelon's treasonous conversation with Marsile) is the diplomatic message. The *Chanson de Roland* opens with a Saracen council scene in which Blancandrin proposes to Marsile the terms of peace which, he thinks, will be acceptable to Charlemagne; when it has been decided that this indeed is the best course, Marsile appoints Blancandrin to deliver the message, and relates it to him *even though it was Blancandrin who originally formulated it.* In the French camp the opposite process occurs: Blancandrin delivers the terms to Charlemagne, who in turn calls a council of the principal French lords and recounts the message to them. The terms of peace are spelled out four times, in formulas which have little use outside the message motif. The following verses from these four laisses constitute the core of the message, and provide an example of the kind of variation the formulas undergo to conform to assonance. The hemistichs in italics are those which, allowing for assonantal variation, recur within the sequence itself.

> Blancandrin's original proposal, laisse 3:
> "Vos li durrez urs e leons e chens,
> *Set cenz camelz e mil hosturs muers,*
> *D'or e d'argent .IIII.C. muls cargez,*
> *Cinquante carre qu'en ferat carier:*
> *Ben en purrat luer ses soldeiers.*
> En ceste tere ad asez osteiet;
> *En France, ad Ais, s'en deit ben repairer.*
> *Vos le sivrez* a la feste seint Michel:

*Si recevrez la lei de chrestiens,*
*Serez ses hom par honur e par ben.*
*S'en volt ostages, e vos l'en enveiez. . . ."*

Marsile's instructions to the messengers, led by Blancandrin,
laisse 6:
    Si me direz a Carlemagne, le rei,
    Pur le soen Deu qu'il ait mercit de mei.
    Ja einz ne verrat passer cest premier meis,
    *Que jel sivrai od mil de mes fedeilz,*
    *Si recevrai la chrestiene lei,*
    *Serai ses hom par amur e par feid;*
    *S'il voelt ostages,* il en avrat par veir."

Delivery of the message by Blancandrin, laisse 9:
    *Iço vus mandet* reis Marsilies, li bers:
    Enquis ad mult la lei de salvetet,
    *De sun aveir vos voelt asez duner,*
    *Urs e leuns e veltres enchaignez,*
    *Set cenz cameilz e mil hosturs muez,*
    *D'or e d'argent .III. cenz muls trussez,*
    *Cinquante care que carier en ferez;*
    Tant i avrat de besanz esmerez
    *Dunt bien purrez voz soldeiers luer.*
    En cest pais avez estet asez;
    *En France, ad Ais, devez bien repairer;*
    *La vos sivrat,* ço dit mis avoez."

Charles reports Marsile's terms to his council, laisse 13:
    Li reis Marsilie m'ad tramis ses messages;
    *De sun aveir me voelt duner grant masse,*
    *Urs e leuns e veltres caeignables,*
    *Set cenz cameilz e mil hosturs muables,*
    *Quatre cenz mulz cargez del or d'Arabe,*

> Avoec iço *plus de cinquante care;*
> *Mais il me mandet* que en France m'en alge:
> *Il me sivrat* ad Ais, a mun estage,
> *Si recevrat la nostre lei plus salve.* . . .

These laisses provide examples of most of the ways in which formulas can be varied to serve different syntactic and assonantal needs. Some require no change whatsoever: *set cenz cameilz, d'or e d'argent, cinquante carre, en France ad Ais,* and *de sun aveir.* In several the change in point of view necessitated a change of person or number:

| | | |
|---|---|---|
| *ben en purrat* | to | *dunt bien purrez* |
| *vos le sivrez* | to | *que jel sivrai, la vos sivrat, il me sivrat* |
| *si recevrez* | to | *si recevrai, si recevrat* |
| *serez ses hom* | to | *serai ses hom* |
| *iço vos mandet* | to | *mais il me mandet* |
| *s'en deit ben repairer* | to | *devez bien repairer* |

Two changes are made which cannot be accounted for by syntactic factors, and which could therefore be stylistic: *en ceste tere* to *en cest pais,* and *s'en voelt ostages* to *s'il voelt ostages.* One formula moves from a second hemistich position to a first, *.IIII.C muls cargez* [*trussez* in laisse 9] becoming simply *quatre cenz muls,* and the first hemistich *cinquante carre* of laisses 3 and 9 is augmented to *plus de cinquante care,* an example of a change in meaning necessitated by metrical considerations alone. Among the second hemistich formulas, alterations of a different kind are effected because of assonantal requirements. Either the final word is changed, as

| | | |
|---|---|---|
| *mil hosturs muers* | becomes | *mil hosturs muables* |
| *par amur e par ben* | becomes | *par amur e par feid* |

or the word order is juggled, as

| | | |
|---|---|---|
| *qu'en ferat carier* | becomes | *que carier en ferez* |
| *luer ses soldeiers* | becomes | *voz soldeiers luer* |

or else both transformations are required:

| | | |
|---|---|---|
| *vos voelt asez duner* | becomes | *me voelt duner grant masse* |
| *la lei de crestiens* | becomes | *la crestiene lei, la nostre lei plus salve.* |

These variations, most evident in message motifs, are by no means restricted to them. The same transformations are carried out in hundreds of formulas throughout the *Chanson de Roland*. Indeed, the flexibility of formulas *in these particular metrical, syntactic, and semantic ways,* within certain easily definable limits, is just as much a character of the oral tradition as is the relative stability of the words themselves.[17] At the same time the substitutions of *muables* for *muez,* as an epithet of *hosturs,* of *veltres caeignables* for *veltres enchaignez,* of *plus de cinquante care* for *cinquante carre* and, later in the plot, of *.VII. C. cameilz, d'or e argent cargiez* (v. 645) for the entire treasure, clearly show that the oral tradition does not place an absolute value upon consistency. A *hostur mué* is one which has already gone through the molting process and is much more valuable as a hunting bird than a *hostur muable,* ready to molt but not yet molted; *veltres caeignables* may not differ at all from *veltres enchaignez,* but no

---

[17] C. W. Aspland views Old French formulas from a syntactic perspective in *A Syntactical Study of Epic Formulas and Formulaic Expressions Containing the -ant Forms in Twelfth Century French Verse* (St. Lucia: University of Queensland Press, 1970), and concludes that "ability to adapt common constructions into various syntactical patterns and not mere repetition of set expressions is the mark of the competent verse maker." (Pp. 34–35) For another treatment of formulaic flexibility in the epic see Renate Hitze, *Studien zu Sprache und Stil,* pp. 99–102, 111–114, 135–141.

exercise in casuistry is capable of transforming *cinquante carre* into *plus de cinquante care*. I do not mean to criticize the poets, for whom literal accuracy may have been a foreign concept. But it does follow from these examples that the scholar should be extremely cautious in placing literary value upon the nuances of discrete words in the *Chanson de Roland*. Exact shade of meaning is a concept indispensable to the intelligent reading of written poetry, but more often than not out of place in the explication of oral epic. To the *Roland* poets, *hostur mué* and *hostur muable* are two variations upon a basic formula for "goshawk," and the apparent nuance conveyed by the change of adjective is semantically nonfunctional.

The message conveyed by Ganelon as a reply from Charlemagne to Marsile is also repeated textually, although not under the same circumstances nor as often as Blancandrin's. Charlemagne is not shown pronouncing the terms of his reply, but when Ganelon attempts to deliver the message to Marsile, he is interrupted by the pagan king, who threatens him with his spear because of the insolence of Ganelon's phraseology. After Marsile's anger has abated, Ganelon insists on speaking the message again, as if he had not been able to finish the first time. His second delivery, more highly embellished than the first, adds only one element of substance, that Roland will share sovereignty over Spain with Marsile if the latter agrees to terms, a revision which is perhaps of Ganelon's own fabrication. Again I have italicized the formulas common to both laisses.

> 33: E dist al rei: "Salvez seiez de Deu,
> Li Glorius, qui devum aurer!
> *Iço vus mandet* Carlemagnes, li ber,
> *Que recevez seinte chrestientet;*
> *Demi Espaigne vos voelt en fiu doner.*
> *Se cest acorde ne vulez otrier,*
> *Pris e liez serez par poested;*

*Al siege ad Ais en serez amenet,*
*Par jugement* serez iloec finet;
La murrez vus a hunte e a viltet."

36:   Si li ad dit: "A tort vos curuciez,
      *Quar ço vos mandet* Carles, ki France tient,
      *Que recevez la lei de chrestiens;*
      *Demi Espaigne vus durat il en fiet.*
      L'altre meitet avrat Rollant, sis nies:
      Mulz orguillos parçuner i avrez!
      *Si ceste acorde ne volez otrier,*
      En Sarraguce vus vendrat aseger;
      *Par poestet serez pris e liez;*
      *Menet serez tut dreit ad Ais le siet:*
      Vus n'i avrez palefreid ne destrer,
      Ne mul ne mule que puissez chevalcher;
      Getet serez sur un malvais sumer.
      *Per jugement* iloec perdrez le chef.
      Nostre emperere vus enveiet cest bref."

*Iço vus mandet* and *que recevez* are the only phrases recurring
from Blancandrin's message sequence, so that, aside from the salu-
tation, one cannot really speak of a set configuration of formulas
employed in the message motif, but only of a pattern of repeating
the terms textually, with formulas which vary according to the
content of each message. The variations from one laisse to an-
other of Ganelon's two deliveries are not so extensive as those
seen in Blancandrin's embassy, owing to the fact that here the
same grammatical person is operative in both laisses. The only
alterations are those brought about by the change of assonance
from *e* (<*a*), *ie* to *ie*, *ien*.

I have insisted at length upon the abundance, in the *Chanson
de Roland*, of formulas which introduce and convey the content
of speech, in order to point out that, while the battle sequence
is the best defined motif in the poem, its formulas do not consti-
tute the most frequently employed category. The impression

might arise that only the battle scenes, regarded as most banal by modern readers, are formulaic. But this is false: the key psychological developments of the epic plot are also constructed formulaically. About two of every five verses in the *Roland* consist of direct discourse of one kind or another, mostly of the types discussed in the preceding pages, and not only are discourse motifs dominant in the poem, but the ambiance of battle, with the boasts which precede it, the cries of defiance and encouragement, the threats, the regrets over the bodies of fallen heroes, and even the message scenes, essential to plot development and conferring poetic meaning upon the battle of Roncevaux, would be impossible without these speech formulas.

The collective persona of the *Roland* singers, including, of course, the poet of the archetype of Oxford, projects itself into the narrative through phrases which constitute a special class of speech formulas. The most intrusive of these is *desor cumencet* (179, 3704, 3747, 3946), by which the beginning of an episode is announced to the audience. Appeals to authority, designed to increase the poets' credibility by making it appear that their source is a written document—always held in high esteem by an oral society moving toward literacy, which regards writing with semireligious awe—are themselves, ironically, formulaic: *il est escrit* (1443, 1684, 3742), *ço dit la geste* (1685, 2095). *Que fereient il el?* (1185, 2812 [*plus*], 2961 [*qu'en*]), *voeillet o nun* (1419, 1659 [*voelent*], 2043, 2168, 2220, 3170), and *de ço qui calt?* (1405, 1806, 1840, 1913, 2411, 3339 [*d'iço, seignurs, qui calt?*]) interject the narrator's commentary on the inevitability of events; *men escientre*, spoken by the poet in one of its occurrences (2073) —it is normally found in the speech of characters (as 524 [*escient*], 539, 552, 756, 768, 1116 [*sun*], 2286) as is the second hemistich variation *par le men escientre* (1791, 1936 [*escient*], 3591)—conveys a tone of uncertainty. The singers supplement their own presence by drawing the audience into symbolic participation through *la veisez* (349, 1655, 3388), *ki lui veist* (1341, 1970), and *ki puis veist* (1680, 3473). These occasional interventions, most of them common to other *chansons de geste*, break the poem's objective veneer. Their collective effort is to express the poets' attitudes toward their material: authoritative and at the same time fallible, but never detached from the events which are being recounted. Above all the narrator participates with his characters in the fatalistic stance essential to the heroic ideal.

Of the remaining types of predicate formulas, those found in battle motifs are the most abundant single group. They have also, however, received the most attention: Jean Rychner used expressions denoting the idea "to spur one's horse" for his analysis of the relationship between first and second hemistich formulas,[18] and Renate Hitze has consecrated a thoroughly researched book to the battle formulas of eight selected *chansons de geste*.[19] The battle laisse is probably the oldest motif in the *Roland* tradition, for it is the closest in subject matter to those *chants d'actualité* concerning historical battles which led to the development of a full-blown epic in tenth and eleventh-century France and probably formed the core of the earliest versions of *Roland*, whose historical antecedent is the ambush of Charlemagne's army on August 15, 778. Because of the extent of previous treatments, I shall not treat combat formulas in the same detail as those of speech, but no description of Roland's formulaic style would be complete without at least a brief account of the standard phrases employed to represent battle.

There are fixed phrases for references to battle, and for the realization that battle is approaching: *ceste bataille* (8 occurrences), *une bataille* (vv. 589, 813), *tantes batailles* (4 examples), *por granz batailles* (2243, 2889), *bataille avrez* (1044, 1130), *bataille avrum* (1460, 3304, 3321), *en tel bataille* (1361, 1887), *en la bataille* (1875, 3251). The disposition and size of armies, their appearance perceived as masses of armor and weapons seen from a distance, and the sound of the musical instruments of warfare

---

[18] *La Chanson de geste: essai sur l'art épique des jongleurs* (Geneva: Droz, 1955), pp. 141–146.
[19] *Studien zu Sprache und Stil.*

and of battlecries, are all communicated in formulas: *granz sunt les oz* (6 occurrences), *od sa grant ost, li ber* (2149, 2444), *justees sunt* (3347, 3384), *luisent cil elme* (1031, 1452, 3306), *helmes laciez* (712, 1042, 3079), *halbercs vestuz* (683, 711, 3088, 3858 [*vestent osbercs*]), *e cil escuz* (1032, 1453, 1810), *e cez escuz* (3307; also in general battle scenes: 2538, 3485), *escuz unt genz* (998, 1799, 3090), *e cil espiez* (1032, 1811, 3308 [*cez*]), *ceintes espees* (684, 3089), *sunent cil graisle* (1004 [*mil*], 1832, 3118, 3309), *funt mil grailles suner* (700, 2443 [*fait ses grailles suner*], 3301 [*i fait suner ses greisles*]), *sunez voz graisles* (2110, 3136), *fait suner ses taburs* (852, 3137 [*funt lur taburs suner*]) and *grant est la noise* (1005, 1455, 2151).

Before battle, the knights must arm, sometimes upon command (*adubez vos!* 1793, 3134), and this is represented either as a collective scene or as individuals dressing in defensive armor and taking up their weapons: *ad vestue sa brunie* (384 [*out*], 2988, 3079 [*e vestues lor bronies*]), *d'osbercs e de helmes* (1798, 1809 [*osbercs e helmes*]), *lacet sun helme* (996 [*lacent lor elmes*], 2500 [*laciét sun elme*] 2989, 3142), *ceignent espees* (997, 3866), *pent a son col* (2991, 3149), *tient sun espiét* (2992, 3152), *e gunfanuns blancs e blois e vermeilz* (999, 1800 [*e vermeilz e blois*]), *e le dragon* (3330, 3550). They mount their horses: *es destrers muntent* (1001, 1801), *puis sunt muntez* (8 occurrences, of which 4 are outside arming scenes), followed twice by *sur lur curanz destrer* (1142, 3869 [*en*]); kings are aided by subordinates: *l'estreu li tint* (4). When a single combat scene follows immediately, the horse is tested: *fait sun eslais* (2997, 3166).[20]

Battles in the *Chanson de Roland*, as in the *chanson de geste* in general, are depicted as a series of single combats, punctuated by cries of encouragement and defiance, with an occasional pause in the sequence of duels, during which the conflict is seen from a

---

[20] *Roland's* arming scenes are intelligently discussed by Michael Holland, "Rolandus Resurrectus," pp. 400–403, who finds that the order hauberk, helmet, sword, shield, lance, pennant, horse is only departed from when the troops are described as already armed.

more distant point of view in what may be called the "general
battle" motif. There are relatively few of these moments in
*Roland*, with the result that the formulas employed in them are
not particularly abundant: *Franc e paien* (1187, 1397, 3561),
*Franceis i fierent* (1438, 1654, 1662), *mult ben i fiert* (1413, 3481
[*fierent*], 3543), *e li Franceis* (followed by *i fierent e si caplent*,
1347, and *i fierent comunment*, 1416), *e cez escuz* (2538, 3307,
3485), *a colps pleners* (2463, 3401), *en la grant presse* (1967,
2057, 2070, 2090, 2129), *moerent paien* (1348, 1417), *paien sunt
morz* (1439, 3648), *l'un mort sur l'altre* (1971, 3372), and *les
enchalcerent Franc* (1660, 2460 [*ben les enchalcent Franc*]). Most
of these are collective expressions, as is to be expected. For gen-
eral qualification of the battle scene, the formula is *la bataille est*
followed by an adjectival phrase containing the word *merveillus*
in six cases (1320, 1412, 1653, 1661, 3381, 3420) and *dur* or
*aduree* in the other two (1396, 3393), the exact form of the second
hemistich varying according to assonance. Four out of eight times
*la bataille est* begins a laisse (laisses 104, 109, 110, and 125) and
once it ends one (laisse 245).

The configuration of the single combat motif, which occupies
36 separate laisses in the *Roland*, the overwhelming majority
recounting one combat between two knights, is particularly styl-
ized. In a typical combat, the hero who will win the battle is
generally mentioned in the first verse, spurs his horse—*bro-
che[n]t le[s] bien* (6 occurrences), *brochent ad ait* (vv. 1184,
1802, 3350, 3541), *brochent amdui a ait* (1381), *puis brochet le
cheval* (3341, 3430 [*ben*]), *sun* [or *le*] *cheval brochet* (14 occur-
rences)—strikes a blow with his lance—*vait le ferir* (7 occur-
rences), *si* [or *e* or *il* or *puis*] *vait* [or *vunt*] *ferir* (16 occurrences)—
breaks his opponent's shield—*l'escu li frein[s]t* (12 occurrences),
*tute li freint* (1263–3361)—and hauberk—*de sun osberc li rompit
la ventaille* (1293, 3449 [*li desrumpt*]), *e sun osberc rumput e des-
mailet* (2079, 2158), *e mis osbercs desmailet e rumput* (2051),
*e l'osberc li derumpt* (7 occurrences including various assonantal
variations), *de sun osberc li ad rumput les pans* (1300, 1601 [*li*

*ad les pans rumput*]), *de sun osberc les dous pans li desaffret* (3426), *de sun osberc li derumpit les dubles* (1284, 3466 [*les pans*])—kills him—*que mort l'abat* (14 occurrences), *si l'ad mort abatut* (1957, 3929), *l'abat mort des arçuns* (1229, 1577), *mort le tresturnet* (1357, 1385), *el camp mort le tresturnet* (1287, 1541) —, and finally insults the dead body or shouts encouragement to his companions.[21]

While these are the basic elements of *Roland's* single combat motifs, others vary or ornament the action. I shall treat them in order of their occurrence within the configuration of the single combat motif, but, when the occasion arises, instances where they occur outside the motif will be included.

In the second wave of battles at Roncevaux, every other laisse from 114 to 122 contains, as an embellishment of the single combat motif, between the naming of the knight and his spurring forward to begin striking, the formula *siet el cheval,* followed, on four occasions, by the horse's name in the second hemistich, and an additional verse commenting on the animal's fitness for battle:

> *Siet el cheval* qu'il cleimet Barbamusche,
> *Plus est isnels* que esprever ne arunde (vv. 1534–1535).
> *Siet el cheval* qu'il cleimet Gramimund,
> *Plus est isnels* que nen est uns falcuns (1571–1572).
> *Siet el cheval* qu'il cleimet Saltperdut,
> *Beste nen est* ki poisset curre a lui (1597–1598).
> *Siet el cheval* que il cleimet Mormorie,
> *Plus est isnels* que n'est oisel ki volet (1615–1616).

The first of this series of laisses is an expanded version, with Turpin's horse as its subject:

> Li arcevesque cumencet la bataille,
> *Siet el cheval* qu'il tolit a Grossaille;

Ço ert uns reis qu'il ocist en Denemarche.
Li destrers est e curanz e aates,
Piez a copiez e les gambes ad plates,
Curte la quisse e la crupe bien large,
Lungs les costez e l'eschine ad ben halte,
Blanche la cue e la crignete jalne,
Petites les oreilles, la teste tute falve;
*Beste nen est nule* ki encuntre lui alge.
Li arcevesque brochet par tant grant vasselage (1487–1497).

Between the naming of the horse Turpin is riding and the formula *beste nen est (nule)*, which is the form this particular ornamentation takes at its least elaborate, the tradition has developed a highly embellished account, the only ornamented description of a horse in the entire poem. The two essential formulas, *siet el cheval* and *beste nen est (nule)*, neatly frame the detailed description to form a graphic representation of how the technique of elaborative expansion sometimes operated in the *Roland* tradition. The additional verses are inserted between these two phrases: *siet el cheval* is a flexible opening formula, allowing for further embellishment without actually necessitating it; *beste nen est* is similarly a graceful conclusion, summing up the steed's worth in a comparison with other horses independently of the preceding verse. The pattern for elaboration upon a horse is thus latent in the tradition as a quality of the single combat motif. That the Oxford poet chose to activate it only once is a measure of his stylistic restraint.[22]

The technique of elaboration is not nearly as transparent in other cases. The four laisses in which descriptions of horses are restricted to only two verses also contain embellishments upon the knight himself, but without the telltale framing formulas. In-

---

[22] The formula *siet el cheval* also appears in two later combat motifs: *siet el cheval qu'il apelet Gaignun* (v. 1890) and *siet el cheval qu'om cleimet Veillantif* (v. 2127), but without any verses of further qualification.

stances of this submotif vary considerably in length, from one additional verse,

> Margariz est mult vaillant chevalers,
> E bels e forz e isnels e legers (vv. 1311–1312),

or

> Grandonie fut e prozdom e vaillant
> E vertuus e vassal cumbatant (1636–1637),

to eight verses, as in the cases of Valdabrun,

> Celoi levat le rei Marsiliun.
> Sire est par mer de .IIII. .C. drodmunz;
> N'i ad eschipre quis cleimt se par loi nun.
> Jerusalem prist ja par traïsun,
> Si violat le temple Salomon,
> Le patriarche ocist devant les funz.
> Cil ot fiance del cunte Guenelon:
> Il li dunat s'espee e mil manguns (1563–1570),

or of Baligant, whose description follows directly upon his arming in laisse 228. The other examples, in laisses 94, 95, 116, 120, 121 and 122, fall between these two limits.

A third type of expansion at the beginning of a single combat is the shout of defiance (*enquoi perdrat France dulce sun los*, 1194; *encoi perdrat France dulce s'onur*, 1223), which inspires the French knight to attack and kill the Saracen, Roland in one case echoing the shout in his answer (*oi n'en perdrat France dulce sun los*, 1210).

In the battle proper, *brocher* forms the base of most of the formulas of riding, but additional expressions are employed on occasion: *laschet la resne* (vv. 1381 [*laschent lor resnes*], 1617, 2996, 3349 [*laschent les resnes*]), *si li laschet la resne* (1290), *parmi le camp chevalchet* (1338, 3421), *l'ad enchalcet asez* (2785,

2796 [*asez l'ad enchalcet*]), *laiset curre a esforz* (1197, 3547 [*ad espleit*]), *laiset le cheval curre* (1281, 3541 [*lor cevals laissent curre*]).

When Oliver or Roland is in the scene, the name of the hero's sword is occasionally mentioned: *tient Durendal* (1339, 1583, 1870) and *tient Halteclere* (1550, 1953). Instead of breaking the enemy's shield, a knight may land his blow on the helmet; *sur l'elme a or agut* (1954, 1995 [*a or gemet*]), *sur l'elme d'acer brun* (3603, 3926). Details of the wounds or their effects may be specified: *trenchet la teste* (1586, 1956, 3617), *desur le frunt* (2248 [*desuz*], 3919), *entre les dous furceles* (1294, 2249), *entresque a la charn* (1265, 3436), *parmi le cors* (2052, 2080), *de sun cervel le temple en est rumpant* (1764, 1786 [*rumput en est li temples*]), *li sancs tuz clers* (1342, 1980, 3925). An especially strong blow, the "*coup épique*," splits the head and body of the opponent, his saddle, and, in three cases out of four in *Roland*, the horse's backbone. The formulas shared by the single combat motifs which represent this mighty and fabulous blow (laisses 104, 107, 119, and 124) are: *la bone sele* (1373, 1587), *e al cheval* (1374, 1588, 1649), *parfundement le dos* (1588, 1649 [*le dos parfundement*]) and *ambure ocit* (1588, 1650). A syntactic system—*trenchet* plus a part of the anatomy—is also operative here: *trenchet le chef* (1327), *trenchet l'eschine* (1333), *trenchet le cors* (1372), *trenchet la teste* (1586, also found in 1956, 3617, outside this motif), *trenchet le nes* (1646).

On two occasions a blow literally knocks the eyes out of the stricken person's head: *fors de la teste li met les oilz ansdous* (1355); *amsdous les oilz del chef li ad mis fors* (2290). Once Oliver's eyes are turned from a blow he has received, in a formula related to the preceding: *ansdous les oilz en la teste li turnent* (2011).

The technique of striking is embodied in numerous formulaic variations. For a sword, *brandist sun colp* (1552, 1957, 3929) indicates the technical point of shaking the weapon after it has penetrated the enemy's body to ensure that the wound is mortal.

*Pleine sa hanste* (7 occurrences) denotes the practice, still new at the time of the Norman conquest of England, of striking with the lance held straight forward, with the purpose of forcing the opponent from his horse, rather than employing the lance as a throwing weapon.[23] *Empeint le ben* (6 occurrences) shows the knight leaning on his lance after contact has been made. There are two formulas for lances shattering from the shock of encounter: *sa hanste est fraite* (1352, 2050 [*ma*]) and *fruisent cez hanstes* (2539, 3482). Other formulas having to do with striking are: *cascun le fiert* (1824, 3631 [*i fiert*]), *cil i ferrunt* (3051 [*ferrat*], 3199, 3320), *mult ben i fiert* (1413, 3481 [*fierent*], 3543), *a colps pleners* (2463, 3401), *a icest colp* (3365, 3530, 3930), *por itels colps* (1377, 1560), *tanz cols ad pris* (526, 541, 554), *el cors li met* (7 occurrences), *el cors li met la mure* (1285, 1539), *parmi le cors li mist* (1248, 1306), *li ad enz el cors mis* (3356, 3363 [*mise*]), *trestut le cors* (1647, 2020), *tut le fer li mist ultre* (1286, 1540), *si li trenchat* (1328, 1600 [*tut li*], 2720), *cruist li acers* (2302, 2313), and, for a blow which misses its mark, *ne l'ad mie adeset* (1997, 2159 [*unt*]).

When more than one adversary is defeated in a single laisse, the series of battle actions need not be repeated a second time if the formula *pois ad ocis* (4 occurrences) is employed. With the name of the second victim following it in the second hemistich, it constitutes an entire combat in one line.

Although *abatre mort* and *tresturner mort* are the basis of most formulas denoting death on the battlefield, the following expressions also fill that purpose, occasionally being used to describe the few deaths which occur apart from actual combat, such as those of Roland, Marsile, and Alde, or to refer to death in the

---

[23] See D.J.A. Ross, *"Pleine sa hanste," Medium Aevum*, XX (1951), 1–10, and "L'originalité de Turold: le maniement de la lance," *Cahiers de Civilisation Médiévale*, VI (1963), 127–138; also Julian Harris, *"Pleine sa hanste* in the *Chanson de Roland,"* in Kenneth R. Scholberg and Urban T. Holmes, ed., *French and Provençal Lexicography: Studies Presented to Honor Alexander Herman Schutz* (Columbus: Ohio State University Press, 1964), pp. 100–117.

abstract: *ne seit ocis* (vv. 102, 2798), *morz est li quens* (1603, 2021), *morz est Rollant* (2397, 2792, 3802), *il est a mort naffret* (1965 [*qu'il*], 1990 [*ki*], 2771), *que la mort li est pres* (2259, 2270 [*kar*]), *de sun tens n'i ad plus* (1603, 2366, 3840 [*n'i ad mais*]), *est alet a sa fin* (2392, 3723 [*est a sa fin alee*]), *l'anme de lui* (followed by *en portet Sathanas*, 1268; *en portent aversers*, 1533; *as vifs diables dunet*, 3647), *par nun d'ocire* (43, 149), *qu'il i perdent les chefs* (44, 58 [*testes*]). *Deus le guarit* (1316, 3923) indicates that a knight has escaped the immediate attack unwounded. The whole-verse formula *seinz hume mort ne poet estre achevee* (3578, 3914 [*afinet*]) designates the Charles-Baligant and Thierry-Pinabel battles as mortal combats (and perhaps even as judgments of God).

This survey of the means of expression in *Roland's* single combat laisses shows that formulaic style and variety of statement are not incompatible.

Many laisses in *Roland* consist of only single combat motifs, sometimes grouped in series of two or three successive laisses employing the same formulas. There are many examples of this phenomenon,[24] but it is especially evident in the first wave of battles in the Roncevaux episode, which I shall analyse as an example. The first three of these combat laisses, 93–95, have a unity in relation to the rest of the single combat motifs in the poem: all three begin with a Saracen prince, characterized rather than simply named, shouting a defiant challenge to the Franks, and they all end with a shout of encouragement from the victorious knight, exulting over the Saracen's corpse. In their respective laisses Roland, Oliver and Turpin hear the challenge and attack. The characteristic hemistichs or lines of the three laisses follow:

[24] Renate Hitze, *Studien zu Sprache und Stil*, pp. 74–75, gives examples of the sequence of elements in seven *chansons de geste*, showing that groups of successive laisses with similar formulas are not confined to the *Roland*. The phenomenon deserves further study.

| 93 | 94 | 95 |
|---|---|---|
| sun cheval brochet | le cheval brochet | sun cheval brochet |
| vait le ferir | vait le ferir | si l'est alet ferir |
| l'escut li freint | l'escut li freint | l'escut li freinst |
| e l'osberc li desclot | e l'osberc li derumpt | l'osberc li descumfist |
| trenchet le piz | el cors li met | parmi le cors li mist |
| empeint le ben |  | empeint le ben |
| pleine sa hanste | pleine sa hanste | pleine sa hanste |
| del cheval l'abat mort | l'abat mort des arçuns | l'abat mort el chemin |
| ne leserat, ço dit, que n'i parolt | guardet a tere, veit gesir le glutun | guardet a tere, veit le glutun gesir, ne laisserat que n'i parolt, ço dit |
| ultreculvert | de voz menaces, culvert, jo n'ai essoign | culvert paien |
| ferez i, Francs | ferez i, Francs | ferez, Franceis |
|  | "Munjoie!" escriet | "Munjoie!" escriet |

Formal similarities are reinforced by thematic unity. The three laisses represent the three great heroes of the Frankish side, Roland, Oliver, and Turpin, dispatching the first three of the Saracen peers, Aëlroth, Falsaron, and Corsablix, and both knights of a pair have the same function in the two hierarchies. Roland and Aëlroth are both nephews of their respective kings; Turpin and Corsablix—the latter characterized in verse 886 as *mult de males arz*, rendered by Bédier as "[qui] sait les arts maléfiques"[25] —each represent the ecclesiastical function; and Falsaron and Oliver may be regarded as two avuncular figures, Falsaron being the brother of Marsile and therefore Aëlroth's uncle, and Oliver a sage counterpart of Charlemagne.

The next two laisses, 96 and 97, are much briefer and differ from the previous three in that they lack introductory verses embroidering upon the Saracens' identity. In addition, no words are

[25] Turpin later defeats Singlorel, *"l'encanteür ki ja fut en enfer:/Par artimal li cundoist Jupiter"* (vv. 1391–1392). Evidently the archbishop specialized in annihilating practitioners of the black arts.

spoken by the combatants, and the formulas *le cheval brochet*, *pleine sa hanste* and *vait le ferir* are not employed, although a new formula, *sun bon espiét*, is. Again the thematic content corresponds to formal similarities (much less striking than in the previous case, however) in that the victors are Gerin and Gerer, companion knights with alliterating names.

Laisses 98 (Sansun kills the *almaçur*) and 99 (Anseïs overcomes Turgis de Turteluse) both end with a commendation from a third party:

> 98: Dist l'arcevesque: "Cist colp est de baron."
> 99: Ço dist Rollant: "Cist colp est de produme."

Likewise 100 and 101 are marked by a defiant shout over the fallen enemy:

> 100: Aprés li dist: "Turnet estes a perdre."
> 101: Aprés li dist: "Ja n'i avrez guarant."

To end this series of laisses in which ten of the French knights are victorious over an equal number of the pagan peers, laisse 102 stands by itself formally, beginning with Berenger's win over Astramariz, but concluding with three of the seven verses given over to a tally of the enemy dead:

> Des doze pers li dis en sunt ocis,
> Ne mes que dous n'en i ad remes vifs:
> Ço est Chernubles e li quens Margariz (vv. 1308–1310)

These two pagans subsequently suffer opposite fates, Margariz surviving an indecisive attack against Oliver, while Chernuble falls under a tremendous "epic blow" from Roland.

On the basis of the recurrence of first hemistich formulas, the ten laisses are grouped:

93–94–95
96–97
98–99
100–101
102

Recalling that each laisse must have a different assonance from those surrounding it, we see a double pattern at work. In each group the second hemistich formulas *must* change, for assonantal reasons, whence the variations *cist colp est de baron* and *cist colp est de produme* in laisses 98–99, and other similar pairs. But the first hemistich formulas may be identical and serve to unite each group, or, from the composing jongleur's point of view, to facilitate presentation of the series. Just as the use of formulas, less demanding upon the jongleur's creativity than the fashioning of new phrases would be, renders possible rapid improvisation before a critical audience, so employment of similar patterns from laisse to laisse within groups of two or three relieves pressure on the level of successive events.

In addition the singer may well have been satisfying the audience's taste for the fine points of feudal warfare. In the appreciation of other traditional arts, such as the bullfight or the flamenco dance, a neophyte viewer cannot distinguish one type of action from another, but an *aficionado* perceives the nuances of foot emplacement, slight movements of the body, and differences in position which may amount to no more than an inch or two. Likewise the medieval listener, often familiar with the ritual of combat from personal experience, was no doubt attentive to the slight variations in battle technique perceivable in consecutive laisses. If this were not so, the Oxford *Roland* would not contain so many successive single combats. An art which depends totally on public acceptance cannot survive if it is judged boring by contemporary standards. The long sequences of battle motifs, appearing similar to the point of excess to the modern reader, must have been appreciated by the audience of twelfth-century fighting men, and the differences expressed in substitute formulas, or the inclusion and exclusion of typical movements, are no less real for being difficult for us to appreciate. The two or three laisses in each group, joined by a similarity of first hemistich formulas, constitute theme and variation patterns carefully arranged in a tension between nuance and satiation: a theme with two variations for the three great heroes, only one variation in the case of lesser warriors.

Although the formulas employed for the communication of direct speech and those which serve to construct battle scenes provide the two predominant constituents of epic plot, its dramatic personal conflicts and its martial subject, they by no means include even a majority of the hemistichs repeated within the *Chanson de Roland*, for the other formulas of various kinds, taken together, are more numerous than combat and speech formulas combined. Traditional phrases are not confined to a few types of standard action, leaving to the jongleur the "freedom" to fill in the intervening areas of his narrative with original phraseology. On the contrary, formulas are present in nearly every context, and the most banal and seemingly unnecessary gestures, as well as the images and central thematic statements, are at times expressed in hemistichs which recur within *Roland*.

This myriad of "miscellaneous" formulas is difficult to classify adequately into meaningful groups, and the reader will understand that the semantic fields into which they can be divided are not as clearly delimited as those of speech and battle.

The largest single category of action formulas after those already treated is that which designates movement from one place to another, such as riding: *icil chevalchent* (vv. 1920, 3054), *puis si chevalchent* (5 occurrences), *tant chevalchat* (2818, 2842, 3697), *tant chevalcherent* (402, 405, 2689), *chevalchet l'emperere* (706, 3316), *paien chevalchent* (710, 3265); flight: *paien s'en fuient* (5 occurrences); pursuit: *apres le vait sivant* (1160, 2649), *la vos siurat, ço dit* (136, 153); return: *ja returnerunt Franc* (1072, 1704), *s'en deit ben repairer* (36, 135 [*devez ben*]), *Carles repairet* (2133, 2145, 2149); coming and going: *atant i vint* (617, 634), *venuz i est* (798, 3935), *Guenes i vint* (178, 674), *i est Neimes venud* (230, 774), *en France irai* (2681, 2732, [*irat*]), *aler i volt* (2226, 2548), *seignurs, vos en irez* (79, 360), *ki est as porz passant* (1071, 1703, 1766); and turning back: *Rollant s'en turnet* (2184, 2200). Related are those showing a change of position or other movement not requiring displacement, such as standing up: *en piez se drecet* (195, 218, 2234 [*sur piez*]), *se drecent sur lur piez* (3884), *met sei en piez* (2277, 2298 [*sor piez*]); sitting down: *alez sedeir* (251, 272); lying down: *si est culchet adenz* (2358, 3097 [*si se est*]), *culchet sei a tere* (2449, 2480); or mounting and dismounting: *muntet li reis* (3112, 3679), *descent a piet* (2013, 2878), *descendirent a pied* (120, 1746 [*i descendrunt*]), and *Franceis descendent* (4 occurrences).

Among actions of a religious nature is the appeal for, or the promise of, conversion, a paramount ideological concern in the *Roland*, generally couched in the idiom *receivre la lei* whose verb occupies the first hemistich:

| | |
|---|---|
| si recevrez | la lei de crestiens (v. 38) |
| si recevrai | la crestiene lei (85) |
| si recevrat | la nostre lei plus salve (189) |
| puis recevrat | la lei que nus tenum (225) |
| que recevez | seinte crestientet (431) |
| que recevez | la lei de crestiens (471) |
| si recevrat | la lei que vos tenez (695) |
| si recevrat | seinte crestientet (2620) |
| e ne guerpisset | la lei de crestiens (2683) |

*Si recevez* is found only once outside this combination, during Ganelon's message scene when Charles calls him forward:

Ço dist li reis: "Guenes, venez avant,
Si recevez le bastun e lu guant!" (319–320).

In addition to those hemistichs introducing prayers,[26] other liturgical actions represented in formulas include penitence: *cleimet sa culpe* (2239, 2364, 2383); the blessing of absolution: *l'ad asols e seignet* (340, 2205, 3859 [*e asols e seignez*]); simple benediction: *lievet sa main* (2194, 2848); and assistance at mass: *messe e matines ad li reis escultet* (164, 670).

Governmental, diplomatic and tactical matters are represented sporadically: *ses barons mandet pur sun counseill fenir* (166, 169), *out sun cunseil finet* (62), *puis se baiserent es vis e es mentuns* (as a sign of alliance: 626, 633 [*es buches e es vis*]), *funt les enguardes* (548, 561), *n'avrez mais guere* (595, 872), *mais n'i avrai guarant* (329, 1303 [*ja n'i avrez*]), *i ad fait aprester* (for preparation of ships: 2624, 2627), *cil tient la tere* (956, 1215, 3313), *que Carles tient* (2308, 2334, 2353), *branches d'olives en voz mains porterez* (72, 80), *dunez mei l'arc* (767, 780 [*dunez li*]), *jo vos cumant* (2673, 2815 [*jo te*]), *se jo nel vos cumant* (273, 2659 [*ne li*]), *par vostre dun* (224, 246, a rare four-syllable second hemistich), *qu'il ait mercit de mei* (82, 239 [*qu'aiez mercit de lui*]).

Some verbal formulas of a general nature do not fit into any of these categories: *Rollant reguardet* (1851, 1978, 1998 [*l'ad Rollant reguardet*], 2086), *fierement le reguardet* (745, 3423), *ja savez vos* (3413, 3825), *ço set hom ben* (287, 293), *pur Deu vos pri* (1177, 1516, 1741), *jo vos durrai* (75, 3207), *soürs est Carles* (549, 562), *se li reis voelt* (258, 295), *que nos aidez* (623, 630 [*si nos*]), *si la tramist* (967, 1503 [*li*]), *ne lesserat* (859, 1206, 1931), *est remes en estant* (2459, 2655 [*sunt*]), *puis sil laissums ester* (2154, 2162 [*laisent*]), *Franceis se taisent* (217, 263), *s'en cuntienent plus queit* (3555, 3797 [*se cuntienent*]), *Carles se dort* (718, 724, 736, 2525, 2569), *est par matin levet* (163, 669), *nes poet guarder* (9, 95), *puis que il sunt* (896 [*il est*], 1095, 3858), *cum jo serai* (2910, 2917), *qu'il ert en France* (726, 2556), *quant ert il mais* (528, 543, 556), *n'i ad celoi* (6 occurrences), *n'i ad icel* (1845, 3540), *n'i ad paien* (22, 854), *n'i ad Franceis* (571, 3789), *s'il troevent ou* (3004, 3025), *asez est mielz* (44, 58, 1518, 1743

26 See above, pp. 128–129.

[*si est il asez melz*]), *un dener ne li valt* (1262, 3338 [*lur*], 3435), *icil ert frere* (880, 1214), *iert i sis niés* (575, 585), *asez i ad* (2427 [*qu'asez*], 2633, 2643, 2694, 2955, 3795), *l'unt Francs recumencet* (1677, 1884), *passet li jurz* (3560, 3658, 3991), *la noit est aserie* (717, 3658, 3991), *e apert la clere albe* (737, 3675 [*si apert le cler jor*]). This concludes the inventory of verbal formulas in the *Chanson de Roland*, by far the largest category of repeated hemistichs.

Formulas containing substantival subjects and objects transcend the boundaries of particular motifs, since the persons, places, and objects which they designate are not generally confined to particular types of actions.

The most utilitarian type of substantival formula is the proper name, which at first view may not appear to be a formula at all, but which is commonly arranged in combination with other words so as to constitute a four or six syllable combination.[27] By this means the jongleur retains the option of using the proper name or leaving it understood, a choice he would not have if proper names were integrated into first or second hemistich formulas denoting specific actions. There are such formulas, but all but a few of them involve verbs of speaking, as *respunt dux Neimes* or *dist Oliver*, and their number is limited in comparison with the quantity of autonomous name-hemistichs. Since proper name formulas are of little intrinsic interest, I will omit the citation of line numbers for them (except in the case of epithets) and indicate only the number of occurrences.

Some personal names need only the addition of a toponym of origin to be metrically sufficient: *Gefreid d'Anjou* (7), *Malprimis de Brigant* (2), *Oger de Denemarche* (3), *Tedbald de Reins* (3), *Turpin de Reins* (2), *Turgis de Turteluse* (2), *Karles de France* (2). Two and three syllable personal and proper names must be combined with particles: *e! Durendal* (3), *e Berenger* (2), *e Blan-*

---

[27] Only the exotic Estramarin (vv. 64, 941) and the toponym Tere Maior (vv. 600, 952, 1532, 1667, 1784) fit into the hemistich without augmentation of any kind.

*candrins* (2), *e Bramimunde* (4), *e Oliver* (14), *ne Oliver* (3), *de Carlemagne* (4), *de Durendal* (3), *de Guenelun* (4) *de Mahumet* (2), *de Sarraguce* (6), *en Sarraguce* (7), *qu'en Sarraguce* (2), *a Charlemagne* (3), *que Guenelun* (2), *pur Pinabel* (2), *devers Ardenne* (2). Occasionally, in a second hemistich, proper names are combined into pairs: *Oliver e Rollant* (4), *Rollant e Oliver* (2), *Gibuins e Loranz* (2), *Carlun e France dulce* (2), *Tervagan e Mahum* (2). All of these pairs are persons or entities which belong together in a natural relationship, either as companions, as gods of the same religion, or as ruler and land. The inclusion, then, of the names *Guenes e Blancandrins* (402, 413) in one hemistich, from the moment they pledge their mutual aid, may be regarded as symbolic of a new and nefarious *compagnonnage*.

Most often, the word which fills in the remaining syllables to constitute, with the proper name, a complete hemistich, is a noun of title, blood relationship, or friendship, placed in apposition with the name: *bel sire Guenes* (3), *cumpainz Rollant* (2), *ami Rollant* (5), *Oliver frere* (3), *l'arcevesque Turpin* (5), *seint Gabriel* (5), *sun cumpaignun Gerer* (2), *le cunte Guenelun* (3), *Tierris, li dux d'Argone* (2), *li emperere Carles* (3), *li paien Baligant* (2), *uns paiens Estorgans* (2), *un paien Valdabrun* (2), *mais li quens Guenes* (2), *e li quens Jozerans* (2), *li quens Oger* (2), *e li quens Oliver* (2), *li quens Rabels* (2), *li quens Rollant* (34), *li quens Rollant, li riches* (2), *le rei Marsiliun* (3), *al rei Marsiliun* (4), *li reis Marsilie* (20), *Carlemagne li reis* (2), *Carles li reis* (4), *Guenes li quens* (5), *e Jozeran le cunte* (2), *Neimes li dux* (11), *Sansun li dux* (3). Epithets may also serve this purpose, both for toponyms and for personal names, although for the latter there are rather less than one might expect for an epic: *e Anseïs li fiers* (105, 796, 2408), *Carles li magnes* (703, 841, 905, 1195, 1404, 1732, 1949, 3329), *Carles li velz* (929, 970), *Guenes li fels* (844, 1457, 3735), *de Jurfaleu le blund* (1904, 2702), *reis Marsilies li bers* (125, 680), *Richard li velz* (171, 3050, 3470), *al bon vassal Rollant* (1777, 3185); *e! France dulce* (1985, 2928), *vers dulce France* (702, 706), *en dulce France* (360, 573, 1054), *en France dulce* (1064 [*ne*],

2661, 3673), *de dulce France* (109, 2379, 2431 [*France dulce*]), *trestute Espaigne* (2703, 2721), *demie Espaigne* (432, 472), *Espaigne le regnet* (697, 1029, 2787), *en France la lur tere* (50, 804 [*de France, nostre tere*], 808 [*de France*]). To designate the emperor's court, two nouns are needed: *en France ad Ais* (36, 135), *ad Ais a sa capele* (52, 726 [*a sa capele ad Ais*], 2917 [*em ma capele*], 3744 [*a la capele*]).

Common nouns, designating persons, animals, objects, or abstractions, are subject generally to the same adaptations as personal names, with the addition of numerical elements joined to some: *li dui message* (2704, 2765), *quatre perruns* (2268, 2272), *en dis escheles* (3192, 3237 [*e dis*], 3314 [*les dis*]), *li doze per* (15 occurrences), *des doze cumpaignuns* (858, 878 [*as doze*]), *e tuz les doze pers* (903, 2776), *des doze pers* (1308, 2515), *e vint hostages* (646, 679), *ensembl'od lui tels trente* (1410, 3781 [*out trente*], 3766 [*trente ki od lui sunt*]), *tels quatre cenz* (2092, 2120), *mil chevaler* (2442, 3677), *od mil Franceis* (808, 3661 [*a mil*]), *quinze milie de Francs* (3019, 3196), *vint milie Francs* (587, 789, 827, 3461 [*tels vint milie Franceis*]), *plus de vint milie humes* (13, 2578 [*ad plus de vint mil humes*]), *vint milie sunt* (3039, 3046), *cent milie Francs* (842, 2907, 2932, 3124), *plus de cent milie* (3000, 3402), *quatre cent milie* (715, 851). For the sake of convenience I have deferred until now the mention of certain verbal formulas which also contain numerical elements. A series of ordinal formulas marks the formation of the thirty Saracen divisions before the final battle between the Franks and the pagans under Baligant's command: *la premere est* (3220, 3238, 3253), *e la terce est* (3224, 3285), *e la quarte est* (3225, 3241, 3255), *e la quinte est* (3226, 3242, 3256), *e la siste est* (3227, 3243, 3257), *e la sedme est* (3228, 3244, 3258), *e la disme est* (3230, 3246, 3260). The ordinal *tut premerein* (879, 1189, 2424, 3373) denotes the lead action of a series. Cardinal numbers are represented in Marsile's amazed contemplation of Charlemagne's legendary longevity, *dous cenz anz ad passet* (524, 539 [*dous cenz anz ad e mielz*]), and in the sonorous line which sets forth the temporal background of Charlemagne's campaign in Spain, *set anz tuz pleins* (2, 197 [*ad pleins*], 2610).

Common nouns, especially titles, often stand by themselves, with only the addition of an article, conjunction, preposition, or possessive adjective to support them: *branches d'olives* (72, 80), *e l'estandart* (3267, 3552), *li amiralz* (22 occurrences), *li algalifes* (505 [*e l'algalifes*], 1943), *li arcevesque* (10 occurrences), *e l'arcevesque* (6 occurrences), *l'une meitiet* (1264, 3433), *la rereguarde* (6 occurrences), *e Peitevin* (3702, 3794, 3961), *e Sarrazins* (1030, 1186), *li empereres* (55 occurrences), *quant l'empereres* (2870, 3975), *si Arrabiz* (3011, 3081), *de bachelers* (3020, 3197)), *de Sarrazins* (1007, 1929), *sur tuz les altres* (823, 3119), *sun cumpaignun* (1160, 1994), *de ma maisnee* (1820, 2937), *de ses parenz* (1410, 3766, 3781).

Like proper names, common nouns are accompanied by toponyms, appositional designations of religion, nationality, or blood relationship, and titles of address, or are joined in pairs by coordinating conjunctions: *ja cil d'Espaigne* (1081, 1745), *des jaianz de Malprose* (3253, 3285 [*Malpreis*]), *paien d'Arabe* (2810, 3555), *li reis de France* (1168 [*nuls reis*], 3334), *de cels de France* (9 occurrences), *des plus feluns* (69, 3248 [*de plus*]), *les Sarrazins d'Espaigne* (1083, 1847), *li Sarrazins espans* (612, 2828 [*dui*]), *barons Franceis* (4 occurrences), *cist Franceis chevalers* (1688, 3890 [*cil*]), *bel sire niés* (784, 881), *bel sire reis* (863, 876, 3824), *le filz seinte Marie* (1473, 2938), *e! gentilz hom* (2177, 2252), *sire cumpainz* (1113, 1146, 1546, 1672, 1693, 1868, 1976, 2000, 2027), *seignors barons* (13 occurrences), *Franc e paien* (1397, 3561), *Baivers e Saisnes* (3700, 3793), *alques de legerie* (206, 513), *ne mul ne mule* (480, 757), *palefreid ne destrer* (479, 757), *mun ami e mun per* (362, 1975 [*sun . . . sun*]), *ne ses sainz ne ses angles* (1089, 3718), *e les vals e les munz* (856, 2434, 3695), *les destreiz e les tertres* (805, 809), *carbuncles e lanternes* (2633, 2643 (*lanternes e carbuncles*]), *le bastun e le guant* (268, 320, 2727 [*sun . . . sun*]), *as chevals e as armes* (1095, 2986, 3040 [*e de chevals e d'armes*], 3857 [*lur chevals e lur armes*]).

Finally, adjectives are found in combination with nouns: *d'un palie alexandrin* (408, 463), *de cele gent averse* (2630, 2922 [*e tante*], 3295 [*la meie*]), *de bons vassals* (939, 1986), *sun bon cheval* (1344, 1610), *sun bon cheval curant* (1153, 3047 [*e bons cevals curanz*]), *de sun cheval curant* (1302, 3112 [*en sun*], 3468), *de sa main destre* (340, 770), *le destre braz del cors* (597, 1195), *sun destre guant* (2373, 2389, 3851), *el destre poign* (484, 2678, 2719 [*le*], 2781 [*le*]), *dreiz emperere* (308, 766, 2441), *par la franceise gent* (396, 2515 [*de*]), *li gentilz reis* (2479, 3642 [*e!*]), *ses grandes pels de martre* (281, 3940 [*od ses granz*]), *mult grant damage* (1885, 2037), *mult grant eschec* (99, 2478), *meillor vassal* (5 occurrences), *mult merveillus turment* (1423, 3104 [*de merveillus*]), *li nostre deu* (1907, 2600, 3277), *nostre Franceis* (1255, 1746), *felun paien* (1057, 1068, 1098), *del rei paien* (692, 845), *vers la paiene gent* (2360, 3367 [*vers la gent paienie*]), *gent paienor* (1019 [*cele gent paienur*], 2639), *de la gent paienur* (2427, 2694), *le rei persis* (3204, 3354), *li reis poësteïfs* (460, 2133), *tanz riches reis* (527, 542, 555), *a trestute sa gent* (614, 2362 [*e trestute*]), *vaillant chevaler* in various combinations (1311, 1547, 2657, 2861), *veire paterne* (2384, 3100), and *vostre olifan* (1101, 1171). What is most unexpected in this group is the relatively limited number of noun-epithet combinations.[28]

Purely descriptive phrases are rare in the *Chanson de Roland*, for the poem is, as is well known, spare in its descriptions. Few characters are singled out for detailed descriptions, and even for them only the most general characteristics are provided: *gent ad le cors* (118, 3115)) is said of Charlemagne, *corps ad mult gent* (895, 1159) of the *amurafle* of Balaguez and Roland, *cors ad gaillard* (2895, 3763) of Roland and Ganelon, and *granz est e forz* of Malpramis and Pinabel. The head is the only feature focussed upon in formulas: *mult par out fier lu vis* (142, 283 [*e mult fier lu visage*]), is said of both Charlemagne and Ganelon,

---

[28] The addition of epithets composed of entire hemistichs (see below, p. 156 and of epithets qualifying proper names (above, pp. 152–153) does not alter this judgment.

while whiteness of beard, not confined to Charlemagne alone but ascribed also to the other great emperor, Baligant, seems to signify a figure of authority, worthy of respect: *blanche ad la barbe* (3173, 3503), *ki la barbe ad canue* (2308, 2353 [*flurie*]), *ki ad la barbe blanche* (2334), *tresqu'en la barbe blanche* (3618), *a la barbe flurie* (970, 2605 [*od la*], 3654 [*canue*]), *ki est canuz e vielz* (538, 551 [*e blancs*]). These same imperial beards call forth several of the rare images in the *Roland*, also formulaic: Charlemagne's is white *cume flur en avrill* (3503), while both Baligant's beard, white *ensement cume flur* (3173) and *cume flur en espine* (3521) and his hair, white *cume flur en estet* (3162) are graced with comparisons. Thus even the similes, among the few stylistic features of the poem which resemble classical figures of rhetoric and might thus be ascribed, although inaccurately so, to an ancient source, are formulaic. No one descriptive characteristic is confined to one character alone. Only Oliver has a double formulaic epithet: *e Oliver, li proz e li curteis* (176 [*e li gentilz*], 576, 3186 [*e li vaillanz*], 3755). Horses *e curanz e aates* (1490, 3876 [*sunt curanz*]), swords *enheldees d'or mier* (966 [*ki d'or est enheldie*], 3866, 3887), battle flags *blancs e blois e vermeilz* (999, 1800 [*e vermeilz e blois*]), a saddle *ki a or est gemmee* (1373, 1587), [*est gemmee ad or*]), a shield *ki est a flurs e ad or* (1276, 1354 [*ad or e a flur*]), and helmets *as perres d'or gemmees* (1452, 3306), *ki ad or sunt gemmez* (1031, 3911 [*ki sunt a or*]), *ki gemmet fut ad or* (1585, 2288), *ki est a or gemmet* (2500, 3142 [*ad or est*]) complete the list of entities endowed with formulaic epithets making up an entire hemistich. *Clers fut li jurz* (1002, 2646 [*est*], 3345), *e li soleilz luisant* (2646, 3345) and *halt sunt li pui* (814, 1755, 1830, 2271), the latter a powerful evocation of the rearguard's isolation among the Pyrenean passes, are the only formulaic descriptions of landscape.

Adverbial formulas, designating time, place, accompaniment, and manner, are far less dependent on the thematic content of the episode in which they appear than are other types of formulas.

The poet presents the emperor dismounting from his horse *sur l'erbe verte* (v. 2448) to pray that the sun stop in the sky so as to facilitate his pursuit of the fleeing pagan army, the blood of a combatant dripping *sur l'erbe verte* (1665, 3453, 3972), Roland lying *sur l'erbe verte* awaiting death (2358), a silken cloth being spread *sur l'erbe verte* for Baligant's council scene (2652), or a prefiguration of the duel between Thierry and Pinabel *sur l'erbe verte* (2565). Even the most common battle and speech formulas, such as *dient Franceis, si vait ferir, ço dit li reis, sun cheval brochet, que mort l'abat, e dist al rei,* and *Guenes respont,* each occurring 14 times or more and all specifically attached to particular motifs or characters, have none of this flexibility. Indeed they are useful *because* they denote a specific action of frequent occurrence, unlike *Roland*'s adverbial formulas whose utility derives from the fact that they fit widely varying contexts. *Roland*'s adverbial formulas are:

Time:

icele noit (2495, 2498)

d'ures en altres (2843, 3371)

apres iço (230, 774)

a trestut mun vivant (323, 2662)

a tute vostre vie (212, 595 [en])

Place:

sur l'erbe verte (671, 1612 [desure l'herbe verte], 1665, 2175, 2236, 2269, 2273, 2358, 2448, 2565, 2573, [sur la verte herbe], 2652, 2876, 3097, 3453, 3972)

cuntre le ciel (1156, 1596, 2015, 2240, 3912)

en cest païs (17, 134, 266, 2800)

desuz un pin (114, 165, 2357, 2375)

en ceste tere (35, 1908, 2736, 2797)

devers Espaigne (1021, 2266, 2367, 3128)

encuntre tere (1981, 2416, 2422)

par tut le camp (2947, 2999, 3525)

de tutes parz (1378, 1511, 2065)

desur sa bronie (1843, 3122)

ki est enmi un camp (2651, 3968)

en la citet (101, 3736)

ultre ses campaignuns (2236, 2565)

dedevant sei (2964, 3266)

dedevant lui (2300, 2576)

e derere e devant (1832, 3118)

enz el verger (501, 510)

ja mais en tere (930, 2023)

as porz d'Espaigne (824, 1152)

en sa cambre voltice (2593, 2709
   [la], 3992)
d'ici qu'en orient (401, 558, 3594,
   [oriente])
par tantes teres (525, 540, 553)
en sun visage (2218, 2299)
d'altre part est (7 occurrences)

el premer chef devant (3018, 3195)
es puis de Haltoie (209, 491 [as
   puis])
en seintes flurs (1856, 2197)
par tute la cuntree (709, 1455)
entre sa brace (1721, 3939)

Contiguity, relationship:
ensembl'od els (175, 1896, 2395,
   3196, 3461)
unt en lur cumpaignie (587, 827
   [unt en la lur cumpaigne]
apres icels (3021, 3198)

ensembl'od lui (104, 1410, 1805,
   1839, 2130, 2578, 2817, 3637,
   3936)
encuntre mei (1559, 2921)
ja devers els (3030, 3071)

Manner:
par amur e par feid (86, 3460,
   3801, 3893), par feid e par amur
   (2897, 3770, 3810)
isnelement (2085, 2453, 2536,
   2766, 2988, 3575, 3884)
par grant vertut (1246, 1551,
   1754, 2851, 3878)
par poestet (477, 3653)
mult dulcement (2026, 2176, 2343,
   2886 [tant])
mult fierement (219, 2984, 3316,
   3536)
u altrement (494, 1880)

par amistiet (622, 1530)
par grant saveir (369, 426)
par jugement (436, 482)
cumfaitement (581, 1699)
cumunement (1836, 3416)
ireement (733, 762)
e menut e suvent (1426, 2364)
par merveillus ahan (2474, 3963)
en quel mesure (146, 631 [par])
de mult fiere raisun (875, 1231
   [par])
mult haltement (3270, 3300)
a si grant tort (1899, 3592 [a
   mult])

While not nearly as obvious to the reader as phrases found only
in combat scenes, adverbial formulas deserve as much scholarly
attention as the latter, and perhaps even more, since their very
lack of attachment to specific contexts makes them an excellent
index of style regardless of the subject of the works in which
they appear.

   In their contextual adaptability, the adverbial formulas exhibit
to the highest degree that flexibility of the formulas which is an

indispensible counterpart to their semantic fixity. Both qualities must be appreciated before a full understanding of the texture of this style can be attained. In general, it appears that the less a formula type is adaptable by its meaning to different contexts, the more likely it is to contain open syllables whose content can be varied for syntactic flexibility. Thus while both speech formulas and proper names undergo frequent slight modifications, the former by the free substitution of particles such as *e* and *ço* when the names contained in them are insufficient for the proper syllable count, and the latter by the addition of toponyms of origin and various nouns in apposition, the adverbial formulas, at the opposite pole, need to be modified relatively little from occurrence to occurrence, their extremely general meaning rendering them highly mobile.

The variety of the *Chanson de Roland's* formulas is extraordinary: every kind of action, from the most "epic" battle stroke to the rare comparison, is represented in semantically patterned phrases. Intuitional judgments have led some scholars to generalize about the extent of the formulaic language, but only detailed analysis can reveal its range and scope. The formulaic language is by no means confined to speech and battle hemistichs, frequent as these may be and obvious as they may appear to a casual observer. They constitute only a minority of *Roland's* formula tokens. Neither are formulas limited to peripheral or unimportant scenes: at times they signal the most important plot developments. Furthermore, as was previously demonstrated, the most appealing scenes, taken as a whole, are slightly more formulaic than the rest of the work. The inventory presented in these pages only includes phrases repeated within the confines of the poem itself, thereby eliminating, albeit necessarily, formulas shared by other poems in the tradition but which occur only once within the 4002 lines of the Oxford manuscript. Still it is obvious that the *Chanson de Roland* is, not incidentally or superficially, but essentially, a product of oral tradition, which is the only process known to result in creation through formulaic style.

# 5: *Roland's* Motifs and Formulas and the Evolution of Old French Epic Style

THE *Chanson de Roland's* style is fundamentally formulaic. But if this style is common to the *chansons de geste* as a whole, how can one account for the fact that the *Roland* stands apart artistically from the other epics of the late eleventh and twelfth centuries, and is universally recognized as superior to them in literary quality, even to the moving *Chanson de Guillaume* and to what we have of the archaic *Gormont et Isembart*? Can the differences in esthetic appeal be accounted for by the evolution of formulaic style and composition by motif within the epic genre during the course of the twelfth century?

Let us take as a first example a well delineated motif, the *planctus* or pronouncement of funereal regrets upon the body of a fallen hero. Paul Zumthor,[1] in a study which isolates the essential characteristics of the *planctus*, notes that all of the *Chanson de Roland's* seven major examples (vv. 1851–1868, 2022–2032, 2186–2199, 2200–2221, 2246–2258, 2399–2417, and 2885–2944) are pronounced by combatants. He distinguishes six fundamental elements, with corresponding textual references, in the most complete set of regrets, those spoken by Charlemagne over

[1] "Etude typologique des *planctus* contenus dans la *Chanson de Roland,*" *La technique littéraire des chansons de geste: Actes du Colloque de Liège (septembre 1957),* Bibliothèque de la Faculté de Philosophie et Lettres de l'Université de Liège, CL (Paris: Société d'Edition "Les Belles Lettres," 1959), pp. 219–234; see also, by the same author, "Les *planctus* épiques," *Romania,* LXXXIV (1963), 61–65.

Roland's body on the battlefield of Roncevaux: 1) the narrative
link, including two parts, the finding of the dead hero (*veit sun
nevold gesir*) and the announcement of the dirge (*a regreter le
prist*); 2) direct address of the corpse (*amis Rollant*); 3) prayer
for the soul of the deceased (*Deus metet t'anme . . . en pareis*);
4) a statement of praise, expressed either directly as a characteri-
zation (*unques . . . tel chevaler ne vit*), or indirectly as the hero's
death reflects upon Charlemagne's misfortunes (*la meie honor est
turnet a declin*); 5) the external signs of mourning, either on the
part of Charlemagne himself (*Carles se pasmet*) or of his army:

> Cent milie Francs en unt si grant dulur
> n'en i ad cel ki durement ne plurt;

and 6) an indication of interior grief (*jamais n'ert jurn de tei
n'aie dulur*). To these six he adds four more not present in the
initial laisses of Charlemagne's *planctus* but inserted in later
laisses: 1) allusion to the distant homeland (*cum jo serai a Loün,
cum jo serai a Eis*); 2) the *ubi est* topic in which friends who re-
mained at home will ask for the deceased either directly (*ven-
drunt li hume . . . demanderunt: U est li quens cataignes?*) or in
indirect discourse (*vendrunt li hume, demanderunt noveles*); 3)
the answer to this question (*il est morz en Espaigne, morz est
mis niés*); and 4) the narrative conclusion, which closes the
motif and provides a transition to the main *récit* (*dist dux Naimes:
Or ad Carles grant ire*).

The other six of *Roland's planctus*, three pronounced over the
bodies of the ensemble of dead knights, two on Oliver, and one
on Turpin, contain no new elements, and all the elements of
Charlemagne's regrets are found in them, although to varying
degrees of completeness. The phrase *mare fustes*, expressing
the fatality of the victim's death, occurs once in the prayer ele-
ment (*mare fustes, seignurs*, v. 2195) and once in a passage of
praise (*tant mar fustes hardiz!* v. 2027). Unlike the *vantance*
motif, the order of *planctus* elements varies, but certain tenden-

cies are discernible: the motif normally opens with the narrative
link, followed, five times out of six, by the external signs of
mourning or the announcement; five times out of six the apostro-
phe is placed either in the expression of praise or in the expression
of interior grief.

On the basis of an examination of the *planctus* in other *chan-
sons de geste*, and in order to facilitate the study of *planctus*
formulas in particular, I shall make the following modifications
in Professor Zumthor's classification: the first of his fundamental
elements can be divided into two distinct entities, the narrative
link and the announcement, as can the fourth, praise of the de-
ceased expressed directly as a characterization or hyperbolic
comparison, and the misfortune of his surviving comrades, in-
cluding the person who is pronouncing the dirge but not neces-
sarily limited to him; appended to this latter element one may
find an enumeration of the dangers to which his death exposes
them. In addition, further amplifications are sometimes present:
an identification of the killer, with pledge to avenge the death,
and an expression of desire to follow the deceased into death.

Professor Zumthor also notes that, aside from the *planctus*
motif proper, there are two classes of phrases—I shall term them
"submotifs"—which, although extremely brief, are related to
the *planctus* and share many of its formulas. He calls them anti-
cipatory *planctus* (*planctus annonciateurs*) and narrative *planc-
tus*. The first type anticipates the battle of Roncevaux in words
which evoke the possibility of the rear-guard's destruction, and
the second consists of brief narrative passages reporting the grief
of a knight when he learns of the death of one of his companions.

An ideally reconstituted and complete motif would contain all
these elements, although not necessarily in the same order in
each instance. The elements are listed below, accompanied, when
applicable, by formulas taken from *Roland's planctus* motifs
and submotifs. The line references to verses occurring in motifs
proper are in italics.

1. NARRATIVE LINK: *veit gesir sun nevold* (2876, 2885 [*sun nevold gesir*], 2894; *iloec trovat* (2186, 2188); *guardet a tere* (2885, 2894); *Rollant reguardet* (1851, 1978);

2. ANNOUNCEMENT: *mult dulcement a regreter le prist* (2026, 2886);

3. EXTERNAL SIGNS OF MOURNING: *ne poet muer* (773, 2517); *ne poet muer n'en plurt* (823, 841,  2193, 2517, 2873); *plurent des oilz* (2415, 2943); *.c. milie Francs* (842, 2907, 2932); *pluret si se demente* (1404, 1836 [*n'i plurt e se dement*], 2517 [*n'en plurt e nes dement*]); *n'i ad celoi* (1814, 1836), *ki durement ne plurt* (1814, 2419, 2908); *encuntre tere* (2416, 2422);

4. APOSTROPHE: *sire cumpainz* (1983, 2027); *ami Rollant* (2887, 2898, 2909, 2916, 2933);

5. PRAYER FOR THE SOUL OF THE DECEASED: *e prient Deu* (1837, 2518); *de tei ait Deus mercit* (1854 [*de vos*], 2887, 2933), *tutes vos anmes* (1855, 2196), *en pareïs* (2197, 2899);

6. INTERIOR GRIEF: *si grant doel ad* (2219, 2929, 2936), *ja mais n'ert jurn* (2901, 2915); *de doel e de pitet* (1748, 2206 [*le doel e la pitet*]); *e li Franceis dolenz e curuçus* (1813, 1835 [*curuçus e dolent*]);

7. PRAISE: *ja mais n'iert hume* (1984, 2254); *tant mar fustes hardiz* (2027, 2221 [*ber*]); *veincre e esmaier* (2211, 2213);

8. MISFORTUNE OF THE SURVIVORS;

9. UBI EST: a. PLACE: *cum jo serai* (2910, 2917);
    b. QUESTION: *u est* [plus proper name] (2403, 2404, 2405, 2409);
    c. ANSWER: *jo lur dirrai* (2913, 2919 [*jes*]), *de ço qui calt*, an assertion of the futility of answering (1405, 1840, 2411);

10. REFERENCE TO THE KILLER SOMETIMES WITH PLEDGE OF VENGEANCE;

11. SPEAKER'S DESIRE TO DIE;

12. NARRATIVE CONCLUSION.

Eight of these twelve elements are represented by phrases re-
peated within the limits of the *Chanson de Roland*. The others
are present but not formulaically: the desire for death (*si grant
doel ai que ne voldreie vivre*, 2936), misfortune of the survivors
(*la meie honor est turnet en declin*, 2890, and *cum decarrat ma
force e ma baldur*, 2902), the enumeration of the enemies who will
revolt against Charlemagne now that Roland is no more (vv.
2921–2924) as well as a reference to the killers (*ki tei ad mort*,
2935).

Charlemagne's regrets on his nephew's death, occupying five
laisses, is the only *planctus* to contain all of these elements in
the *Roland*:

| | |
|---|---|
| CCVI Li empereres de pasmeisuns revint. | *External sign of mourning* |
| Naimes li dux e li quens Acelin, | |
| Gefrei d'Anjou e sun frere Henri | |
| Prenent le rei, sil drecent suz un pin. | |
| 2885 Guardet a la tere, veit sun nevod gesir. | *Narrative link* |
| Tant dulcement a regreter le prist: | *Announcement* |
| "Amis Rollant, de tei ait Deus mercit! | *Apostrophe, prayer* |
| Unques nuls hom tel chevaler ne vit | *Praise* |
| Por granz batailles juster e defenir. | |
| 2890 La meie honor est turnet en declin." | *Misfortune of survivor* |
| Carles se pasmet, ne s'en pout astenir. AOI. | *External sign of mourning* |
| CCVII Carles li reis se vint de pasmeisuns; | |
| Par les mains le tienent .III. de ses barons. | |
| Guardet a tere, vei gesir sun nevuld: | *Narrative link, with* |
| 2895 Cors ad gaillard, perdue ad sa culur, | *elaboration* |
| Turnez ses oilz, mult li sunt tenebros. | |
| Carles le pleint par feid e par amur: | *Announcement* |
| "Ami Rollant, Deus metet t'anme en flors, | *Apostrophe, prayer* |
| En pareïs, entre les glorius! | |
| 2900 Cum en Espaigne venis a mal seignur! | |
| Jamais n'ert jurn que de tei n'aie dulur. | *Internal grief* |
| Cum decarrat ma force e ma baldur! | *Misfortune of survivor,* |
| N'en avrai ja ki sustienget m'onur; | *with elaboration* |
| Suz ciel ne quid aveir ami un sul! | |
| 2905 Se jo ai parenz, n'en i ad nul si proz." | |

| | |
|---|---|
| Trait ses crignels, pleines ses mains amsdous; | *External sign of mourning* |
| Cent milie Franc en unt si grant dulur | *Internal grief* |
| N'en i ad cel ki durement ne plurt. AOI. | *External sign of mourning* |
| CVIII "Ami Rollant, jo m'en irai en France. | *Apostrophe* |
| 2910 Cum je serai a Loün, en ma chambre, | *Ubi est: place* |
| De plusurs regnes vendrunt li hume estrange; | |
| Demanderunt: 'U est li quens cataignes?' | *Ubi est: question* |
| Jo lur dirrai qu'il est morz en Espaigne. | *Ubi est: answer* |
| A grant dulur tendrai puis mun reialme: | *Misfortune of survivor* |
| 2915 Jamais n'ert jurn que ne plur ne n'en pleigne." | *External signs of mourning* |
| CCIX "Ami Rollant, prozdoem, juvente bele, | *Apostrophe* |
| Cum jo serai a Eis, em ma chapele, | *Ubi est: place* |
| Vendrunt li hume, demanderunt noveles; | *Ubi est: question* |
| Jes lur dirrai, merveilluses e pesmes: | *Ubi est: answer* |
| 2920 'Morz est mis nies, ki tant me fist cunquere.' | |
| Encuntre mei revelerunt li Seisne, | *Misfortune of survivor* |
| E Hungre e Bugre e tante gent averse, | *with enumeration of* |
| Romain, Puillain e tuit icil de Palerne, | *dangers* |
| E cil d'Affrike e cil de Califerne; | |
| 2925 Puis entrerunt mes peines e mes suffraites. | |
| Ki guierat mes oz a tel poeste, | |
| Quant cil est [morz] ki tuz jurz nos cadelet? | |
| E! France, cum remeines deserte! | |
| Si grant doel ai que jo ne vuldreie estre!" | *Speaker's desire to die* |
| 2930 Sa barbe blanche cumencet a detraire, | *External signs of mourning* |
| Ad ambes mains les chevels de sa teste. | *with elaboration* |
| Cent milie Francs s'en pasment cuntre tere. | |
| CCX "Ami Rollant, de tei ait Deus mercit! | *Apostrophe, prayer* |
| L'anme de tei seit mise en pareïs! | |
| 2935 Ki tei ad mort France ad mis en exill. | *Reference to killer* |
| Si grant dol ai que ne voldreie vivre, | *Speaker's desire to die,* |
| De ma maisnee, ki pur mei est ocise! | *with elaboration* |
| Ço duinset Deus, le filz sainte Marie, | |
| Einz que jo vienge as maistres porz de Sirie, | |
| 2940 L'anme del cors me seit oi departie, | |
| Entre les lur aluee e mise, | |
| E ma car fust delez els enfuïe!" | |
| Ploret des oilz, sa blanche barbe tiret. | |
| E dist dux Naimes: "Or ad Carles grant ire." | *External signs of mourning* |
| AOI. | *Narrative conclusion* |

Literary qualities which distinguish the *Chanson de Roland*
as a whole are present in this scene, which takes place after Char-
lemagne has pursued the remnants of Marsile's army and spent
the night on the banks of the river Sebre, but before he is aware
of Baligant's arrival in Spain. Tenderness of feeling for Roland
(*tant dulcement a regreter le prist*) is embodied in the terms of
endearment by which Charlemagne addresses his nephew, *ami
Rollant, juvente bele,* and in the delicate image of paradise, *Deus
metet t'anme en flors.* His grief, on the other hand, approaches
violence as he tears his hair and beard (vv. 2906, 2930–2931,
2943). The *planctus* moves gradually from a contemplation of
Roland's person—dwelt upon in the two similar laisses which
open the motif with praise of the dead hero, a brief description of
his body introduced by the highly ironic *cors ad gaillard,* and the
prayer that he be granted salvation—to a preoccupation with the
living, who must "turn to their affairs" without Roland's protec-
tion. The misfortune of the survivor is mentioned in the second
laisse, both in hierarchical terms, *n'en avrai ja ki sustienget
m'onur,* and in an expression of personal isolation, *suz ciel ne
quid aveir ami un sul.* It is subsequently expanded upon in a laisse
dominated by the *"ubi est"* element which suggests Roland's far-
flung reputation, *vendrunt li hume estrange,* but focuses again
upon the difficulty of ruling an empire without the hero's support,
*a grant dulur tendrai puis mun reialme.* The fourth laisse elab-
orates still more upon the emperor's misfortune by ornamenting
it through the enumeration of dangers, the peoples who will now
revolt against their defenseless monarch. The final stage, in laisse
CCX, centers on an affective conclusion, Charlemagne's wish to
join his *maisnee* in the tomb and in heaven. Thus while every
laisse contains external signs of mourning, an apostrophe to
Roland, and mention of the survivor's misfortunes, the variable
elements are structured symmetrically and progressively:

CCVI: PRAISE                    CCVII: PRAYER
CCVIII: UBI EST                 CCIX: UBI EST, ELABORATED
CCX: PRAYER, DEATH WISH

Naime brings the emperor back to the world of practical consid-
erations in laisse CCXI by recommending burial of the rear-guard
in a common grave. Charlemagne never again wishes for death,
transforming his grief into action in the episode of Baligant (cf.
especially vv. 2983–2986). But the tension between delicacy of
affection and violent reaction to the loss, which attains its fullest
expression in this *planctus,* surfaces again on two occasions:
when the Frankish army, riding into battle against Baligant, weeps
at the sound of Roland's horn, blown now by Guineman, and in
the episode of Alde *la bele,* itself a brief but intense *planctus*
which ends with the fulfillment of the fiancee's death wish. No-
where else in the poem, however, is the elegaic quality of the
*Chanson de Roland* so effectively expressed as in this passage,
which combines symmetry, tension, and affective development
with the technique of similar laisses.

To conclude, however, on the basis of this scene's artistry that
it must be the creation of a learned poet, schooled in the technique
of written composition, would be erroneous. Those very elements
whose combination makes Charlemagne's *planctus* so effective
are, as indicated in the schematic reconstruction of the motif on
p. 163, formulas employed in other passages of *Roland.* The
whole-verse announcement *tant dulcement a regreter le prist*
recurs *ipsissimis verbis* in Roland's *planctus* for Oliver (v. 2026).
The delicate image *Deus metet t'anme en flors* echoes Roland's
two prayers for his men:

> Tutes vos anmes otreit il pareïs!
> En seintes flurs il les facet gesir! (1855–1856),

and

> Tutes vos anmes ait Deus li Glorius!
> En pareïs les metet en seintes flurs! (2196–2197).

The ironic formula *cors ad gaillard,* recalling the former life-
force of this lifeless body, now drained of its very color, *perdue*

*ad sa culur*, is employed later to designate, of all people, Ganelon the traitor, in v. 3763, which also includes the association with color: *cors ad gaillard, el vis gente color*.[2] In this case the poet has developed a striking irony not by relinquishing his formulaic language, but by manipulating it well. There is nothing stylistically original either about the expression of mourning, the feelings of grief, or the *"ubi est"* element (see vv. 2403–2409). As effective as Charlemagne's *planctus* is, then, it is nevertheless constructed with standard phrases which are part of the *Roland* tradition's stock of formulas.

The *planctus* motif recurs in similar configurations elsewhere in the *chansons de geste*, and the *Prise d'Orange* contains a particularly well developed version. Bertran, nephew of Guillaume and brother of Guïelin, believing falsely that his two kinsmen have been killed by the Saracens in Orange, regrets their passing:

| | |
|---|---|
| Li cuens Bertran s'est par matin levé, | |
| 1660 Monte el palés Otran le deffaé | |
| Qu'il ot conquis par sa ruiste fierté. | |
| As granz fenestres s'est li cuens acoté; | |
| Il regarda contreval le regné, | |
| Vit l'erbe vert et le rosier planté, | |
| 1665 Et l'orïol et le melle chanter. | |
| Lors li remembre de Guillelme au cort nes, | *Narrative link* |
| De Guïelin son frere, l'alosé, | |
| Molt tendrement commença a plorer, | *External sign of mourning* |
| Or le regrete, com ja oïr porrez: | *Announcement* |
| 1670 "Oncle Guillelme, tant feïs foletez | *Apostrophe, reproach* |
| Quant en Orenge alas por regarder | |
| Com pautonnier einsi atapiné: | |
| Guïelin frere, com vos estïez ber! | *Apostrophe, praise* |
| Or vos ont mort Sarrazin et Escler; | *Reference to killer* |
| 1675 Ge sui toz seus en cest païs remés, | *Misfortune of the Survivor* |
| Si n'i voi hom de mon grant parenté | |
| A cui ge puisse bon conseill demander, | |

[2] The V4 jongleur, in the corresponding verse, retains the irony but leans on it rather heavily, employing the same phraseology which Oxford uses to describe Ganelon: *cor a gaiardo, lo viso gente collor*.

Or revenront ceste part li Escler,      *With enumeration of*
Et Goulïas et li rois Desramez      *dangers*
1680 Et Clarïaus et son frere Acerez
Et Aguisanz et li rois Giboëz
Et li aufins de Rëaumont sor mer,
Li rois Eubrons et Borreaus et Lorrez
Et Quinzepaumes et ses freres Gondrez,
1685 Li .XXX. roi qui d'Espaigne sont né.
Chascuns avra trente mile adoubé,
Si m'assaudront a Nymes la cité,
Si me prendront par vive poësté;
Ge serai mort, ocis ou afolé.
1690 Mes d'une chose me sui ge porpensé:
Ge ne leroie por l'or de .X. citez      *Ubi sunt: place*
Que je ne voise el regne dont fui nez,
Si remenrai avec moi mon barné,
Que amena Guillelmes au cort nes.
1695 Quant ge venrai a Paris la cité
Ge descendrai au perron noielé;
Venront encontre serjant et bacheler,
Qui de Guillelme me vorront demander,      *Ubi sunt: question*
De Guïelin, mon frere qui est ber.
1700 Helas, dolent, n'en savrai que conter,      *Ubi sunt: answer*
Mes qu'en Orenge les ont paien tüez!"
.IJ. foiz se pasme sor le marbrin degré,      *External sign of mourning*
Quant le barnage le corut relever.      *Narrative conclusion*
LVIII Li cuens Bertrans fu molt grains et dolanz      *Interior grief*
Por Guïelin et Guillelme le franc,
Il les regrete bel et cortoisement:      *Announcement*
"Oncle Guillelme, tant feïs folement      *Apostrophe, reproach*
Quant en Orenge alas si faitement
Com pautonnier en atapinement.
1710 Guïelin frere, com vos estïez franc!      *Apostrophe, praise*
Or vos ont mort Sarrazin et Persant;      *Reference to killers*
Ge sui toz seus el regne des paiens,      *Misfortune of survivor*
N'ai ovec moi ne cosin ne parent.
Or revenra rois Tiebauz d'Aufriquant      *With enumeration of*
1715 Et Desramez et Goulïas le grant,      *dangers*
Li .XXX. roi o lor efforcement;
Si m'assaudront a Nymes ci devant.
Ge serai morz et livrez a torment.

Mes, par l'apostre que quierent peneant,
1720 Ge nel leroie por les menbres perdant,
Que ge ne aille a Orenge la grant,
Si vengerai le duel et le torment            *Pledge of vengeance*
Que Sarrazin ont fet de noz parenz.
Helas, chetis, que vois ge atendant,
1725 Que ge mon cors ne lor met en present!"[3]

The laisse structure of this *planctus* is not as well delineated as
is that of Charlemagne's regrets. It begins in the twenty-first
verse of laisse LVII, after the narration of how Guillaume and
Guïelin have ejected their Saracen adversaries from Gloriette,
Orable's palace in Orange. In *Roland* the laisses contain no other
element than the motif in question. Bertran's *planctus* is situated
between the voyage of a messenger, Guillebert, to Nîmes and
his arrival before Bertran, which provides a narrative conclusion
to the motif at the beginning of laisse LIX. The motif in the
*Prise d'Orange* is a remarkable counterpart to Charlemagne's
dirge: it contains ten of the twelve fundamental elements, dis-
pensing only with a prayer for the souls of Bertran's kinsmen
and the speaker's death wish. It modifies only one element, re-
placing praise for Guillaume with a reproach to the hero for his
foolhardy adventure which, Bertran believes, has cost him his
life. The element of praise is retained, however, for Guïelin.
While the *planctus* of the *Prise d'Orange* occupies only two
laisses, it is three lines longer than Charlemagne's, and thus of
approximately the same dimensions. It too repeats formulas
within the scene, although the formulas it employs differ in every
case from those found in *Roland: oncle Guillelme* (PO 1670,
1707), *Guïelin frere* (PO 1673, 1710), *tant feïs foletez* (PO 1670,
1707 [*folement*]), *quant en Orenge* (PO 1671, 1708), *com vos
estïez ber* (PO 1673, 1710 [*franc*]), *or vos ont mort* (PO 1674,
1711), *Sarrazin et Escler* (PO 1674, 1711 [*et Persant*]), *ge sui toz*

---

[3] The text is taken from Blanche Katz, ed., *La Prise d'Orenge* (New York:
King's Crown Press, 1947), and is identical to the corresponding passage of
Professor Régnier's edition.

*seus* (PO 1675, 1712), or *revenront* (PO 1678, 1714 [*revenra*]),
*li .XXX. roi* (PO 1685, 1716), *si m'assaudront* (PO 1687, 1717),
*ge serai mort* (PO 1689, 1718), *ge ne leroie* (PO 1691, 1720). In
spite of the variance in formulaic repertory, there are several
similarities of phrasing:

| element | Roland | Prise d'Orange |
|---|---|---|
| Announcement | mult dulcement | molt tendrement |
| Reference to killer | ki tei ad mort | or vos ont mort |
| Misfortune of survivor | suz ciel ne quid aveir ami un sul | ge sui toz seus en cest païs remés |
| | se jo ai parenz, n'en i ad nul si proz | n'ai ovec moi ne cosin ne parent |
| | encuntre mei revelerunt li Seisne | or revenrunt ceste part li Escler |
| Ubi est: place | cum jo serai a Eis, cum je serai a Loün | quant je venrai a Paris la cité |
| Ubi est: question | vendrunt li hume | vendrunt encontre |

Even though their respective performances are generations apart,
the poets behind Oxford and the performance of the *Prise
d'Orange* extant in French manuscript 774 of the Bibliothèque
nationale, Paris, each had access to a traditional technique of
the *planctus*. They differ in stylistic details, but the similarity
of elements in the two configurations is impressive.

Not that the two *planctus* are artistically indistinguishable.
"Traditional" does not signify "uniform." The two laisses of the
*Prise d'Orange*, like the first two of Charlemagne's regrets, ex-
hibit the technique of similar laisses, but not with the same result:
laisse LVIII repeats the content of the preceding laisse in a quite
monotonous way, changing the first hemistich formulas very
little, and altering only the assonating words in the second hemi-
stichs, so that what is said to Guillaume and Guïelin in vv. 1707–
1718 is nearly identical to the words as first spoken in vv.
1670–1689. The sole exception worthy of note is a rearranging
and foreshortening in the enumeration of enemies to whom

the kinsmen's deaths have exposed Bertran. At that point the
second laisse diverges from the first. The adversative *mes* leads
Bertran's imagination on the one hand to Paris, where the *"ubi
sunt"* takes place, and on the other to Orange to avenge Guillaume
and Guïelin. The texture of the *planctus'* poetic diction does not
vary from one poem to the other: there is no greater frequency of
weak verses, of fillers, of needless elaboration in one version than
in the other. But both the structure and the tone of Bertran's
*planctus* are remarkably less effective. *Roland's* balanced symme-
try, one laisse in counterpoint with the next, traces the develop-
ment of Charlemagne's grief from a contemplation of the dead
hero to the desire for death. The *Prise d'Orange* presents us with
no particular development at all, unless it be Bertran's decision,
trivial in comparison with Charlemagne's death wish, to wreak
vengeance upon the Saracens of Orange. In addition the affective
gulf between Bertran's speech and the words of Charlemagne
wishing that Roland be granted salvation among the heavenly
flowers is, literarily, substantial. The emperor's sorrow is inti-
mately felt in the five almost incantatory evocations of *ami
Rollant,* the touching apostrophe *juvente bele,* and the extreme
gesture of pulling out his own hair. Moreover, one feels that the
tragedy of his grief is unadulterated, for never does he utter a
word of reproach about his nephew's motives, whereas an accu-
sation of foolhardiness is substituted, in Bertran's address, for a
traditional element of praise. While I cannot agree with Professor
Régnier's evaluation of the *Prise d'Orange* as a *"chef-d'oeuvre
d'humour,"*[4] it appears to me that, through an unimaginative
use of the *planctus* and other epic motifs, it approaches self-
parody. But all the differences of tone and structure discussed
here can be accounted for by a more skillful domination of the
traditional motif by the jongleur whose work has come down
to us in the Oxford text, or by a longer and more intense process
of filtration on the part of generations of jongleurs who trans-
mitted the Roland legend in poetic form. The disparities are

---

[4] *La Prise d'Orange,* (Paris: Klincksieck, 1969), p. 31.

every one a matter of degree and not of essence, and all remain within the province of composition by formula and motif.

There are many other *planctus* in the twelfth-century *chanson de geste*, but the motif does not appear in every epic nor is it ever again as complete as in *Roland* and the *Prise d'Orange*. Among the other eight epics treated in Chapter II, the *planctus* motif proper is found in *Gormont et Isembart* (vv. 466–488, 529–542), the *Chanson de Guillaume* (vv. 1930–1948, 1988–2023, 2179–2193), *Raoul de Cambrai* (vv. 1503–1520, 2546–2561, 3165–3200, 3307–3309, 3376–3383, 3479–3495, 3557–3576, 3665–3695), and the *Moniage Guillaume* (vv. 6264–6279). The *Charroi de Nîmes*, the *Couronnement de Louis*, the *Siège de Barbastre*, and the *Pèlerinage de Charlemagne* have none. In addition to the motif proper, many shorter passages depict the announcement of death to the deceased's next of kin, cries of vengeance, general expressions of regret, and reminiscences of dead heroes, or those presumed to be dead; these shorter passages, analogous to the anticipatory and narrative *planctus* described by Professor Zumthor, are, in general, more varied than those found in *Roland*.

Among the twelve *planctus* elements as they are present in the other *chansons de geste*, the most constant is the apostrophe to the dead person, which appears in all but one *planctus* (*Raoul de Cambrai*, vv. 3307–3309). Next are the narrative link, usually containing the verbs *trover* or *veir*, and the announcement of the motif, frequently including the verb *regreter*. The warrior's praise, mention of the killer, the external signs of mourning, and the misfortune of survivors appear with moderate frequency, while the other elements are seldom seen in the motif proper.[5] There is a definite evolution away from the full *planctus* as found in *Roland* and the *Prise d'Orange* toward a less schematized and more varied structure. The only new element, if indeed it merits that designation, is the practice of kissing the corpse, but it ap-

---

[5] See Zumthor, "Les *planctus* épiques." Note that the key-words and phrases cited by Professor Zumthor occur in both the motif proper and in the briefer submotifs.

pears only in *Raoul de Cambrai* (vv. 2550, 3711). Even though
they retain the other elements, the later poets never include as
many and sometimes interrupt the motif with narrative, as in
this example from *Raoul de Cambrai*:

| | |
|---|---|
| Il regarda leiz .j. bruellet plaignier, | *Narrative link* |
| Son fil vit mort; le sens quide changier. | |
| De ci a lui ne fine de broichier; | |
| A pié descent de son corant destrier, | |
| 2550  E tot sanglant le commence a baissier: | *(Kiss)* |
| "Fix," dist li peres, "tan vos avoie chier! | *Apostrophe* |
| Qi vos a mort, por le cors s. Richier, | *Mention of killer* |
| Ja de l'acorde ne vuel oïr plaidier | |
| Si l'avrai mort et fait tot detranchier." | *Pledge of vengeance* |
| 2555  Son fil vost metre sor le col del destrier, | |
| Qant d'un vaucel vit lor gent repairier. | *Interruption* |
| G[uerri] le voit, n'i a qe corecier; | |
| Sor son escu rala son fil couchier. | |
| "Fix," dist li peres, "vos me covient laissier, | *Apostrophe* |
| 2560  Mais, ce Dieu plaist, je vos quit bien vengier. | *Pledge of vengeance* |
| Cil ait vostre arme qi le mont doit jugier!" | *Prayer* |

In this instance, the motif is more narrative than lyric: in the
*Chanson de Roland* all action ceases during each *planctus*, and
nothing is permitted to interrupt the expression of anguish. The
result of this loosening of contours in *Raoul* is a more fluid inter-
play of motif and narration. The impression is of a continuous
flow of action in *Raoul de Cambrai*; in *Roland* the motifs func-
tion as whole blocks, set off from the narrative around them.

The sole occurrence of a *planctus* in the *Moniage Guillaume*
confirms the impression that in later *chansons de geste* the motif
tends to melt into the narrative.

| | |
|---|---|
| La oïssiés de Turs grant plorison, | *External signs of mourning* |
| 6265  Lor puins detorgent s'ont lor cevax derous, | |
| Pasmé en chïent set mile des archons. | |
| Sovent maudïent Tervagant et Mahon: | *Announcement: prayer* |
| "Ysorés sire, chi a trop grant dolor! | *element reversed* |
| Que feront ore vo prince et vo contor? | *Apostrophe* |

6270 Ja en vo terre mais ne retornerons."           *Misfortune of survivors*
     As tentes vient mout tost ceste raisons     }
     Que mors estoit Ysorés l'Arragons.          }   *Interruption*
     Lors fisent doel, ainc n'oïstes grignor:        *Interior grief*
     Il le regretent entour et environ.              *Announcement (?)*
6275 Au cors en vienent poignant tout a bandon       *Narrative resumes*
     Tels trente mile, qui si effreé sont
     Qu'a paines sevent dire n'oïl ne non.
     Franc les esgardent, qui estoient au pont,
     Voient le doel que li Sarrasin font.

In this passage the verb *regreter,* used consistently to begin the
motif with the announcement element, has been displaced to
the very end. The *planctus* is interrupted by the observation
that news of Ysoré's death has reached the Saracen tents. It is
difficult to say whether this is a true interruption, for what fol-
lows those verses is so amorphous, in comparison with the un-
mistakable contours of the earliest motifs, that the motif may
have ended with the direct discourse in v. 6270.

In the *Moniage Guillaume* and *Raoul de Cambrai,* latest in date
of the six *chansons de geste* containing the *planctus,* the motif
has all but lost its definition. The *Chanson de Roland* holds the
sole literarily effective example of the genre, and has no suc-
cessors in this respect. Viewed in this light, Bertran's regrets in
the *Prise d'Orange* take on the quality of an archaism, preserved
from one of that poem's earlier versions and transmitted through
oral tradition to the mid-twelfth-century performance extant in
manuscript A. The *planctus* as a semiautonomous traditional
motif disintegrated during the century following Oxford.

To the reader it may seem that I have devoted an inordinate
amount of attention to one motif, out of proportion with the im-
portance of this type of scene in the poem. I do not believe that
this is so, for the *planctus* and related submotifs together consti-
tute one of the most significant sets of formulas in the *Chanson
de Roland* and serve, more than any other motif, to set the unique
tone which separates this work from the rest of the *chanson de
geste* tradition. The high tragedy of the *Roland* lies not in the

loss of an army of twenty thousand men nor in the hero's death itself, but in the frequently expressed *awareness*, on the part of key protagonists, of impending death and of the losses it will bring to the Frankish nation and its emperor. Both Roland and Charlemagne have premonitions of the rearguard's fate, Roland vaguely through Ganelon's transparent statements and ominous actions, and Charlemagne more clearly through a dream. The tone of regret permeates the entire first half of the poem and is established as a major presence long before the first *planctus* proper is pronounced.

Ganelon himself, from the time of his designation by Roland to carry the message, has the possibility of death present in his mind. His request that the Franks see to his son's future well-being, since "*ja nel verrai des oilz*" (v. 316) draws a reproach from Charlemagne which might well be applied to all the French knights: "*tro avez tendre coer*" (v. 317), for the French themselves find a pretext for pessimism in Ganelon's clumsiness as he drops the glove, symbol of authority. Admittedly the French are right in their augury, "*De cest message nos avendrat grant perte*" (v. 335), but no more right than was Ganelon in making arrangements for his son's upbringing. He will expose himself to death in Marsile's camp, and the embassy will eventually lead to his own destruction, although not in the manner he foresees at this point in the action. His own men see him off on the expedition with a *planctus*-like speech, complete with external signs of mourning, apostrophe, the phrase *tant mare fustes*, praise of his accomplishments, and an oblique threat of revenge against Roland:

> La veïsez tant chevaler plorer,
> Ki tuit li dient: "Tant mare fustes, ber!
> En cort al rei mult i avez ested,
> Noble vassal vos i solt hom clamer.
> Ki ço jugat que doüsez aler
> Par Charlemagne n'er guariz ne tensez.

Li quens Rollant nel se doüst penser,
Que estrait estes de mult grant parented" (vv. 349–356).

Far from attempting to hide his apprehension before the prospect
of death, Ganelon repeats his reference to his family and asks
that they be greeted in his name. This scene is both a premature
*planctus* upon Ganelon and a declaration of final wishes. Traitor
though he will become, Ganelon is without rival the most mag-
nificent figure in the first theme, and this anticipatory *planctus*
adds to his stature as a great lord, conferring upon him an honor
later reserved for the martyrs of Roncevaux.

Charlemagne's awareness of his nephew's approaching death
is apparent in two scenes. He seems to have an intuition of fate
while he is presiding over the transfer of authority to Roland:

"Dreiz emperere," dist Rollant le barun,
"Dunez mei l'arc que vos tenez el poign.
Men escientre nel me reproverunt
Que il me chedet, cum fist a Guenelun
De sa main destre, quant reçut le bastun."
Li empereres en tint sun chef enbrunc,
Si duist sa barbe e detoerst sun gernun;
Ne poet muer que des oilz ne plurt (vv. 766–773).

The emperor is perhaps weeping at the sheer bravura of Roland's
taunt, but he also knows that this symbolic act of transmission
will take his nephew to his grave. Naimes must step forward, as
he does later upon hearing Roland's horn blast, to move the em-
peror to action. The previous night Charlemagne has dreamt
two symbolic scenes, the first of which concerns Roland: at the
pass Charles stands holding an ash spear; Ganelon seizes it and
shakes it so furiously that the splinters fly up toward the sky
(vv, 717–724). He later recalls this vision to Naime, amidst a
scene of general anguish and anticipation in the French army:

LXVI  Halt sunt li pui e li val tenebrus,
       Les roches bises, les destreiz merveillus.
       Le jur passerent Franceis a grant dulur;
       De .XV. lius en ot hom la rimur.
       Puis que il venent a la Tere Majur,
       Virent Guascuigne, la tere lur seignur,
       Dunc le remembret des fius e des honurs,
       E des pulcele e des gentilz oixurs:
       Cel nen i ad ki de pitet ne plurt.
       Sur tuz les altres est Carles anguissus:
       As porz d'Espaigne ad lesset sun nevold.
       Pitet l'en prent, ne poet muer n'en plurt. AOI.
LXVII  Li .XII. per sunt remés en Espaigne.
       .XX. milie Francs unt en lur cumpaigne,
       N'en unt poür ne de murir dutance.
       Li emperere s'en repairet en France;
       Suz sun mantel en fait la cuntenance.
       Dejuste lui li dux Neimes chevalchet
       E dit al rei: "De quei avez pesance?"
       Carles respunt: "Tort fait kil me demandet!
       Si grant doel ai ne puis muer nel pleigne.
       Par Guenelun serat destruite France:
       Enoit m'avint un avisiun d'angele,
       Que entre mes puinz me depeçout ma hanste,
       Chi ad juget mis nes a rereguarde.
       Jo l'ai lesset en une estrange marche!
       Deus! se jol pert, ja n'en avrai escange!" AOI.
LXVIII  Carles li magnes ne poet muer n'en plurt.
       .C. milie Francs pur lui unt grant tendrur,
       E de Rollant merveilluse poür.
       Guenes li fels en ad fait traïsun.
       Del rei paien en ad oüd granz duns,
       Or e argent, palies e ciclatuns,
       Muls e chevals e cameilz e leuns.
       Marsilies mandet d'Espaigne les baruns,

> Cuntes, vezcuntes e dux e almaçurs,
> Les amirafles a les filz as cunturs:
> .IIII.C. milie en ajustet en .III. jurz (vv. 814–851).

In this magnificent scene, the traditional technique has surrounded Charlemagne's words of remorse with two brilliant laisses assonating in *u*. The first joins evocation of the imposing mountain landscape with a feeling of foreboding captured in the assonating words which designate sound (*rimur*), darkness (*tenebrus*), the affective state of the knights (*merveillus, dulur, plurt, anguissus*) and the objects of their concern (*seignur, oixurs, nevold*). Laisse 68 leads from Charles, to his men who weep for Roland, to Ganelon, traitor against Roland, and finally, through those intermediate steps, to Marsile and his army's preparations for battle: the gradual transition approaches perfection. Between the French retreat and the Saracen advance, the emperor communicates to Naime his foreknowledge, terrible and accusing in its clarity since, despite the dream, Charles has done nothing to prevent the disaster: "*Jo l'ai lesset en une estrange marche!*" He has not himself verbalized his motive for inaction, but Naimes may have done so for him when he stated the futility of opposing Roland's determination:

> La rereguarde est jugée sur lui:
> N'avez baron ki jamais la remut (vv. 778–779).

Nevertheless in his great *planctus* over Roland's body, Charlemagne reproaches himself for having allowed the fatal situation to develop, when he addresses his nephew with the plaintive phrase: "*Cum en Espaigne venis a mal seignur!*" (v. 2900) This passage, laisses 66–68, is the major elegiac expression of tragic anticipation in a thoroughly elegiac poem. Its landscape reappears (v. 1830) at the poem's climax, when the sound of Roland's horn calls the French back from their mountain journey. It is the fullest statement of Charlemagne's guilt.

In the battle of Roncevaux, between the two waves of Saracen forces, the first led by Marsile's nephew Aëlroth and the second by the Saracen emperor himself, there is a series of three laisses, 109–111, dominated not by the fighting itself, but by reflection upon the disaster. Each begins with an evocation of the battle in general terms, but ends on a more reflective note:

> CIX  . . . Tant bon Franceis i perdent lor juvente!
> Ne reverrunt lor meres ne lor femmes,
> Ne cels de France ki as porz les atendent. AOI.
> Karles li magnes en pluret, si se demente.
> De ço qui calt? N'en avrunt sucurance.
> Malvais servise le jur li rendit Guenes
> Qu'en Sarraguce sa maisnee alat vendre. . . . (vv.
>     1401–1407)
> CX  . . . Franceis i perdent lor meillors guarnemenz;
> Ne reverrunt lor peres ne lor parenz,
> Ne Carlemagne, ki as porz les atent.
> En France en ad mult merveillus turment:
> Orez i ad de tuneire e de vent,
> Pluies e gresilz desmesureement;
> Chiedent i fuildres e menut e suvent,
> E terremoete ço i ad veirement.
> De seint Michel del Peril josqu'as Seinz,
> Des Besençun tresqu'as port de Guitsand,
> N'en ad recet dunt del mur ne cravent.
> Cuntre midi tenebres i ad granz;
> N'i ad clartet, se li ciels nen i fent.
> Hume nel veit ki mult ne s'esspoant.
> Dient plusor: "Ço est li definement,
> La fin del secle ki nus est en present."
> Il nel sevent, ne dient veir nient:
> Ço est li granz dulors por la mort de Rollant. (vv.
>     1420–1437)
> CXI  . . . Vunt par le camp, si requerent les lor,

>Plurent des oilz de doel e de tendrur
>Por lor parenz par coer e par amor.
>Li reis Marsilie od sa grant ost lor surt. AOI (vv.
>1445–1448).

In each laisse mention is made of the relatives and friends, never again to be seen, who await the doomed knights in France or at the Pyrenean passes. Just as Charlemagne's grief was singled out for emphasis in the earlier series of three elegiac laisses, so here the centerpiece of the scene is the spectacle of nature itself groaning in anticipation of Roland's death with the same combinatory elements: darkness, sound, and affective state, although with a more dramatic effect secured by the substitution of an actively mourning nature, in the form of a terrible storm and earthquake in France, for the passive evocation of mountain landscape. The full significance of this awesome scene is summed up in the reaction of the populace. The poet-persona's commentary culminates in a majestic alexandrine verse which confers full mythic significance upon the hero, raising him above the level of ordinary mortals: *Ço est li granz dulors por la mort de Rollant.* The brief interlude during which the French search out the dead and weep for their relatives is interrupted by Marsile's attack.

The full *planctus* scenes begin to occur toward the end of the second wave of battles at Roncevaux, after Turpin, anticipating the arrival of the main army at Roncevaux, depicts the French mourning over the fallen bodies:

>Truverunt nos e morz e detrenchez,
>Leverunt nos en bieres sur sumers,
>Si nus plurrunt de doel e de pitet,
>Enfuerunt nos en aitres de musters (vv. 1747–1750).

Subsequently Roland regrets the deaths of his own men (laisses CXL and CLXII), of Oliver (CLI, CLXIII), and of Turpin (CLXVII), before Charlemagne, arriving at the battlefield, pronounces a *planctus* over his rearguard (CLXXVII) and the full set of regrets over Roland (CCVI–CCX). The poem's final set of regrets, not a *planctus* proper according to Professor Zumthor's definition since it is not pronounced in the presence of Roland's body, is the episode of Alde, which is nothing less than the actualization of the *ubi est* scene. This question and Alde's death wish are the only two elements which concern Roland's death, but both are raised from rhetoric to the level of action since Alde actually asks the question and is immediately granted her wish to follow her fiancee to the grave. Charlemagne takes her lifelessness to be an external sign of mourning (*quidet li reis que el se seit pasmee*, v. 3724), feels grief over her loss (*pitet l'en prent, sin pluret l'emperere*), and finally realizes she is dead (*quant Carles veit que morte l'ad truvee*, v. 3728). The *planctus* elements are thus shared between Roland and Alde in this short and poignant episode.

In the *Chanson de Roland* the *planctus* is not a perfunctory motif. No other *chanson de geste* is permeated to this degree by a sense of the loss suffered when great heroes die.[6] The dominant tone is achieved through the traditional formulas and configurations of phrases expressing grief, of which the *planctus*

---

[6] The *Chanson de Guillaume* approaches the *Roland* most closely in this respect, and contains some poignant scenes of loss such as, for example, Guillaume's address to the empty hall, once filled by his men who have now died at Saracen hands:

> "Ohi haltes tables, cum estes levees!
> Napes de lin vei desure getees,
> Ces escuiles emplies e rasees
> De hanches e d'espalles, de nuieles e de obleies.
> N'i mangerunt les fiz de franches meres,
> Qui en l'Archamp unt les testes colpees!"
> Plure Willame, Guiburc s'est pasmee. (*CG*: 2402–2408)

This elegiac character of two of the most archaic *chansons de geste* leads one to conjecture that the ninth and tenth-century songs, for whose existence there is much persuasive historical evidence, may have been primarily elegiac in nature.

proper is the most clearly structured example. If death were portrayed as annihilation, then the song would be pessimistic, but other moments of defiance, expectation, and regret surround the moment of death. The combatants come to terms with their fate, and the survivors look back upon them in admiration. The regrets of Charlemagne and Alde and the havoc in the cosmos itself contribute to the mythification of Roland, a transcendent hero whose death causes a hundred thousand men to weep, a woman to die, and a whole nation to stand in wonder. But the means of expressing this transcendence belongs to a traditional technique, shared by other singers and used by them, though in a less effective way. The elegiac tone contributed by the *planctus* formulas, submotifs, and motifs is by no means the sole reason why the *Chanson de Roland* surpasses the other French epics, but the all-pervasive atmosphere which it creates extends from the French council scene to the last verse of the poem,

"Deus," dist li reis, "si penuse est ma vie!"
Pluret des oilz, sa barbe blanche tiret.

This tone is one of the elements most instrumental in setting the *Chanson de Roland*, esthetically, apart from and above all the other creations of its period and genre.

Another motif, of less frequent occurrence than the *planctus* but present in the earliest epic texts, is the hero's death. It is absent from *Le Pélerinage de Charlemagne* and the cyclic poems *Le Couronnement de Louis*, *La Prise d'Orange*, *Le Charroi de Nîmes*, *Le Siège de Barbastre* and *Le Moniage Guillaume*, for the simple reason that in these songs the hero does not die in battle. This trait may simply reflect a change in nature of the epic subject in the twelfth century, for *Raoul de Cambrai* and *Gormont et Isembart*, which belong to no epic cycle, as well as the *Chanson de Guillaume* and the *Chanson de Roland*, which form the primitive nuclei of cycles, all tell of a great hero's death. The essence of a cycle is the exploits of the hero's manhood, and later poets who wish to elaborate upon his deeds with new material are forced to tell of his birth, childhood, youth, and old age, as well as the lives of his ancestors and descendents, the hero's death itself having already been preempted in more ancient songs. Unlike *Raoul de Cambrai, Gormont et Isembart*, and the *Roland*, the *Chanson de Guillaume* relates the death not of the eponymous hero, but of his nephew Vivien. This motif's traditional character can be seen when its occurrences in the three earliest poems are compared.

Like all the high points of the *Chanson de Roland* outside of "Baligant," Roland's demise is recounted in a series of three similar laisses, the second and third of which develop the narrative slowly by the addition of important details. Roland's soul is borne away by angels in the last line of the final laisse.[7]

| | | |
|---|---|---|
| CLXXIV | Ço sent Rollant que la mort le tresprent, | *[Introduction]* |
| | Devers la teste sur le quer li descent. | |
| | Desuz un pin i est alet curant, | *Situation* |
| | Sur l'erbe verte s'i est culchet adenz, | |
| | Desuz lui met s'espee e l'olifan; | *Disposition of arms* |
| 2360 | Turnat sa teste vers la paiene gent; | *Stance* |
| | Pur ço l'at fait que il voelt veirement | |
| | Que Carles diet e trestute sa gent, | |
| | Li gentilz quens, qu'il fut mort cunquerant. | |
| | Cleimet sa culpe e menut e suvent; | *Mea Culpa* |
| 2365 | Pur ses pecchez Deu en puroffrid lo guant. | *[Glove]* |
| | AOI. | |
| CLXXV | Ço sent Rollant de sun tens n'i ad plus. | *[Introduction]* |
| | Devers Espaigne est en un pui agut; | *Situation* |
| | A l'une main si ad sun piz batud: | *Mea Culpa* |
| | "Deus, meie culpe, vers les tues vertuz | *Mea Culpa, apostrophe* |
| 2370 | De mes pecchez, des granz e des menuz | *Mention of sins* |
| | Que jo ai fait des l'ure que nez fui | |
| | Tresqu'a cest jur que ci sui consoüt!" | |
| | Sun destre guant en ad vers Deu tendut: | *[Glove]* |
| | Angles del ciel i descendent a lui. AOI. | *[Angles]* |
| CLXXVI | Li quens Rollant se jut desuz un pin; | *Situation* |

[7] I have already shown that this scene is highly formulaic. See above, pp. 56–58.

| | |
|---|---|
| Envers Espaigne en ad turnet sun vis. | *Stance* |
| De plusurs choses a remembrer li prist: | *[Review of* |
| De tantes teres cum li bers cunquist, | *accomplishments]* |
| De dulce France, des humes de sun lign, | *[Survivors]* |
| 2380 De Carlemagne, sun seignur, kil nurrit. | |
| Ne poet muer n'en plurt e ne suspirt. | |
| Mais lui meïsme ne volt mettre en ubli, | |
| Cleimet sa culpe, si priet Deu mercit: | *Mea Culpa, prayer* |
| "Veire Patene, ki unkes ne mentis, | *Apostrophe* |
| 2385 Seint Lazaron de mort resurrexis, | *Credo* |
| E Daniel des leons guaresis, | |
| Guaris de mei l'anme de tuz perilz | |
| Pur les pecchez que en ma vie fis!" | *Mention of sins* |
| Sun destre guant a Deu en puroffrit; | *[Glove]* |
| 2390 Seint Gabriel de sa main l'ad pris. | |
| Desur sun braz teneit le chef enclin; | *Bodily posture* |
| Juntes ses mains est alet a sa fin. | *[Death]* |
| Deus tramist sun angle Cherubin, | *[Angels]* |
| E seint Michel del Peril; | |
| 2395 Ensembl'od els sent Gabriel i vint. | |
| L'anme del cunte portent en pareïs. | *Soul leaves body* |

The bracketed elements occur only in *Roland*; the others recur in at least one other death scene. The prayer for remission of sins forms the core of this type scene: its key words are *meie culpe,* the essential phrase in the liturgical *confiteor,* punctuated by beating of the breast in the liturgy as well as in *Roland* (v. 2368). This prayer forms a crescendo during the course of the three similar laisses. Stated in laisse CLXXIV, *cleimet sa culpe e menut e suvent,* it takes on a definite form in the succeeding laisse, through direct discourse, including an apostrophe to God, the words *meie culpe,* and the mention of the hero's sins. It reaches its fully expanded state in the final laisse, where it is ornamented with the "epic *credo,*" an affirmation of faith accomplished through a series of clauses each of which mentions one mystery of faith or article of common Christian belief. The two other principal narrative elements are used as framing devices: at the beginning the situating of the scene, Roland recumbent on the grass under a pine tree, and at the end the parting of soul from body.

The three laisses begin in a similar way, placing Roland in scene; mention of approaching death, present in the first two, is omitted in the third, in which the hero actually dies. The final elements replace description and explanation of Roland's physical land offers his glove to God, and in the following laisse the angels descend from paradise to accept it, taking Roland's soul back to heaven with them in the last laisse. Like the confession of sins, the angels are dwelt upon increasingly as the episode progresses, emphasizing that God will receive Roland into paradise. These elements replace description and explanation of Roland's physical state, the advance of death from his burst temple toward his heart, his situation prostrate[8] upon the green grass under a pine, the disposition of his sword and horn, and his defiant attitude, face turned toward the enemy as a conqueror in fulfillment of a promise previously made to Charlemagne and recalled by him when he arrives at Roncevaux to search for his nephew's body (vv. 2863–2867).

The Oxford poet's outstanding virtue in this representation is his rhetorical restraint. Ornamentation is held to a minimum. Roland's exploits, reviewed in detail just before the death scene, in laisse CLXXII, here occupy only one verse (2378). As a leader of men, he thinks only of his emperor, his country, and his lineage. In performances recorded later in the middle ages, this restraint in ornamentation is no longer observed. The late-thirteenth or early-fourteenth-century manuscript of Châteauroux is typical of this trend. For Oxford's

De dulce France, des humes de sun lign,
De Carlemagne, sun seignur, kil nurrit,

[8] For the meaning of *adenz*, see Mario Roques, "L'attitude du héros mourant dans la *Chanson de Roland*," *Romania*, LXVI (1940), 357n, and G.J. Brault, "Old French *adenz, endenz*, Latin *ad dentes, in dentes*," *Romania*, LXXXV (1964), 323ss.

it reads

> De Durendart, dont terres conquis tant;
> De douce France et d'Aude la vaillant,
> Niece Girart de Viene la grant;
> De Charllomeine, qi est as poz passant,
> Qi le nosri soef por bon talant,
> E d'Oliver qe il laissa gisant
> Les l'arcivesqe, desoz le pin sanglant (Ch., vv. 4142–4148).[9]

The five-verse *credo* of laisse CLXXVI, with its two clauses recalling the saving of Lazarus and Daniel, is, in Cambridge, ornamented to nine verses, including clauses devoted to the three children in the fiery furnace, Mary Magdalen, and the crucifixion and burial of Christ. Châteauroux adds recollections of two saints and the Old Testament Jonas:

> Lors reclama le Glorios puissant
> Qi de la Virgine nasqi en Balliant:
> "Si voirement, comme je sui creant,
> Qe covertis seint Feron lo tirant,
> Saint Policarf qi de mal fasoit tant,
> De la fornas ou furent li enfant,
> Tuit sain et sauf s'en issirent joiant,
> Et a Jonas qi aloit preïchant,
> Qe la balene transgloti en estant
> Al port d'Orcaise, desoz Lagarillant,
> Soz Niniven ou errent mescreant,
> La le geta une aube aparant;
> Vostre miracle furent aparissant:
> Saint Lazaron, qi ere vostre servant,
> De mort a vie lo feïstes parllant.
> Damedeu pere, tot issi voiremant,

---

[9] All citations of the *Roland*'s manuscripts follow Raoul Mortier's *Les Textes de la Chanson de Roland* (Paris: Editions de la Geste Francor, 1940–1943).

Come gel croi et sai a esciant,
Garisez m'arme par le vostre commant" (Ch., vv.
    4156–4173).

In these later versions the majesty of Roland's death is diluted
in the maudlin effects of superfluous expansions. The slow, lyric
development of the prayer and the angelic assistance become
progressively blurred as time passes.

In the other epics, the death scene which most resembles Ro-
land's, although still different in character and style, is, ironically,
that of the apostate Isembart in *Gormont et Isembart*. Unfortu-
nately the Brussels fragment breaks off before the scene ends,
leaving us with no way of knowing Isembart's last gestures, but
despite this truncation the contours of the traditional motif are
apparent.

|  |  |
|---|---|
| La u chaï li Margaris, | *Situation* |
| al quarefor de treis chemins, | |
| 630 lez un bruillet espés foilli, | |
| de Damne Deu li membra si | |
| que ja dira li frans gentilz | |
| par quei il dévret bien guarir: | |
| "Sainte Marie, genitrix, | *Apostrophe* |
| 635 mere Deu, dame," Isembarz dist, | *[Prediction fulfilled]* |
| "e! jal me dist uns Sarrazins, | |
| ultre la mer, qui en sorti, | |
| si jeo veneie en cest païs, | |
| que jeo sereie u morz u pris. | |
| 640 Or sai jeo bien que il veir dist. | |
| Aïe! pere Deus," dist il, | *Apostrophe* |
| "qui enz en sainte cruiz fus mis, | *Credo* |
| a vendresdi mort i sofris, | |
| dont tut tun pueple reensis, | |
| 645 en saint sepulchre fustes mis, | |
| a al tierz jorn resurrexis. | |
| Si veirement cum ceo feïs, | *Prayer* |
| si aiez vos de mei merci. | |
| La meie mort pardoins icil, | *[Pardon for killers]* |
| 650 por vostre amor, qui m'unt ocis. | |
| Sainte Marie, genitrix, | *Apostrophe* |

mere Deu, dame," Isembarz dist,
"depreiez en vostre bel filz,                    *Prayer*
qu'il ait merci de cest chaitif!"
655  Guarda aval, en un larriz,
e vit un olivier fuilli.                         *Situation*
Tant se travaille qu'il i vint;
sor la fresche herbe s'est asis;
contre orïent turna sun vis;                     *Stance*
660  a terre vait, culpe bati;                   *Mea Culpa*
puis se dreça un sul petit                       *Bodily posture*
.  .  .

Isembart's death scene begins by a copse, and is then transferred
to the *fresche herbe* under an olive tree,[10] where he confesses
his sins in a prostrate position (*a terre vait*, GI 660), recalling
Oxford's vv. 2357–2358 in which Roland runs from the *quatre
perruns . . . de marbre fait* (vv. 2267–2268) to the pine tree and
prostrates himself on the *erbe verte*. Like Roland, Isembart faces
the enemy, toward the east, for he has debarked from England in
this attempt to take his former homeland by force. As in the
*Chanson de Roland*, the prayer, with *credo* and *mea culpa*, is the
core of this motif, and an especially significant thematic develop-
ment, since Isembart is returning at the moment of death to the
Christian faith of his birth. But the prayer is fragmented and
garbled in this instance. The first apostrophe to the Virgin Mary
leads not to the plea for her intercession on Isembart's behalf,
as one would expect, but to the mention of a previous prediction
of Isembart's disastrous end, almost a *non sequitur*. The prayer
for intercession occurs eighteen lines later, after a verbatim repe-
tition of the same apostrophe to the Virgin; between the two is
the "epic *credo*," of moderate length and ornamented with refer-
ences to Christ's life. The second part of the motif, beginning
with the new situation in vv. 655–658, does not occupy a new
laisse, and it is unlikely, given the extent of the material already

[10] Alphonse Bayot took this olive tree as evidence of traditional language
in *Gormont et Isembart* deriving from "ces chants épiques dont quelques
rares témoignages attestent dès la seconde moitié du XIe siècle," in "Sur
*Gormont et Isembart*," Romania, LI (1925), 273–290.

presented, that it went on to another laisse in the integral manu-
script. Some elements of *Gormont et Isembart*'s death scene are
new, namely the inclusion of the old prediction and the request
that God pardon the killers, hardly applicable in Roland's case,
but the same basic configuration operates here as in the *Chanson
de Roland*. Once again, however, the Oxford poet's sense of
structure raises his creation above the level of perfunctory ac-
tualization of the motif. His treatment of Roland's death in similar
laisses, rather than in one, with slow elaboration of the main
themes, confession of sins, and God's acceptance of Roland's
contrition, produces a meditation which is substantially more sat-
isfying than the essentially narrative spectacle of Isembart's death.

The circumstances of Vivien's death in the *Chanson de Guil-
laume* are radically different from those of Isembart and Roland,
and not a little disconcerting. Vivien, abandoned by his allies
Tiébaut and Estourmi but supported by a small band of followers,
must face one hundred thousand enemy Saracens at the Archamp.
After a fierce battle, he finally succumbs: a berber strikes him on
the head, so that his brains spill out onto the grass; a crowd of
Saracens falls on the body and hacks at it, then carries it away
so that the Christian reinforcements will not be able to recover it
(*CG*: 913–928). Meanwhile Vivien's cousin Girard, who has
gone to Barcelona for help, returns with Guillaume and thirty
thousand knights. After a four-day battle Guillaume is the sole
survivor, but upon returning to the city he finds that his wife
Guibourc has assembled another army of thirty thousand, having
told the knights that they must avenge Vivien's death (*CG*,
1373). This time Guillaume is victorious after defeating the
Saracen king Dérame in a single combat: *Ore out vencu sa
bataille Willame* (*CG*, 1980). Searching the battlefield, he suc-
ceeds in finding Vivien's body:

CXXXI . . . Vivien trove sur un estanc,                     *Situation*
    A la funteine dunt li duit sunt bruiant,
    Desuz la foille d'un oliver mult grant,
    Ses blanches mains croisies sur le flanc,

Plus suef fleereit que nule espece ne piment.
Par mi le cors out quinze plaies granz;
De la menur fust morz uns amirailz,
U reis u quons, ja ne fust tant poanz (*CG:* 1988-1995).

Guillaume begins to pronounce a *planctus* over the body, which takes up the last five verses of the laisse and all ten verses of the following. Laisse CXXXIII contains the death scene proper, for Vivien, despite the explicit details of the earlier section, is still holding on to life. The laisse begins with a *reprise* of Guillaume's regrets, some of which I have omitted as irrelevant to the present question.

| | |
|---|---|
| XXXIII A la funtaine dunt li duit sunt mult cler, | *Situation* |
| Desuz la foille d'un grant oliver, | |
| Ad bers Willame quons Vivien trové. | |
| Par mi le cors out quinze plaies tels, | |
| 2015 De la menur fust morz uns amirelz. | |
| Dunc le regrette dulcement e suef: | *Planctus* |
| "Vivien, sire, mar fustes unques ber. . . . | |
| Dites, bel sire, purriez vus parler | |
| 2025 E reconuistre le cors altisme Deu? | |
| Si tu ço creez, qu'il fu en croiz penez, | |
| En m'almonere ai del pain sacré, | |
| Del demeine que de sa main saignat Deus; | |
| Se de vus le col en aveit passé, | |
| 2030 Mar crendreies achaisun de malfé. | |
| Al quons revint e sen e volenté, | |
| Ovri les oilz, si ad sun uncle esgardé. | |
| De bele boche començat a parler: | *Apostrophe* |
| "Ohi, bel sire," dist Vivien le ber, | *[to Guillaume]* |
| 2035 "Iço conuis ben que veirs e vifs est Deu | *Credo* |
| Qui vint en terre pur sun pople salver, | |
| E de la virgne en Belleem fu nez, | |
| E se laissad en sainte croiz pener; | |
| E de la lance Longis fu foré, | |
| 2040 Que sanc e eve corut de sun lé. | |
| A ses oilz terst, sempres fu enluminé; | |
| 'Merci!' criad, si le pardonad Deus. | |
| Deus, mei colpe, des l'ore que fu nez, | *Apostrophe,* |
| Del mal que ai fait, des pecchez e dé lassetez! | *Mea Culpa* |

2045 Uncle Willame, un petit m'en donez."
"A," dist le cunte, "a bone hore fui nez!
Qui ço creit ja nen ert dampnez."
Il curt a l'eve ses blanches mains a laver,          *[Communion]*
De s'almosnere ad trait le pain segré,
2050 Enz en la boche l'en ad un poi doné.
Tant fist le cunte que le col en ad passé.
L'alme s'en vait, le cors i est remés.               *Soul leaves body*
Veit le Willame, comence a plurer.
Desur le col del balçan l'ad levé,
2055 Qui l'en voleit a Orenge porter.
Sur li corent Sarazin e Escler. . . .

Note that Guillaume's *planctus* intervenes between the situation,
under a tree as in *Roland* and *Gormont et Isembart* (an olive as
in the latter), and the "epic *credo*," which is not addressed di-
rectly to God but is, rather, an answer to Guillaume's question
posed in vv. 2024–2025. Five elements concord with Roland's
death scene, and four of them recur in *Gormont et Isembart*, the
last possibly occurring in the lost section of the Brussels frag-
ment: the situation, the apostrophe, the "epic *credo*," the *mea
culpa*, and the parting of soul from body. Many of the other
elements would be out of place because of the peculiar situation
in the *Chanson de Guillaume*, such as the hero's stance facing
the enemy (the enemy has here been defeated by Guillaume, at
least temporarily), the disposition of arms (Vivien's body has
been moved by the pagans, and there is no indication that he still
has his weapons), and the prayer that the killers be pardoned
(they are heathens, unlike those responsible for Isembart's death).
The *credo* tells the story of Longinus, common in later epic in
this type of prayer,[11] but that slight modification of the pattern
of *Gormont et Isembart* and *Roland* is negligible compared to
the moving scene of the Eucharist administered by Guillaume to
his dying nephew. The nearby stream, in which Guillaume washes

[11] See Edmond-René Labande, "Le *credo* épique: à propos des prières
dans les chansons de geste," *Recueil de travaux offert à M. Clovis Brunel*
(Paris: Société de l'Ecole des Chartes, 1955), II, 62–80.

his hands before feeding Vivien the consecrated bread, reminds one of the stream at Roncevaux from which Turpin attempts to fill the olifant with water before falling exhausted on the grass, where he soon dies. The communion scene lifts Vivien's death to the level of pathos of certain episodes from the *Chanson de Roland*, such as Roland's attempt to destroy his sword Durendal or Charlemagne's *planctus*. Still, the technical perfection of the *Roland*'s similar laisses has no rival here. The strophic structure of this tableau is extremely unbalanced: the first laisse contains both the situation of the death scene and the beginning of Guillaume's *planctus*, the second the *planctus* alone, and the third a lyrical *reprise* of the situation, the conclusion of the *planctus*, the death scene proper, and a passage of 35 verses which recounts a new attack by the Saracens, who capture Guillaume's nephew Gui. Measured thematic development is Oxford's technical strong-point, and there is not a single instance in it of such a gross intrusion of new material upon a major scene. Once again Oxford shows its superiority through proportioned use of traditional means, and not through any device which must be accounted for by the hypothesis of a written intervention.

Raoul de Cambrai's death scene contains only four elements: the apostrophe to God, an affirmation of previous ability perhaps analogous to Roland's review of his former accomplishments, a one-line prayer to the Virgin Mary, and the parting of soul from body, *l'arme s'en part del gentil chevaler* (RC, 3156), separated from the preceding element by 24 lines recounting Bernier's remorse at having dealt the disabling blow, and Ernaus' *coup de grâce*, delivered on the already expiring Raoul. As with the *planctus*, the hero's death is integrated into the narrative, in the only late-twelfth-century example to be found among the *chansons de geste* treated here, and ceases to be an autonomous moment in the epic narration.

As with the *planctus* too, the death scenes of *Roland*, the *Chanson de Guillaume*, and *Gormont et Isembart* are all formulaic,[12] but very few formulas are shared among them. Vivien's confession,

> Deus, mei colpe, des l'ure que fu nez,
> Del mal que ai fait, des pecchez e dé lassetez!

resembles Roland's

> Deus, meie culpe, vers les tues vertuz
> De mes pecchez, des granz e des menuz
> Que jo ai fait des l'ure que nez fui,

but, strictly speaking, the two passages share only one unmistakable formula, *Deus, meie culpe*. Likewise Vivien's posture, *ses blanches mains croisies sur le flanc* (*CG*, 1991), recalls Turpin's *cruisiedes ad ses blanches [mains], les beles* (*R*, 2250), but the similarity is not literal enough to be called formulaic without further evidence. On the other hand, the traditional character of the hero's death scene is apparent. *Gormont et Isembart*, the *Chanson de Roland* and the *Chanson de Guillaume*, despite their common Anglo-Norman scribal traits, may have been recorded in widely separated areas and sung by jongleurs formed in independent traditions; this might account for the relative lack of common formulas in the scenes I have examined, but it is hardly compatible with the stability of the configurations of idea-patterns which stand behind the motifs. One conclusion would account for both the variety of formulas and the stability of motifs: in the Old French epic tradition—I have no reason at present to think that this conclusion can be extended beyond the French genre— the formulas commonly employed for key narrative motifs appear to move vertically, one might even say diachronically, within the tradition of a given song, and pass rather seldom from song to song or from singer to singer independently of the song. The sing-

---

[12] The *Guillaume*'s is 37 percent formulas, *Gormont et Isembart*'s 26 percent.

er would tend, in performing a work which he had heard from the lips of another jongleur, to retain the same formulas. Naturally some cross-pollenization of these formulas would occur, but relatively little, if our material is a guide. The motival configurations, however, are shared horizontally, or synchronically, by the confraternity of jongleurs, who then actualize them with formulas traditional to the song which they happen to be singing. That, aside from the forms which occur in *Roland,* the most archaic *planctus* motif should be found in the *Prise d'Orange,* while the most archaic death scene appears in *Gormont et Isembart,* should not surprise. Whatever the exact dates of composition of these poems, *Roland* is consistently the most primitive (the word is used in its temporal sense) of the *chansons de geste* in its technique. Fragmentary relics of the eleventh-century art have subsisted, in isolated scenes, in other epics, and the two motifs in question provide unmistakable examples.

The essential verticality of the narrative formula tradition is confirmed by an examination of the relationship between the hero's death scenes in two extant performances of the *Chanson de Roland.* Here is the final laisse recounting Roland's death as it appears in the fifteenth-century Cambridge manuscript (the actual performance is undoubtedly much earlier), juxtaposed with Oxford, whose attested formulas are in italics.[13]

| CAMBRIDGE | OXFORD |
|---|---|
| Ly duc se geut soubz .I. pin fielluz; | *Li quens Rollant* se jut desuz un pin; |
| Devers Espaigne avoit tourné sun vis. | *Envers Espaigne en ad turnet sun vis.* |
| 2025 De moult de choses a dementer c'est prins: | De plusurs choses a remembrer li prist: |
| De tant de terre que il avoit conquis, | *De tantes teres* cum li bers cunquist, |
| De France douce, du seignouri païs, | *De dulce France,* des humes de sun lign, |
| De Charlon son oncle o le cler vis. | *De Carlemagne,* sun seignur, kil nurrit. |

[13] For the evidence for these formulas, see note 45 of chapter 2, beginning on page 56 above.

Le cueur du ventre ly est moult attendris,

2030 Mez ly mesmez ne voult mettre en oublis.

Il bat sa coupe, si crie Dieu mercis:

"Vray doux Pere, qui onc ne mentis,

Saint Lasaron de mort resurrexis

Et Daniel du leon garantis,

2035 Les .III. enfans qui furent en feu mis,

A Marie ses pechez demeis,

Par nos pechez fus en la croix mis

Et en sepulchre fustez ensevelis!

Si com c'est voir, beau Pere Jhesu Cris,

2040 Gardez moy l'ame des infernaux peris!"

*Ne poet muer n'en plurt e ne suspirt.*

*Mais lui meïsme ne volt mettre en ubli,*

*Cleimet sa culpe, si priet Deu mercit:*

*"Veire Patene, ki unkes ne mentis,*

Seint Lazaron de mort resurrexis,

*E Daniel des leons guaresis,*

Guaris de mei l'anme de tuz perilz

*Pur les pecchez que en ma vie fis!"*

*Sun destre guant a Deu en puroffrit;*

*Seint Gabriel de sa main l'ad pris.*

A cest mot est ly duc esvenoys,

Son elme enbronche, ses mains met sur son piz;

L'ame s'en part, le corps est enpalis.

Dieu y tranmist .I. angre cherubis

2045 Et saint Michiel est en pres lui assis:

L'ame du conte portent en paradis.

*Desur sun braz teneit le chef enclin;*

*Juntes ses mains est alet a sa fin.*

Deus tramist sun angle Cherubin,

*E seint Michel del Peril;*

*Ensembl'od els sent Gabriel i vint.*

L'anme del cunte portent en pareïs.

The motif's basic structure is followed in Cambridge, although the "epic *credo*" has been expanded and the transference of Roland's glove to God through the angel Gabriel omitted. Of the 24 formulas attested within the limits of Oxford, 9 are present in the later text and 5 more are in verses omitted in Cambridge. In addition 6 phrases which are found only once in Oxford have also been retained in the oral tradition until the performance reflected in Cambridge: *saint Lazaron, de mort resurrexis, Dieu y tranmist, .I. angre cherubis, l'ame du conte, portent en paradis,* and constitute formulas in the context of the *Roland* tradition. Other hemistichs share one or two words only:

| CAMBRIDGE | OXFORD |
|---|---|
| soubz .I. pin fielluz | se jut desuz *un pin* |
| *de* moult de *choses* | *de* plusurs *choses* |
| *a* dementer c'est *prins* | *a* remembrer li *prist* |
| que il avoit *conquis* | cum li bers *cunquist* |
| *du leon* garantis | *des leons* guaresis |
| gardez *moy* l'ame | guaris de *mei* |
| des infernaux *peris* | l'anme de tuz *perilz* |

indicating an evolution in the poem's language, through the centuries, gradual enough to have resulted in the preservation of a few words even in phrases otherwise modified. Only four verses are changed in their entirety: 2029 and 2041–43, which seem to be a gloss on the content of Oxford's *desur sun braz teneit le chef enclin.* On the other hand, in vv. 2027–2028, two epithets, extremely common in the later *chansons de geste,* have been employed by the poet of Cambridge in place of phrases present in the earlier tradition as attested by Oxford: *du segnouri país* and *son oncle o le cler vis.* The Cambridge laisse, then, differs from Oxford in the ornamentation of the "epic *credo,*" in three complete verses, and in much of the phraseology of several other verses. It resembles Oxford in that the basic narrative content is unchanged, and the two versions share 16 formulas, of which 9 are attested as formulas within Oxford. The hero's death scene in Cambridge resembles, formulaically, that of Oxford much more closely than Oxford's resembles those of *Gormont et Isembart* or the *Chanson de Guillaume.* I have chosen this one example out of hundreds of possibilities. One has only to compare any later *Roland* manuscript with Oxford, with the aid of the line concordances established by Raoul Mortier in his edition of the various manuscripts, to see that, protean as it is, the oral tradition of the *Roland* is highly cohesive when its formulas and motifs are placed together against those of any other song. The jongleurs who performed in the years between the writing down of Oxford and that of Cambridge have improvised somewhat in this scene, but they have also kept the form and much of the language of their predecessors. Memory has played an essential role, but it has been the memory of a whole pattern, unencumbered by the concern for literal reproduction—the memory of an oral tradition of singers and not of a society whose mode of thought is literate.

The formulas found in the *planctus* and the hero's death scenes are generally of the type that directly advance the action of the epic plot, because they belong to motifs essential to the particular tone and meaning of these works. On the other hand, formulas whose purpose is basically ornamental may present a quite different profile than those attached to particular motifs. In Cambridge and Châteauroux the "epic *credo*" has been ornamented with additional articles of faith: two clauses suffice to make a *credo*, or perhaps even one, but the number can be expanded indefinitely to fit the jongleur's taste and the audience's perseverance. The Oxford manuscript is the least ornamented; it is compact and gets on with the basic incidents of the plot more quickly than the later performances. That this evolution toward longer, less tightly woven, more highly ornamented plots is present in the *chanson de geste* as a whole and not just in the *Roland* tradition is no new insight. But no study of formulaic texture would be complete without a comparative analysis of just *how* ornamental formulas are used in the *Roland* and the later *chansons de geste*.

Certain formulas seem to have been current in the epic language expressly because they were suited for use in ornamentation. Four types stand out in particular: the epithet occupying an entire hemistich, benedictions or maledictions visited upon epic characters, oaths sworn upon the invocation of saints, and phrases indicating alacrity. Because the *Roland* is less ornamented than other *chansons de geste*, I shall analyse these formulas in the *Moniage Guillaume*, comparing it to *Roland*.

Many of *Roland*'s epithets do not stand by themselves in separate hemistichs, but are integrated with the person or object which they characterize: thus in the first hemistich position *Guenes li fels, de dulce France*, and *sur l'erbe verte*, and at the assonance *e Anseïs li fiers* and *de Jurfaleu le blund*. Those which do occupy entire hemistichs are more versatile for the singer to use, because they are syntactically more flexible. These are of three types: phrases composed largely of adjectives and coordinating conjunctions, such as *li proz e li curteis*; relative clauses, such as *ki ad la barbe blanche* and *ki a or est gemmee*; and, closely related to this last type, prepositional phrases, such as *a la barbe flurie* or *as perres d'or gemmees*. There are 48 epithets occupying a whole hemistich in the *Chanson de Roland*.

In the *Moniage Guillaume*, 85 such epithets are distributed in an extraordinarily concentrated fashion, with 21 characterizing the hero Guillaume alone, and 39 modifying the name of God. The remaining 25 are partitioned among five other characters, the saints who are invoked in oaths, the land of Provence, and various plants and objects. Ornamentation of God's name was obviously of particular use to the jongleurs of the *Moniage Guillaume* tradition, on a quantitative basis nearly twice as useful as the characterization of the poem's hero, Guillaume, through epithets. The reason for this is not that the *Moniage Guillaume*'s subject is religious—for it is so only superficially—but that references to God provided the jongleurs with an extensive system of second hemistich ornamentation adaptable to many situations. The most predictable use is in prayers. Thus before Guillaume's combat with the giant, he implores God's help:

"Dieus," dist Guillaumes, "qui tout le mont formastes,
Secorés moi, biaus pere esperitables!" (*MG*: 2600–2601)

But the mention of God's ornamented name can be simply an introduction to a rhetorical question,

> "Dieus," dist li famles, "qui el ciel fais vertus,
> Mes gentieus sire que est il devenus?" (MG: 1620–1621),

or an exclamation,

> "Diex," dist Guillaumes, "qui el ciel fais vertus,
> Ains que g'i viegne, crien qu'il ne soit vencus" (MG: 5165–5166),

or an oath,

> "Par celui Dieu qui tout a a garder,
> Ja por larron ne me quier a celer" (MG: 1197–1198),

or a reflection that the characters' fate depends on God,

> Se Dieus n'en pense, qui en crois fu penés,
> Mar commencha li famles a canter (MG: 1206–1207).

These uses are of such general nature that they might be inserted at will in the most disparate of situations. In accordance with their generality, such epithets, all occurring in the second hemistich, are available in a multiplicity of assonances. *Qui estoras le mont* (MG 1681) is inappropriate for a laisse assonating in A, but the word order can be modified to *qui le mont estora* (MG 4070). *Qui tout as a jugier* (MG: 2391, 6521 [*tout a a*]) becomes, for an I.E assonance, *qui tout a en baillie* (MG: 647, 4721 [*as*]). Fourteen of the poem's nineteen assonances, accounting for all but 274 of the 6629 verses, are represented in this second hemistich system:

> A                    qui tout le mont forma (6587, 6607 [as])
>                      qui le mont estora (4070)

| A.E | qui me fist a s'image (2259) |
| | qui Noé mist en l'arce (2595, 5467) |
| | qui tout le mont formastes (2600, 5457) |
| AI | qui fait croistre le glai (843) |
| AN, EN | ou la moie ame apent (375) |
| AN.E | qui fist et home et feme (1164) |
| É | qui en crois fu penés (1206, 5373) |
| | qui tout a a garder (1197) |
| É.E | qui fist ciel et rousee (2886) |
| | qui mainte ame a sauvee (2902) |
| I | qui onques ne menti (38, 5678) |
| | qui en la crois fu mis (3691) |
| I.E | qui tout a en baillie (647, 4721 [as]) |
| IÉ | qui le mont dois jugier (160, 4176, 3050 [doit]) |
| | qui tout a a baillier (180) |
| | qui tout as a jugier (2391, 6521 [a]) |
| Ó, ON | qui estoras le mont (1681) |
| | qui soufris passion (3249, 3982 [soufri]) |
| O.E, ON.E | qui fist et mer et onde (4224) |
| OI | qui haut siet et lonc voit (1875, 2552, 6446, 6488) |
| U | qui el ciel mains lassus (104) |
| | qui el ciel fais vertus (138, 1620, 5165) |

That this system is not, like the corresponding Homeric phenomenon, endowed with "economy" (the existence of one formula for any given set of semantic, syntactic, metrical, and, here, assonantal, requirements) does not detract from its effectiveness. The Old French versification is less exigent than the Greek hexameter and, because of this, does not require "economy." These second hemistich formulas, as well as those attached to heroes' names (such as, for Guillaume, *a la ciere hardie, au cort nes le baron* [or *le marcis*], *a la fiere persone* [or *poissance*], *au corage aduré, qui cuer ot de baron* [or *de lion*], *qui mout a fier talent,*

or *qui tant amé nos a*), places, plants, and objects, are superfluous
to the informational content of the passage in which they occur,
for they express a quality intrinsic to the noun they modify. But
they give the jongleur the opportunity for an easy assonance and
contribute to that aura of perfection so common in epics of the
most disparate geographical origin.

Another, similar, second hemistich system in the *Moniage
Guillaume* involves the swearing of oaths, usually invoking the
name of a saint chosen for its sound rather than for any particular
appropriateness to the situation. The patterns *par le cors saint . . .*
(*Denise, Eloi, Fagon*, etc.), *foi que doi saint . . . , par les sains
de . . . (Bretaigne, Polise), por sainte . . . (carité, patrenostre)*,
and such unvarying formulas as *par la loi que jou tieng* and *par
les iex de mon cief*, a total of 63 occurrences, appear in 13 of the
*Moniage Guillaume's* 19 assonances and constitute a means of
ornamentation as versatile as the epithets. There is no trace of
this system of oaths in the *Chanson de Roland*, whose characters
swear by their right hands or their beards alone (cf. *par ceste
barbe: Roland*, vv. 249, 261, 3954).

Invocations of divine power, Christian or Muslim, for male-
diction or blessing, form a third major ornamental system of
assonating hemistichs. They take the form of a wish,

> "Qui es tu? va, Mahoumet te maldie!" (*MG* 3830)
> "Fil a putain, Dieus vous doinst mal torment!" (*MG* 371)

or of an oath introduced by *se*, somewhat analogous to the Eng-
lish construction "So help me God" or "As God is my witness":

> "Mais jou quit bien, se Dieus me beneïe,
> Qu'en l'ermitage estes mors, biaus dos sire" (*MG*: 4728–
> 4729).

Here is the system of the *Moniage Guillaume*, analysed according
to the verbs employed and the syntactic types:

| verb | independent clause | dependent clause |
|---|---|---|
| *maleïr,* | Jhesus le maleïe (638) | que Jhesus maleïe (292, 625, 2179) |
| *maldire* | Mahoumet te maldie (3830) | qui Mahon maleïe (3381) |
| *beneïr,* | | que Jhesus beneïe (3010) |
| *benir* | | se Dieus me beneïe (283, 2168, 3421, 3833, 4728, 6365 [te], 6415) |
| | | se Mahom me benie (3407) |
| *pooir* | Dieus le puist beneïr (1784) | cui Diex puist beneïr (4606) |
| *(plus verb)* | Dieus le vous puist merir (4501, 4570) | qui te puist beneïr (5872) |
| | | qui Diex puist honorer (2070) |
| | Dieus vous puist honorer (1094) | que Dieus puist maleïr (1744, 2808) |
| | | cui Dieus puist vergoignier (1451) |
| | | cui Dieus puist craventer (1137) |
| | | se Dieus me puist aidier (196, 5601 [te]) |
| *doner* | Dieus vous doinst mal torment (371) | cui Dieus doinst mal estraine (1167) |
| *(plus object)* | li cors Dieu mal te donst (2601, 3964) | que Dieus doinst mal entente (2982) |
| *aveir mal dehé* | tu aies mal dehé (3524, 6041) | dont aie mal dehé (3572) |
| | ses cors ait mal dehé (1279) | |
| *faire mal* | Mahoumet mal te face (4005, 6097) | que li cors Dieu mal fache (3146, 4629 [qui]) |
| *craventer* | li cors Dieu vous cravent (353) | que Damedieus cravente (1137) |
| *otroier (mal)* | | que Jhesus mal t'otroit (1833) |
| *destorner (de mal)* | | cui Dieus destort de mal (4044) |
| *sofraindre* | | cui Damedieus sofraigne (1146) |

The complexity of this system is contingent upon the alternatives present in its constituent elements: they can express positive or

negative wishes or oaths, from either the Christian or the Saracen
point of view, in dependent or independent clauses. Thus the
Islamic "god" can be called *Mahoumet* or *Mahon*, the Christian
divinity, *Dieus, Jhesus, Damedieus*, or even *li cors Dieu* accord-
ing to the syllable count of the other words in the hemistich. The
predicates are of two syllables (*mal fache*), three (*maleïr, vergoig-
nier, craventer, beneïr, honorer*), or four (*puist* plus a three-
syllable infinitive, or *doinst* plus a three-syllable complement).
The alternative forms *maleïr* and *maldire, beneïr* and *benir*, are
also accounted for by this need for verbal flexibility; *maldie* and
*benie* contain one less syllable than their counterparts *maleïe*
and *beneïe*.[14] The more versatile the standard components, the
more easily the jongleur can adapt them to each other in a given
situation. He can utilize this system with the name of any char-
acter and in the speech of any character: Saracens bless their
coreligionists and damn the French, Christians wish their ene-
mies to perdition and call upon God to succor their allies. But
for all its usefulness, there is little more than a trace of this
system in the *Chanson de Roland* (see vv. 1608, 1632, 1667,
1906, 3641).

The three systems considered up to this point have all shown
dependency on nouns, generally on the name of God or of an
epic character. The most extensive system of assonantal orna-
mentation for actions in the *Moniage Guillaume* expresses the
idea "he did not hesitate." Its nature is sufficiently general—
it is almost devoid of meaning—to be inserted after just about
any first hemistich containing an action. Thus the last part of

De lui s'en part si n'i fist nul demor (*MG* 3988)

adds little, if anything, to the sense of the line. I have listed
elsewhere[15] the formulas of alacrity in the *Couronnement de*

---

[14] The epic language contains many such alternate forms, many of which
may be explained through the needs of various formula systems.
[15] "Formulas in the *Couronnement de Louis*," *Romania*, LXXXVII (1966),

*Louis*, which contains a strikingly similar system, in which 45 such phrases occur, 23 of them in conjunction with adverbial expressions of place of the type *De ci a Rome ne se sont aresté*. The seven assonances into which they are inserted account for 89 percent of the *Couronnement de Louis'* verses. There are 50 such phrases in the *Moniage Guillaume* distributed among 13 assonances. In *Roland* I can only find seven (vv. 338, 1415, 2021, 2805, 3140, 3366, 3519).

That these four systems of ornamentation all function in the second hemistich position is easily explained: the informational content of the Old French epic is generally carried in the first hemistichs. A jongleur's anticipation from the *Moniage Guillaume* with several phrases of the type I have just analysed illustrates this principle:

> Hui mais orrés une fiere canchon,
> Tele ne fu trés le tans Salemon,
> Comme Guillaumes, QUI CUER OT DE LION,
> Fu puis hermites, SI CON LISANT TROVONS,
> Dedens Provence, CEL ESTRANGE ROION,
> Et com paien, LI ENCRIEME FELON,
> Le tinrent plus de set ans en prison,
> Dedens Palerne, en la tor Synagon (*MG*: 1722–1729).

The tale anticipated in this text is told mostly in the first hemistichs. In lines 1724–1727 the second hemistichs, in small capitals above, are superfluous to the narrative, for the idea would come across even if textual damage had deprived us of them: *comme Guillaumes . . . fu puis hermites . . . dedens Provence . . . et com paien . . . le tinrent plus de set ans en prison*. Four out of eight

---

331–332. See, in the *Moniage Guillaume*, vv. 53, 106, 568, 823, 924, 945, 981, 1124, 1291, 1294, 1322, 1366, 1528, 1541, 1628, 1707, 1709, 1721, 1885, 2181, 2293, 2456, 2707, 2873, 2899, 2961, 2981, 3179, 3202, 3209, 3230, 3464, 3870, 3984, 3988, 4133, 4414, 4452, 4740, 4851, 5188, 5489, 5534, 5615, 5649, 6039, 6221, 6225, 6281.

assonating hemistichs are decorative (three epithets and an affir-
mation of *auctoritas*), but all eight of the first hemistichs are
essential.

The esthetic effect of this style upon a modern reader is often
unfortunate. In the following scene from the *Moniage Guil-
laume*, the beginning of Guillaume's return to the abbey after he
has fulfilled his mission of buying fish for the monks, a number
of second hemistichs, written in small capitals, could be dispensed
with without detracting from the plot:

> Vait s'ent Guillaumes, QUI PLUS NE VOLT ATENDRE,
> 1125 Lor voie aqueillent ENTRE LUI ET SON FAMLE,
> Et li boins ostes a Jhesu le comande,
> Qui le conduie ET ENCOR LE RAMAINE,
> Qu'a lui servir vauroit metre s'entente.
> Vait s'ent li quens, QUI DE L'ESPLOITIER PENSE,
> 1130 Que a Aignienes puisse repairier tempre,
> Et a ses freres delivrer la vïande.
> Ne mais anchois qu'en l'abeïe rentre,
> Avra le cuer dolent DEDENS LE VENTRE
> Et grant paor qu'il ne perde les menbres;
> 1135 N'i vauroit estre POR TRESTOUT L'OR D'ESPAIGNE,
> Se de son cors ne puet faire deffense,
> Car li larron, QUE DAMEDIEUS CRAVENTE,
> Sont ens el bos, QUI LES GENS I MEHAIGNENT.
> Ancui feront Guillaume grant tormente,
> 1140 Il l'ociront, SE DIEUS DE LUI NE PENSE,
> Car li ber n'a ne espee ne lance,
> Ne arme nule DONT IL SE PUIST DESFENDRE,
> Et cil sont quinse qui ens el bos l'atendent.
> Or le conduie li gloriouse dame
> 1145 QUI DIEU PORTA NUEF MOIS DEDENS SON VENTRE,
> Car li convens, CUI DAMEDIEUS SOFRAIGNE,
> Vauroient bien qu'il fust mors sans atente.
> Et si ne sevent cele ocoison ou prendre:

Ainc ne lor fist anui NE TART NE TEMPRE,
1150 Ne lor toli VAILLANT UNE CASTAIGNE,
Fors por itant que trop lor fait despendre.
Tant va li quens ENTRE LUI ET SON FAMLE,
Qu'en la valee entra sans demorance:
Grant sont li caisne et li fau et li tramble,
1155 Li destrois fors, la valee soutaigne.
Li quens i entre, de Damedieu se saine;
Dist ses vallés: "Sire, par sainte Elaine,
Mes cuers me dit c'on vos asaura tempre,
Li cors me tramble SI ME FALENT LI MEMBRE.
1160 J'amasse mieus, PAR LES SAINS DE BRETAIGNE,
Tous li covens fust ars EN FU DE LAIGNE,
Que nous fuissiens venu sans armes prendre."
Et dist Guillaumes: "Frere, ne t'espaente,
Car se Dieu plaist, QUI FIST ET HOME ET FEME,
1165 Bien passerons parmi le val soutaigne."
Hui mais orrés de Guillaume d'Orenge
Et des larrons, CUI DIEUS DOINST MALE ESTRAINE.

The ornamental hemistichs do not harm the narrative, but for a modern reader they slow it down considerably. There is no real need to say at this point, for example, that the thieves attack people in the forest (this is already known from the previous laisse), that Guillaume will die if God does not help him, that Guillaume is with his valet, that God created man and woman, or that the monks should be burned in a wood fire rather than any other kind. These phrases simply reflect the desires of the medieval audience: that God crush the thieves or give them what they deserve, that he abandon the perfidious monks. Still, the passage was originally meant to be heard, and the ornamentation must be considered in this light, as primarily auditory rather than narrative. It supplies the sound patterns of the assonance essential to the conventions of this poetry. When the jongleur, performing before a present audience, is at a loss for a second hemistich which carries narrative meaning, he simply uses an ornamental phrase.

The resulting dilution of texture is disagreeable to readers accustomed to the modern literary esthetic, and such hemistichs as these have been termed clichés, *chevilles,* or fillers, but they are an indispensable aid to oral composition. Even the *Chanson de Roland,* generally compact in its narration, has epithets occupying an entire second hemistich, invocations of divine power, or formulas of alacrity. Several other types of ornamental hemistichs found in the *Moniage Guillaume* are not unknown to the Oxford jongleur, such as the mention of an object of little value for emphasis (*ne lor toli vaillant une castaigne, MG* 1150; *un dener ne li valt, R* 1262, 3338, 3435) or the hyperbolic reference to riches which the character would refuse if he could only have his wish (*por trestout l'or d'Espaigne, MG* 1135; *pur tut l'or desuz ciel, R* 2666; *plus aimet il traïsun e murdrie/qu'il ne fesist trestut l'or de Galice, R* 1475–1476). None of these systems, however, is as extensive in *Roland* as in the later *chansons de geste,* and some cannot even be called systems in the earlier poem, so sparse are their occurrences. But the Oxford jongleur's ornamentation differs in degree and not in essence from that of his fellow jongleurs: his restrained use of this fundamental process of the oral style appeals to modern taste more than does the style of later singers.

All four systems of second hemistich ornamentation grow in extent during the course of the twelfth century.[16] There are no oaths upon the names of saints, of the type described in this chapter, in *Roland, Gormont et Isembart,* or the *Pélerinage de Charlemagne,* all three very early texts and roughly contemporaneous. This assonating system appears for the first time in the *Chanson de Guillaume* with *[fei] que dei saint Simeon (CG* 3429)

16 Gaston Paris attributes the predominance, in the late *chansons de geste,* of second hemistichs which are unnecessary for the narrative to the employment of monorhymed laisses. *Histoire poétique de Charlemagne* (Paris: Franck, 1865), p. 25, quoted in C.W. Aspland, *A Syntactical Study of Epic Formulas* (St. Lucia: University of Queensland Press, 1970), p. 23.

and *par sainte charité* (CG 3483, 3504), continues in the *Charroi de Nîmes* with *par l'apostre saint Jaque* (CN 1343) and the *Prise d'Orange* with three examples, and suddenly blossoms into full glory in the *Moniage Guillaume* and *Raoul de Cambrai*. In the last poem, the characters swear by saints Dennis, Simon, Hilary, Geri, Peter, Amant, Gervais, Richier, Thomas, and the Virgin Mary, for a total of 47 occurrences, to say nothing of oaths sworn *por sainte loiauté* (three), *por sainte charité* (one), *par les sains de Baviere* (one) and *par les sains de Ponti* (one). Invocations of divine power show a similar, although not so spectacular, development. Absent from the *Chanson de Roland* and *Gormont et Isembart*, they first appear in the *Pélerinage de Charlemagne* with *sire, Deus vos guarisset* (PC 305), and *Deus vos i aconduist* (PC 185) and in the *Chanson de Guillaume* with *qui Dampnedeu confunde* (CG 3171, 3187) and *Dampnedeu te maldie* (CG 2598), and expand in the *Prise d'Orange* with five occurrences, *Raoul de Cambrai* and the *Siège de Barbastre* with eight apiece, and the *Charroi de Nîmes* with eleven. Ornamentation of the name of God through second hemistich clausal epithets rises from two examples in the *Roland, ki unkes ne mentit* (1865, 2384 [*mentis*]) and in *Gormont et Isembart, qui ne menti* (GI 177, 208), and none at all in the *Pélerinage de Charlemagne*, to four in the *Chanson de Guillaume*, five in the *Charroi de Nîmes*, fifteen in the *Siège de Barbastre*, twenty-four in the *Prise d'Orange* and fifty-four in *Raoul de Cambrai*. Formulas of alacrity do not appear in *Gormont et Isembart* but are present in all the other texts, including *Roland*, their number growing steadily to thirty-two in *Raoul de Cambrai* and fifty in the *Moniage Guillaume*. In the later poems these systems and others like them dominate the texture of the epic style, converting it into a slower, less compact, more highly decorative vehicle. This gradual transformation must have coincided with a change in public taste, a natural desire on the part of the audiences for more elaborate retellings of their favorite epic tales. I suspect it also reflects the gradual change from a traditional poetry endemic to the population and sung by amateurs,[17] to the development of a professional class of singers, in greater need of the means of elaborating their material at the drop of a coin.

The ornamental formula systems correspond to what Milman Parry and Albert B. Lord call "formulaic expressions," which I prefer to name "syntactic formulas": lines or half lines which "follow the same basic patterns of rhythm and syntax and have at least one word in the same position in the line common with other lines or half lines."[18] This is an accurate description of the relationship between hemistichs in systems like the following:

> qui tout a a baillier (SB 2098, 4018, 4274)
> qui France a a baillier (RC 330 [baillir], 1675, 2105, 4854,
>      5111, 5222; SB 3595, 4481)
> qui tout a en baillie (PO 1275; RC 5286; MG 180; SB 3295,
>      3329, 3339)
> qui France a en baillie (SB 3916, 5168, 5637)
> qui tout a a garder (MG 1197; SB 3681)

[17] The well-known phrase from the chronicler Hariulf (1088) concerning the legend of Gormont et Isembart, which "patriensium memoria quotidie recolitur et canitur," can hardly refer to the performances of a professional class of singers. As late as 1125 the Vita Sancti Wilhelmi mentions that choruses of young people sing about Guillaume d'Orange, and this appears to signify that his legend was sung by amateurs: "Qui chori iuvenum, qui conventus populorum praecipue militum ac nobilium virorum, quae vigiliae sanctorum dulce non resonant et modulatis vocibus non decantant qualis et quantus fuerit?" And yet William of Malmesbury and Wace report, without giving any sign that they consider it unusual, that a jongleur named Taillefer sang about Roland at the battle of Hastings in 1066. Their testimony dates from long after the event, but both professional and amateur singers probably composed heroic poetry during the latter half of the eleventh century. While the dating of Old French epic texts is far from satisfactory, the earliest of our nine songs, Roland, Gormont et Isembart, and the Chanson de Guillaume, may date from the end of the eleventh century, and the Pèlerinage de Charlemagne was probably written down shortly after the year 1100. From the evidence of ornamental style, I would judge it possible that some of these songs, as they have come down to us, could have been sung by non-professionals rather than by jongleurs.

[18] Albert B. Lord, The Singer of Tales, Harvard Studies in Comparative Literature, XXIV (Cambridge: Harvard University Press, 1960), p. 47.

    *qui France a a garder* (CG 826, 1607; RC 120, 3561; SB
                  3132, 3229, 3608, 3644, 3655, 3824)
  *qui tout a a jugier* (PO 395, 1021, 1541, 1572, 1607 [as]; CN
              443; RC 65, 1132, 1740, 1918, 5154;
              MG 2391 [as], 6521; SB 1891, 3589)
*qui tout a a sauver* (SB 3121, 3259)
*qui France a a tenir* (RC 4783)

In schematic form, the system is organized:

$$
\text{qui}\quad
\begin{Bmatrix} \text{tout} \\ \text{France} \end{Bmatrix}
\quad a \quad
\begin{cases}
a \begin{cases} \text{baillier} \\ \text{garder} \\ \text{jugier} \\ \text{sauver} \\ \text{tenir} \end{cases} \\[2ex]
\text{en} \quad \text{baillie}
\end{cases}
$$

These syntactic patterns, often the same word sequences, and many other ornamental hemistichs of the four types treated in this chapter, are shared by many songs in the Old French tradition. Unlike formulas attached to particular motifs, ornamental formulas are common to the confraternity of singers. Like the idea patterns behind the motifs, they tend to be horizontal or synchronic in nature, depending for their propagation not just on the transmission of the particular song in which they happen to occur, but on the exchange of techniques among singers. They may be passed on within the tradition of the song too, but it is less important, and therefore less common, that they be retained from performance to performance than is the case with formulas which embody key plot developments. When one speaks of the spontaneous composition of oral-traditional epics, the spontaneity is much more evident in the ornamental formulas than it is in motival formulas. Memory does play an essential role in oral transmission, but the pattern of these systems is flexible, so that they can be manipulated by the singers at will. They are not mnemonic systems, but improvisational systems.

When the *Chanson de Roland* is viewed within the context of the possibilities open to epic singers in twelfth-century France, the Oxford poet's outstanding qualities are easily distinguishable. And yet for all his merits, one sees again and again that this poet's genius lay not in the employment of new or unique tools, but in his use of traditional techniques.[19] Restraint of ornamentation is a trait shared by the poets of *Gormont et Isembart*, the *Chanson de Guillaume*, and the *Pélerinage de Charlemagne*, and was therefore characteristic of the oral style of his time. The coherence with which he presents the traditional motifs may well spring from the same source. But he possesses a sense of proportion, a facility for constructing a balanced poem. His song is appealing partly because of its elegiac tone, achieved through standard formulas and motifs but striking because of the way those formulas and motifs are ordered. When his formulas are considered analytically, apart from their contexts in the poem, little, perhaps nothing, differentiates them from the formulas of any other decasyllabic Old French epic. But his manner of organizing them sets him apart as a consummate poet. This manner is difficult to seize because it is at work everywhere in the poem, but it is seen at its best in the sequences of similar laisses, such as Roland's death or Charlemagne's *planctus*, and in the dialogues of the council scenes. On the level of detail, of individual hemistichs, the *Roland* poet's style is not his own but the tradition's. When these hemistichs form whole laisses and the laisses are built into scenes, there is a pronounced contrast between the *Chanson de Roland* and the other *chansons de geste* considered here, and it is all to the advantage of the Oxford poet.

---

[19] C.W. Aspland notes that in *Roland* "the formulas are not yet so abundant as to become tiresome." This is an interesting remark, one which mirrors my own *impressions* despite the fact that I know Roland is substantially more formulaic than the *Moniage Guillaume*, whose repetitions, I am sure Dr. Aspland would agree, do often become tiresome. The difference in readers' reactions to the two songs can be accounted for not by the *number* of formulas, but by the heavy incidence, in the *Moniage*, of ornamental formulas. See *A Syntactical Study of Epic Formulas*, p. 149.

# 6: Consequences

IT HAS BEEN my purpose to present concrete evidence that the Oxford *Chanson de Roland* is as much a product of oral tradition as certain other *chansons de geste* of the eleventh and twelfth centuries through a study of its formulaic style in the context of its own genre. The exceptional beauty of *Roland*, its stature as the best-structured and perhaps earliest French epic text, have led some scholars to consider it an anomaly, the creation of a gifted writer or, at least, the end product of a tradition culminating in a *remanieur de génie*. If by *remanieur* one means a literary poet whose means of creation is pen and parchment, nothing in the style of the poem as we have it justifies this point of view, for the *Roland* has the same types of formulas as the major twelfth-century *chansons de geste* even though it is more sparing in ornamental formulas. It is quantitatively more formulaic than seven of the nine epics with which it is most easily compared.

The differences between the *chanson de geste* and the courtly romance are well known. The romance centers on internal psychological analysis of characters, emphasizes personal feelings and individual destinies, appeals to a sophisticated audience, and is usually based upon fictional adventures embroidered with the utmost fantasy. It expresses itself in a fluid versification based upon the riming couplet, which permits a constant change in the desinance of verses and lends itself to nuances of word order, enjambement, and syntactic variety. The *chanson de geste* presents its characters from the outside, through their actions or their dialogue, embodies the aspirations of large corporate bodies (the Christian state against outside invaders or the regional forces working centrifugally against a strong monarch), appeals mainly to a rather unsophisticated public, is based ultimately upon the feats of historical personages, and finds expression in standard formulas, motifs, and themes. What is the reason for the existence of two vernacular narrative genres in an age when the French language is just beginning to find the means of expressing itself in writing? To anyone who understands the theory of oral-formulaic poetry, who knows that the formulaic nature of the Greek and Yugoslavian epic languages is demonstrable, that there is strong evidence of Mycenean historical elements in the *Iliad*, that the paratactic style is a feature of the oral epic of many countries, that there is a decided lack of internal analysis in Homer's characterizations, and who then sees analogous problems and concerns in the Old French epics, the answer is within reach. There are two narrative genres in twelfth-century France because, as Milman Parry was the first to realize, there are two kinds of literature: written and oral. The *chanson de geste* as we have it is the culmination of an oral tradition, a tradition that may have been over three hundred years old by the time the first written ancestor of Oxford was taken down. The twelfth-century romance, on the other hand, represents the earliest literate attempt to create stories with sophisticated entertainment value in the vernacular language of France. These two literatures live distinct lives side by side, although they are not without influence on each other.[1]

The case of the *Siège de Barbastre* and *Buevon de Conmarchis* provides a particularly illustrative example. The plot of *Buevon*,

[1] Jeanne Wathelet-Willem's contention that the analogy between the *Iliad* and the *chansons de geste* is invalid because there is no significant written literature contemporary with the Homeric poems is itself insufficient, for it fails to take the Yugoslavian material into account. The analogy is not only with Homer, but also with singers from living epic traditions. See the special issue of *La Table Ronde*, consecrated to "*l'épopée vivante*," December, 1958.

written around 1280 by Adenet le Roi, is based on a lost manu-
script of the *Siège de Barbastre*. We have only the first 3947
verses of Adenet's work, which correspond to the beginning of
the extant manuscript C of the *Siège de Barbastre*, up to around
verse 2700 of the Perrier edition.[2] Many of Adenet's verses are
frank borrowings from the *Siège de Barbastre*,[3] but he has re-
worked and expanded his source considerably. One would expect
to find fewer formulas in Adenet's work, presumably created in
writing by an author known to have written a romance, *Cleo-
mades*, than in the *Siège de Barbastre*, with its formulas of oral
delivery (*plest vos oïr chançon, ci conmence chançon*, etc.) and
with a textual tradition compatible with oral transmission, for
which one cannot construct a coherent stemma of manuscript
filiation. The expectation is not disappointed; *Buevon*, repetitious
to a degree of 15 percent, only differs from the *Roman d'Enéas*
and the *Roman d'Alexandre* by one or two percentage points.
The *Siège de Barbastre* places with the *chansons de geste* at 23
percent, equal to the *Pélerinage de Charlemagne* and only 1 per-
cent less than the *Moniage Guillaume*. In battle scenes, where
the formulaic style is perhaps most easily imitated, 55 percent of
the *Siège de Barbastre*'s hemistichs are repeated, as against only
18 percent of *Buevon*'s.[4] Thus there are formulas in Adenet's
work, but the mere presence of formulas does not make a work
fundamentally formulaic. Adenet is a transitional poet, an inter-
mediary between the oral tradition, of which he had undoubtedly
heard many representatives, and the written art of the romance.
Without the benefit of exhaustive stylistic analysis, Albert Hen-
ry, editor of Adenet's works, saw that he was dealing with a
hybrid creation: "Pour le fond, nous avons vu qu'elle [i.e. Adenet's

[2] CFMA; Paris: Champion, 1926.

[3] See Erich Röll, *Untersuchungen über das Verhältnis des Siège de Barbas-
tre zum Bueves de Conmarchis von Adenet le Roi, und die Stellung der
Prosafassung* (Greifswald: Hans Adler, 1909).

[4] "Formulaic Language in the Old French Epic Poems *Le Siège de Bar-
bastre* and *Buevon de Conmarchis*," unpublished dissertation, Ohio State
University, 1964, p. 155.

adaptation] oscillait entre la chanson de geste et le roman, sans
se détacher complètement de l'une, sans atteindre délibérément
l'autre. Pour le style aussi, on peut parler d'une souplesse
émasculée."[5] Try as he did to emulate the style of a *chanson de
geste*, Adenet was no more successful in reproducing the qualities
of oral technique than was Virgil in imitating Homeric formulas.
His material was epic, but his style was that of a trained writer.
Not so with the author of *Roland*.

    Jean Rychner, who first compared the *chanson de geste* with
the oral poetry of other lands, was reluctant to include the *Roland*
in the same category as the other *chansons de geste*: "A supposer
qu'il y ait eu des chants épiques sur Roncevaux antérieurs à la
chanson d'Oxford, leur mise par écrit a dû être très créatrice,
coïncider, en fait, avec un acte de création poétique."[6] A few
years after these words were published, Ramón Menéndez Pidal
argued cogently for the existence of such songs; but *Roland's*
formulas, when compared to those of other *chansons de geste*,
show no different technique at work, but only a greater mastery
of the same art, a mastery with the brilliance of the singer and
not of the clerk. The writing down of the version which leads
to the Oxford manuscript was remarkable, not because it in-
volved a creative artistic process, but because it was an early
and isolated example of a phenomenon which became common in
the thirteenth century, the act of committing a living song to
parchment. The scribe who cooperated in this momentous event
was indeed creative, but his genius participates in the curator's
or the collector's craft rather than in the poet's.

    I have already mentioned the reluctance scholars have shown
toward accepting a work of high quality as an oral composition.
This has been true above all of the *Chanson de Roland*, but such a
belief is often a strong force in the discussion of other *chansons*

    [5] *Les Œuvres d'Adenet le Roi*, II: *Buevon de Conmarchis* (Bruges: "De
Tempel," 1953), p. 28.
    [6] *La Chanson de geste: essai sur l'art épique des jongleurs* (Geneva: Droz,
1955), p. 36.

*de geste.* Perhaps one reason is that its acceptance will force us to place in doubt many critical assumptions which have been admitted up until now, as well as some apparent facts which depend for their validity upon the supposition that the relationship between various epic manuscripts is that between written descendants of an autograph original. Most *chansons de geste* have, for example, been assigned dates on the basis of references to some contemporary event. As oral poems, however, the various versions are not reflections of some hypothetical original text, but the recording of different performances of a poetic legend. They each have their own integrity and, unless there is strong evidence of correction by scribes, they should be regarded as equally valid actualizations of the heroic legend, that entity which joins them together. Their divergent readings cannot correct each other, for the relationship between readings is tenuous. An inestimable number of intermediate singers participate in the endless cross-fertilization of versions characteristic of any oral tradition. Each singer makes modifications in the tale: no two recordings of a known oral epic text, even if based on two performances by the same singer, are alike in their details. This makes for a multiplicity and complexity of "variants" which, as Menéndez Pidal has demonstrated,[7] cannot be resolved into a stemma. A reference to a contemporary event which appears in any one version provides merely a *terminus post quem* for that version; it by no means allows the editor to assign a date for the legend as a whole. Thus the stylistic data I have described in Chapter 5 lead me to believe that the chronological relationship of our nine *chanson de geste* texts, as conjectured according to positivistic criteria,[8] is essentially correct for the versions in question, but I am also persuaded to call into doubt the absolute dates if they are meant to apply to each poeticized legend.

An assumption closer to the subject of this book is that the

---

[7] *La Chanson de Roland et la tradition épique des Francs* (Paris: Picard, 1960), Chapter III, "Généalogie des textes conservés."

[8] See above, p. 23.

care with which the *chansons de geste* were written justifies close readings of the *explication de texte* or "new critical" type. No approach could be further from the spirit of these poems. They were delivered by men so unaffected by the revival of letters going on around them that they betray no evidence of the influence of Virgil, Ovid, or Lucan, so unconcerned about consistency that they introduce and eliminate key characters without reference to their antecedents or final destiny,[9] and so innocent of the ideals of a literate rhetoric that they ignore the teachings of the school concerning repetition, but fill their poems instead, on the levels of both hemistich and laisse, with a kind of repetition taught by no *ars poetica* or *ars rhetorica* either of antiquity or of their own epoch. That great crux of French criticism, the origins of the *chanson de geste*, is no less colored by the perception that the genre is oral: for evidence for a Latin oral heroic poetry is not yet forthcoming, but the Germanic peoples, among whom are numbered the Franks and the Visigoths who settled France, are known to have sung tales about their ancestral heroes.

The consequences of this study for the understanding of oral literature in general must not be overstated. My method has been to test the hypothesis that certain eleventh and twelfth-century works were created orally, by comparing those works with others known to have been composed in writing; this was done through a quantitative study of the kinds of phrases which, the hypothesis posits, are typical of oral poetry. Having found the hypothesis to be confirmed, I went on to examine, qualitatively, the use of those phrases in the most artistically composed of the poems in question. The hypothesis verified through quantitative analysis was reinforced in the qualitative study, for even the *Chanson de Roland* was found to surpass the others not by reason of fundamental differences, but because of the skill which its singer exhibited in his mastery of oral technique. I have made no claim to be able to extend these findings to other literatures or to other genres of French literature, but the same method or analogous ones may

[9] As, for example, in *Roland*, Blancandrin and Jozeran de Provence.

prove fruitful for the study of works suspected to be oral on the basis of external criteria, but not generally accepted as such because of difficulties peculiar to the literature to which they belong or to the modern critical material pertaining to that literature. I am thinking, specifically, of Anglo-Saxon studies, the problem of *Beowulf* and the supposed mixture of oral and learned traits in many early English poems, although the present remarks may apply equally well to other literatures. I am confident that the method set forth in this work is applicable to other literary texts of the same kind of tradition as the Old French, namely to poems whose basic metrical unit is the assonating, or even rhyming, line, as is the case for the Old Provençal and Old Spanish epics,[10] but it seems to me that a different set of criteria will have to be developed for Old English poetry, whose versification is based on rhythms rather than on syllable count and, even more important, on alliterative patterns which link one half of the poetic line to the other. The Old French system of ornamentation bears no resemblance to ornamentation in Anglo-Saxon, which is not a second hemistich (or B-verse) ornamentation, but one whose formal traits permeate the entire line, for the alliterative demands of the versification can be satisfied at various points in the line. My remarks about Anglo-Saxon verse must be limited to the opinion that, contrary to the belief of some observers, the theory of oral poetry as it applies to that literature has not been refuted to date. It seems to me that a key to the problems of oral composition in Old English verse may be found through a thorough study of its alliterative patterns rather than through the search for *ipsissima verba* formulas.

Short ballads and lays present still another set of circumstances. Memory plays an important role in the transmission of long nar-

[10] See L.P. Harvey, "The Metrical Irregularity of the *Cantar de Mio Cid,*" *Bulletin of Hispanic Studies*, XL (1963), 137–143; A.D. Deyermond, "The Singer of Tales and Mediaeval Spanish Epic," *Bulletin of Hispanic Studies*, XLII (1965), 1–8; J.M. Aguirre, "Épica oral y épica castellana: Tradición creadora y tradición repetitiva," *Romanische Forschungen*, LXXX (1968), 13–43.

rative poems; its part must be even greater in the ballad tradition, so much so that the term "improvisation" cannot be used in the same sense for the ballad as it has been employed for the epic. When a singer is reproducing a work of a hundred verses or so, it stands to reason that he will, whether he wishes to or not, depend more upon the performance from which he has heard the work than if he is singing a song of over a thousand lines whose telling might even be spread over a period of several evenings. For this reason ballads are notably more conservative in their evolution than is the epic, with correspondingly less need for ornamental systems. On the other hand, some ballads are as extensive as the shorter epics treated here. The Brussels fragment of *Gormont et Isembart* is only 661 verses long, and the *Pèlerinage de Charlemagne* is 870, while the "Gest of Robyn Hode" in the Child collection is over double that length at 1824 verses, although it appears to have been forged from a dozen or so previously existing shorter poems, and the Spanish "El Conde Dirlos" reaches 1366 verses. There is obviously a continuous progression in length between the shortest ballads and the longest epics, but it seems that, in general, for works below a text length which I would estimate at around 400 verses, the phrase-concordance method would be effective in inverse proportion to the shortness of the text. Nevertheless, while my procedure has only limited applicability to ballad studies, the findings are relevant to them indirectly. They indicate the existence of a large body of oral poetry in the middle ages, and ballad traditions ascend in time to the period in which this oral poetry was flourishing and reflect the same sociological and cultural conditions as does the epic.

Does the formula threshold of around 20 percent, found to be a distinguishing point between the *chanson de geste* and the romance, apply to other narrative traditions with metrical versification? Only extensive research can provide the answer to this question. In his *Parallel-Homer*, the nineteenth-century German scholar Carl Eduard Schmidt found that almost exactly one-third of the Homeric diction was made up of repeated lines or half-lines.[11] This figure is based upon the entire Homeric corpus and not just on samples. It is striking that the formulaic density of the *Iliad* and the *Odyssey*, taken together, is only three percentage points higher than the average of the ten Old French epics (30.3 percent) and three percentage points lower than the *Chanson de Roland*.

[11] *Parallel-Homer, oder Index aller homerischen Iterati in lexicalischer Anordnung* (Göttingen: Vandenhoeck and Ruprecht, 1885), p. viii.

# Index

Adenet le Roi: *Buevon de Conmarchis*, 22–23, 25 n., 26, 28; *Cleomades*, 26, 214–216
Aebischer, Paul, 23 n., 69 n., 70 n., 77
*Aeneid*. See Virgil
Aguirre, J. M., 219 n.
Alde, 67, 143, 167, 182–183
*Alexandre, Roman de*, 22–23, 25 n., 26, 28, 38, 215
Anticipation, 38–39, 78–80, 100–101, 162, 173, 176, 177
Aspland, C. W., 132 n., 208 n., 212 n.
Assonance, 11, 134, 138, 147, 179, 200–202, 204, 207, 208
Auerbach, Erich, 105–106

Baligant, 38, 65, 70–82 *passim*, 97, 100, 111, 113, 126, 144, 156, 157, 166, 167; episode of, 63–104, 167, 184
Bayot, Alphonse, 22 n., 189 n.
Becker, Philip-August, 3
Bédier, Joseph, 1, 40, 41, 145
Benson, Larry D., 18, 30–33
*Beowulf*, 219
Blancandrin, 115, 129–130, 133–134, 218 n.
Bloomfield, Morton W., 30
Bramimunde, 38, 71–73, 74, 81
Brault, G. J., 186 n.
*Buevon de Conmarchis*. See Adenet le Roi

Caesura, 11, 17, 67
*Carmen de prodicione Guenonis*, 70
Charlemagne, 38–39, 63, 65, 66, 70–81 *passim*, 99–103 *passim*, 111–117 *passim*, 127–136 *passim*, 144, 145, 149, 153–154, 155–156, 160–161, 164, 166–172 *passim*, 176–179, 181–183, 186, 193
*Charroi de Nîmes*, 2, 22–23, 25 n., 27, 30, 35, 173, 183, 209–211
Chasca, Edmund de, 12–13
Chrétien de Troyes, 109–110
Clichés, 26–27
Composite creation, 3–4, 16, 36–59, 193
Computer-aided method of formula analysis, 7–10, 20–25, 220
*Couronnement de Louis*, 22–23, 25, 27, 30, 35, 173, 183, 204–205
Creed, Robert, 30
Curtius, Ernst Robert, 12, 13 n.
Cynewulf, 31–33

Dating of Old French epics, 23–25, 217
Delbouille, Maurice, 2 n., 7 n., 33 n., 69 n., 74–75, 79, 82–83, 88, 100
De Poerck, Guy, 23 n.
Deyermond, A. D., 219 n.
Diamond, Robert E., 16 n., 18, 31–32

Elegiac tone, 167, 175–176, 179, 181, 182–183
*Enéas, Roman de*, 6, 14, 22–23, 25 n., 26, 28, 60 n., 215

Farnham, Fern, 63, 68
Favati, Guido, 23 n.

Formulas, 28, 173, 183, 194, 214, 216; syntactic, 7 n., 17, 32, 210; definition of, 10–15, 17, 22, 28, 60 n.; and clichés of thought, 12–13; and oral composition, 13 n., 16, 30–33, 60; statistical reality of, 14; description of weapons in, 14 n., 137; description of armies in, 14 n., 136–137; in key scenes, 14, 42–59, 117, 135, 148; in battle scenes, 14, 20, 88, 108–109, 113, 118, 135, 136–148, 157, 215; of speech, 14, 109–136, 148, 151, 157, 159; density of, 16, 18–21, 23, 26, 29, 34–35, 58, 84, 213, 215, 220–221; flexibility of, 17, 98, 106, 116, 132, 144, 158–159; minimum number of occurrences, 17 n.; inadequacy of sampling to detect, 19–21; geographical distribution of, 24; whole-verse, 31–32; distribution of, 37, 42–58, 83–88, 97, 102–103, 159; and literary excellence, 61–62, 107, 160, 168, 172–173, 182–183, 190, 193, 206, 208, 213, 216, 218; in the episode of Baligant, 83–88; most frequent, 89–97; of praise, 125–127; of blame, 127–128; first hemistich, 147–148, 171; of movement, 148–149; of appeal for conversion, 149; miscellaneous verbal, 150–151; substantival, 151–155; ordinal, 153; descriptive, 155–156; epithets, 156, 198–202; adverbial, 156–159; propagation of, 194–195, 211; blessings and maledictions in, 198, 202–204, 208; oaths in, 199, 200, 202, 208–210; of alacrity, 199, 204–205, 208, 209; systems of, 201–202, 203, 208, 210–211; second hemistich, 205–207; of oral delivery, 215
Fragment of the Hague, 101–102
Frappier, Jean, 23 n.
Friedman, Lionel J., 12 n., 30

Ganelon, 38, 63, 66, 68, 78, 79, 99, 100, 103, 111–117 passim, 122, 126, 127, 129, 133–134, 149, 155, 168, 176–179

Garin de Monglane, 70
Gautier, Léon, 77
Gormont et Isembart, 2, 22–23, 25 n., 26, 30, 35, 160, 173, 183–184, 188–190, 192, 193–195, 197, 208, 209, 210 n., 212, 220
Guillaume, Chanson de, 22–23, 25 n., 30, 35, 88, 160, 173, 182 n., 183–184, 190–195, 197, 208–212

Halvorsen, E. F., 70
Hariulf, 210 n.
Harris, Julian, 14 n., 143 n.
Harvey, L. P., 219 n.
Henry, Albert, 22 n., 23 n., 26 n.
Hitze, Renate, 12 n., 30 n., 107 n., 108 n., 132 n., 136, 144 n.
Holland, Michael, 122, 137 n.
Homer, 107, 214; Iliad, 17, 21, 61–62, 214, 221; Odyssey, 17, 21, 61–62, 221
Horrent, Jules, 69, 70 n., 81

Improvisation, 5, 7, 27, 102, 109, 211, 220
Individualism, 2–6

Karlamagnús saga, 70
Katz, Blanche, 22 n., 170 n.
Kellogg, Robert, 12 n.
Knudsen, Charles A., 69 n., 79

Labande, Edmond-René, 128 n., 192 n.
LaDu, Milan S., 22 n.
Laisses: similar, 41, 99, 101–102, 184; parallel, 98, 144–147; structuration of, 98–100, 102, 106, 108, 193
LeGentil, Pierre, 4, 63
Levy, Raphael, 25 n.
Lord, Albert Bates, 5, 12, 15, 17, 18 n., 19–20, 29, 32, 36, 102–103, 106, 210
Lot, Ferdinand, 1, 23 n.
Louis, René, 4

Magoun, Francis P., Jr., 18, 20
Manuscripts of Roland: Oxford, 1–2, 14 n., 34, 59, 103–104, 195–

198, 216; Lyon, 70; Venice IV, 118 n., 168 n.; Cambridge, 195–198; Châteauroux, 198

Marsile, 38, 65, 66, 71–81 *passim*, 115, 118, 122, 129–130, 133, 143, 145, 153, 166, 176, 179, 180, 181

McMillan, Duncan, 22 n.

Memorization, 5, 220–221

Menéndez Pidal, Ramon, 1, 4, 6 n., 12–13, 34, 66 n., 69 n., 76, 101, 102, 216, 217

*Moniage Guillaume*, 22–23, 25 n., 27, 30, 35, 38, 102, 173–175, 183, 199–208, 209–211, 212 n., 215

Mortier, Raoul, 2 n., 34 n., 187 n., 198

Motifs, 5, 10, 28, 106, 173, 174, 175, 183, 194–195, 211, 214; articulation, 65–68, boast (*vantance*), 118–125, 161; exhortation, 125; praise, 125–127, 161, 170, 172, 176; blame, 127–128; *planctus*, 128, 160–183, 191–193, 195, 198; prayer, 128–129, 167, 185, 187–188, 189–199 *passim*; message, 129–134; authority, 135; general battle, 136, 138; battle cry, 137; arming, 137; single combat, 138–148; description of horse, 139–141; *coup épique*, 142; dream, 177; hero's death, 183–198

Nagler, Michael, 10

Naimes, 73, 80, 114, 117, 127, 177–179

Nichols, Stephen G., 34 n.

*Nota Emilianense*, 70

Notopoulos, James A., 106

Oliver, 41, 72–73, 77, 80, 81, 97 n., 103, 111, 113, 122–124, 126, 128, 144, 145, 146, 156, 161, 167, 181

Olrik, Axel, 113–115

Oral dictation, 16, 60

Ornamentation, 139–141, 186, 198–212, 213, 219, 220

Ovid, 218

Parataxis, 105–106, 125

Paris, Gaston, 1, 208 n.

Parry, Milman, 5, 7, 8 n., 12, 15, 16, 17, 20, 32, 36, 60 n., 61, 106, 210, 214

*Pèlerinage de Charlemagne*, 22–23, 25–26, 30, 35, 38, 113, 118, 173, 183, 208, 209, 210 n., 212, 215, 220

Performance, 217; divisions of, 63–68, 74

*Poema de mio Cid*, 126 n.

*Prise d'Orange*, 22–23, 25, 27, 30, 35, 168–172, 173, 175, 183, 195, 209–211

*Pseudo-Turpin Chronicle*, 70

*Raoul de Cambrai*, 2, 22–23, 25 n., 30, 35, 173–175, 183–184, 193, 209–211

Régnier, Claude, 170 n., 172

Riquer, Martín de, 75, 103, 126 n.

Roland, 41, 63, 66–81 *passim*, 97 n., 100, 103, 104, 111, 113, 114, 117, 122, 125, 127, 128–129, 136, 141–145 *passim*, 155, 157, 161, 164, 166, 167, 172, 176–177, 179, 181–190, 192, 193, 195–197, 210 n.

Romance, 26–27, 29–30, 213–216

Roques, Mario, 110, 186 n.

Ross, D. J. A., 143 n.

Ruggieri, Ruggero M., 69 n.

Rychner, Jean, 1, 3, 13 n., 15, 27–28, 33 n., 35, 63–64, 67, 98–99, 102, 136, 216

Schmidt, Carl Eduard, 220

Scholes, Robert, 12 n.

Siciliano, Italo, 1, 3 n., 14, 60 n.

*Siège de Barbastre*, 22–23, 25 n., 26, 27, 28, 30, 35, 38, 173, 183, 209–211, 214–216

Statistical methods, 16 n., 17–33

Structure, 63, 76, 78, 166, 170, 193, 213

Themes, 5, 63–68, 214; and *topoi*, 13 n.

Traditionalism, 2–6

Transitional poet, 6, 215

Turpin, 72–73, 81, 128, 140, 144–145, 161, 181, 193

Vance, Eugene, 14 n.
Versification, 25–26, 28, 29, 31–32
Virgil, 6, 14, 60 n., 216, 218
*Vita Sancti Wilhelmi*, 210 n.

Wace, 210 n.
*Waltharii Poesis*, 126 n.
Wathelet-Willem, Jeanne, 214 n.

William of Malmesbury, 210 n.
Written creation, 2, 3, 6, 16, 35–36, 59, 167, 193

Yugoslavian epic, 5, 36, 214

Zumthor, Paul, 160–162, 173, 182